*SHADOWS*

   *DREAMS*

      *MEMORIES*

by Orest Sergievsky

*MEMOIRS OF A DANCER:*

# Shadows
of the past

# Dreams
that came true

# Memories
of yesterdays

*by Orest Sergievsky*

*DANCE HORIZONS, NEW YORK*

First paperback edition 1982

ISBN 0-87127-129-X

Library of Congress Catalog Card Number 79-87806

Printed in the United States of America

Dance Horizons, 1801 East 26th Street
Brooklyn, N.Y. 11229

*Dedication:*

*To the memory of my Granny, who helped me create*
  *and form my identity,*
*And to my two sisters, Kira and Colette,*
*And to my friends—past and present—*
  *because they were and are part of my life.*


*My life has been fortunate to have a rainbow on*
*its horizons holding back a curtain of the clouds.*
*My friends and the people I loved*
*created that rainbow.*

Thanks to Tom Russell, Dolores Herman-Reinhold and A.J. Pischl; and special gratitude to Richard Philp who corrected, rearranged, and helped me, with heart-felt understanding, to edit my autobiography.

*Why this book? Why have I written it?*

The past is so little known to the nowadays people. I believe a few of them will be interested in having a look into the past. A few individuals will be interested, some will be amused, others will recognize someone they knew or have heard about. Others might even find help in solving or facing their problems. Others, readers just for the fun of it, "armchair travelers," will visit places they have never seen.

But my main reason is to bring to life, or at least to leave an image of the events gone by, to keep alive the memory of people who were, or are, worth knowing.

I do not wish for some of the people I have known and loved to vanish into an empty past without being remembered.

This was written in 1943 on Biak Island, S.W. Pacific, about events which took place in Kiev, Russia in 1919:

*Some time ago they asked me if I would write a book;*
*With chapters of my life, with pages filled with words,*
*With words spoken from the heart.*
*My past is filled with excitement.*
*Events of bygone days still bring pain, joy, and sadness.*
*But if I were to write about my past or present,*
*I could not say all about my beloved friends.*
*Some of them are still alive; I cannot, I have no right*
*To tell all about my yesterdays,*
*Bringing into light some people,*
*Some "other person" or a special friend.*
*Just to write about myself, it is not worth the while.*
*My life without the people I love*
*Would be as empty as a desert isle.*
*Yet, to many young and lonely,*
*Whose road of life has either just begun,*
*Or whose life is full of silent shadows,*
*I can narrate, tell a message clear and true.*
*Then what am I to do?*
*My rich imagination might invent some new names,*
*Other places, to make my narration "story-like,"*
*As if it were true, yet not true.*
*And if someone, sometime, will read my lines,*
*And will find a familiar image there,*
*Forgive me, and forget, and think: it is just a story,*
*Events and places that came out of space and passed on.*
*Passed on to the garden of remembrance so vast and distant*
*That you or I or any other person could be forever lost there.*
*The memory garden is full of flowers,*
*With blossoms of the days gone by,*
*Where air is filled with tender fragrance,*
*With silent echoes, passing shadows.*
*And now, if or when we hear an echo or a sound,*
*Or see a shadow or a flower that takes us back to days gone by,*
*We sigh, and with a wistful smile,*
*We either welcome or chase away*
*The ghosts of our yesterdays.*

Should I start with "Once upon a time, long, long ago,
In the distant land where shadows, clouds, moonbeams dance. . ."?
Or should I tell a story in a simple quiet way,
Which is nearer to my heart?
A story with its beauty, joy, and sorrow.
I can tell about early sunrise, with the glory of bright colors,
Or the everlasting beauty of the sunset,
With the magnificent curtain of the clouds.
But now I must go back, into the past,
To start my story from the beginning.

It starts with words: "As I remember . . .",
But I remember, all at once, so many things:
Tender caresses and soft whispers over my small child's bed. . . .
"Goodnight . . . spokoynoy nochee . . . sleep well . . . God bless you,"
The soft, tender voice of Granny, that I love so much.
Then, in the darkness, my fantasy begins to play,
And follow swiftly my dreams on their flying way.
Yes, as I remember . . . memories of shadows ever changing, ever
        following.
The events remembered as I remember them,
And events and tales remembered as I remember them being told.
It is a strange day,
When it is the first day you become conscious of your shadow.
While the lonely walks, the shadow keeps company.
In the later years, as time goes by, the shadow changes very little.
But then, all at once, comes a realization of
Some lonely moonlit evening.
In how many places, in how many lands and situations
Your faithful friend—the shadow—followed you.
I remember, in my boyhood,
Helped by the richness of my imagination,
The shadow helped me to escape into fantasy land.
Some quickly improvised creation of my imagination
Would do a magic trick,
Giving the effect of what I wanted,
Between the light and a white wall.
Dressed in borrowed clothes and some extra things from Granny's
        closet
I would begin my shadow-play, going on some fantastic journey

*Into the land of make-believe. . . .*
*Then my memory goes back to the reality,*
*To the real shadows on the street.*
*When all the town, dipped in silent darkness,*
*Holding its breath even in its sleep,*
*Was waiting, watching, listening for a shot or sudden scream,*
*Or the nearing thunder of marching feet,*
*And my shadow by my side, accompanying me on the sparkling snow,*
*On a strange journey to the other side of town,*
*On the way to my uncle's hiding place.*
*With a message that was strange, not completely understood*
*By my inexperienced boyhood.*
*The message was: To give this little gun, which was hidden in my coat,*
*To my Uncle Roman. Somehow he and Granny knew what to do,*
*If or when he would be found.*
*Intuition, or overheard, spoken in a whispered conversation,*
*Told my little heart that this strange mission had,*
*Unknown to me, a "shadow,"*
*The shadow which some people called Death.*
*When going back, through silent streets,*
*My own shadow did not follow me.*
*I was frightened, alone.*
*The moon was behind the clouds that drifted like a curtain*
*To cover the starry sky.*
*So I ran, as fast as I could manage,*
*To the little corner, to a warm room,*
*Where Granny was, where was my home.*


*Again, as I remember . . . how many nights or days ago?*
*How many sunsets or starlit evenings. . . .*
*It seems it was so long, long ago. . . .*
*So long ago, I cannot believe it was true. . . .*


*When the day is gone,*
*And the night covers with its mantle the restless world,*
*I begin to think and wonder.*
*What is Life? But a passing shadow.*
*What is Love? Desire and longing.*

*And my heart silently whispers:*
*Love and life are but one when love is life itself.*
*A faded rose . . . a chord of music . . . Aloha . . . parting . . . End.*

During the eleventh century, invading Tartars conquered the newly Christianized Russ, the tribe that was to become the Russian people. For a few hundred years the Russ had to pay homage to the "Infidels." Periodically, officials of the Genghis Khan came to collect the riches of Russia. One of them, Tomash, fell in love with a Russian *Kniajna* (princess); he became a Christian in order to marry her and to live in Russia. Through the centuries, the name changed into my Granny's name, Tomashevskaya.

# PART
# ONE

Shadows
of the past

Orest Sergievsky painted by Saul Bolasni, 1938-1940.

Left: Katherina Tomashevskaya at Smolny Institute in St. Petersburg, 1885. Above left: Vassily Sergievsky. Above right: Katherine Sergievskaya. Below: Gleb, Boris and Roman Sergievsky.

Above left: Boris. Above: Gleb. Left: Roman.

Opposite page:
Above left: Boris (1919). Right: Gleb (1917).
Below: Roman (1918).

Left: Ella and Boris; Kiev, Russia, 1910. Below left: Ella Bergau. Below: Boris Sergievsky.

Opposite page:
Above left: Ella as a bride. Above right: Mother, after the divorce. Below left and right: Orestik, age 3 and 5, taken before the Revolution, in 1914 and 1916.

Top left: Granny and Orest during the Revolution. Above left and right: Last photos taken in Russia of Granny and Orest for passports. Right: Granny in Paris, 1928.

10

Above: Orest, 1932. Photo by Garlanoff.
Below and right: My sisters, Kira and
Colette.

Top: Captain Boris Sergievsky in
the Tzar's Air Corps, 1917.
Above: Father and Charles
Lindberg on test flights in
Stratford, Connecticut, 1931.
Left: Father.

Above left and right: My friends in Russia, Kolia and Irena, 1920-1927. Right: My first choreography to Schubert's *Serenade* with Galia and Orest, 1933. Below: Stratford (Connecticut) High School graduation, 1932.

13

Left: Orest celebrating New Year's Eve, 1936. Below: Last group photo of Boris and Gertrude Sergievsky with Kira, 1970. Below left: Kira, 1945. Bottom: Father as commander of American-Russian Legion in New York City, 1939.

1

*About 1875:*
The dark and unfriendly Smolny Institute, which was later to witness the bloody events of Revolution, opened its doors to admit a little orphan girl, Katherina Tomashevskaya, eventually to become my grandmother. She had no memories of her beautiful mother or the dashing general who had been her father; by nature of her high birth, she was placed in this well-respected finishing school for young ladies.

The story of Katherina's parents' meeting in a carriage on a journey from St. Petersburg to Moscow was related to her later by a great lady of the Court, who was a distant relative. Katherina's mother, my great-grandmother, had been a very beautiful woman, a petite socialite who had become the toast of the capital and admired for her wit and charm. It was no wonder that the gallant general and the vivacious lady found each other's company a pleasure.

Flirtation developed into romance, then into social upheaval—one of them was already married. Due to a fortunate combination of will-power and social connections, a proposal led to a happy marriage. In the social whirl that followed, the striking young couple was the center of attention at every occasion. The birth of Katherina was a great joy, but was saddened by the ill health of the young mother. Upon her death a few months later, the duties of the mother were taken over by a nurse. The widower, General Tomashevsky, my great-grandfather, was occupied with his military duties; a few visits from distant relatives could not warm the young daughter's life, nor have taken the place of a real home.

Before little Katherina was old enough to become self-sufficient, the General suddenly died. Due to the social position of her parents and to the efforts of an aunt, who was also a Lady of the Court, Katherina was admitted to the Smolny Institute, the best school for young ladies. Granny told me years later that through all the years she attended school there she could not "warm her frail body or her lonely heart."

The Institute was under the wing of the Tzar's court, and the Tzar and

Tzarina made occasional visits. During one of these visits the Tzarina presented Katherina with a medallion for good behavior, along with a pat on the head and a soft smile asking the frail girl if she were in good health. At her graduation, Katherina was given a beautiful gold watch by the Tzar, a present which would later, during the difficult year of the Revolution, save us from hunger. During the preparation for that graduation, Katherina had been almost happy: Marius Petipa, the famous choreographer of the Maryinsky Theatre, taught the girls of the Smolny to dance and execute endless curtsies. Granny remembered all this in later years with pleasure, although her legs and knees had ached from all the lessons and rehearsals.

The most exciting and glamorous event of her life occurred just after graduation, when coaches from the Court called at the Institute to take the young ladies to the palace for dinner in the grand malachite room. Amidst the grandeur and splendor of the palace, Katherina was impressed most by the strikingly costumed Negroes who stood behind each chair with a bottle of champagne which was dutifully tilted whenever a glass was almost empty.

The frowning governess-teacher had no effect. For the first time, life was fun and discipline took a back seat. Dark looks lacked the power to force the gloom of duty to descend upon the young hearts. Cadets from the Royal Military Academy partnered young ladies from the Smolny Institute; the ball that followed seemed unreal to my grandmother, and the evening ended too fast, as if it were a dream.

The description of that night at the palace was so vivid when many years later I heard my Granny narrating it that even now I can imagine the malachite columns in that opulent reception room in the Hermitage. Friends of mine who have visited the palace in modern times tend to think that I was there as a result of my vivid "recollection."

The weeks after the ball were occupied with social activities for the youthful Katherina. A distant aunt, that grand lady of the Court who had assured Katherina's entrance into the Smolny, arranged parties and visits to introduce the graduate to the world of society. Having spent her childhood in the shelter of the Institute, Katherina knew little of "outside" life. Invitations to summer homes and other cities were accepted or declined with care; Katherina's opinion was hardly considered. On these visits to distant relatives, she discovered that life could be gay and bright. There were afternoon walks, carriage rides, laughter, new faces, and new feelings.

Years later Granny laughingly related to me an incident which at the time she thought was a disaster: During one of the promenades, she realized with horror that she was losing one of her pantaloons (in those days they wore bloomers down to their knees, covered with lace and frills). It would be disgraceful; she didn't know what to do. Suddenly she had an idea: She slowed down, letting her companions get ahead of her, then, quickly stepping out of her slipping pantaloons, started running after them, calling that one of them must have lost it! Granny always had the ability to deal with difficult situations; but I would never have thought that she could act that way.

Katherina's loneliness had over the years created a seriousness of character, and the disciplines of the Smolny school developed in her a strong willpower, unusual in such a young person. She was also beautiful and found to her surprise that she possessed the power of making people fall in love with her. Many admirers wrote poems and letters: many asked for a kiss at the next Easter.* There were many letters to be re-read with quickened heart, many poems and messages to consider. One admirer in particular, a dashing officer, student, and scientist, flattered her with candies and flowers. He, Vassily, was a promising engineer with connections at Court.

Katherina wanted to continue her studies. She wasn't sure exactly what she wanted to do, but she knew she wanted to be useful to humanity, to enjoy life. But the people around her made the decisions for her. They "knew better" what was the best for her. Some of her admirers, when they called, were discouraged, told that she was not "at home." As a result, one emotional, poetic youth became a monk. Others managed to get urgent pleas to Katherina, threatening to "finish with life." The general decision of friends and relatives was in favor of the promising young engineer, named Vassily Sergievsky, who had just received a commission to direct the construction of the harbor at Odessa. He was to be my grandfather.

After being promised that she would be allowed to continue her studies and to do some social work, Katherina was convinced to accept the offer to become a Sergievsky. She was 18.

Less than a year later in 1888 at Gatchina, near the Summer Palace at Tzarkoe Selo, a short distance from St. Petersburg, Boris Sergievsky, my father, was born.

---

* The practice of giving an Easter kiss was an accepted and eagerly awaited custom which took place on the eve of Easter, at midnight. After three processions around the church, and then opening the church doors and making the joyful announcement "The Christ is risen!", everyone would answer: "Indeed, He has risen," and kiss and be kissed three times. This opportunity was eagerly anticipated and perhaps even abused by younger generations, for here was a legitimate excuse to indulge in the socially forbidden but much desired, wonderful, wicked habit of kissing.

# 2

*About 1890:*

Descriptions of places can be so real, events can be narrated so vividly, that they become a part of us, exactly as if we had experienced them ourselves. There is a popular song from the Soviet Union about a sailor who reminisces: "I can't tell you *all* about Odessa; Odessa is very, very big; but I can tell you about. . . ." And so it is with me.

During the many years of my life spent together with my grandmother—as orphans of the past, surrounded by the hostile ebbs of revolution—Granny related events which were·filled with such details that the very ruins came to life. She caused my imagination to feel and see, and she gave me the strength to face harsh realities—strength drawn from the strong backbone of a proud past.

To this day, I still do not recall exactly how the Black Sea looked to me when I was a child. But in 1968 during a cruise of the Mediterranean our ship, while sailing from Troy to Constantinople, made a slightly off-course approach to the Black Sea, as near as allowed by the Soviets. We, the passengers, took a brief look at forbidden waters. I was there as a child of three and again at four, but I have only a few dream-like memories: How my maternal grandfather was an all-powerful despot, ruling the household like a king; how my Aunt Anna, Mother's sister, danced around a Christmas tree in a fairy costume, bringing me presents; and how "O'Mama," Mother's mother, caressed me and gave me wonderful forbidden sweets.

My mother told me many years later in 1972 while I was visiting her in Edinburgh that the Sergievsky's house in Odessa was big and grand, three stories high, with wide windows and a grand staircase. Granny had told me that when the house was finally finished and the young family moved in, she felt like she was living in a church. The place was so big, the ceilings so high, and she was so inexperienced in running such a castle-like household that she had to have a full staff of servants—maids, cooks, handymen, and so forth—in order to make things run smoothly. She told me of trying to arrange some large plants on the stair landings and in the corners of the big rooms to fill in some empty spaces.

When Father was just a small boy, a miniature Shetland pony called *Malutka* (Little One) was led up the wide stairs as a birthday present for the five-year-old Boris from his father.

The big house was the first to be built on the cliff overlooking the sea. They were to name the street *Sergievskaya*, but then decided it more appropriate to call it more impersonally *Tchernomovskaya* (Black Sea Street). Although the house was massive, with thick walls, it was bright. Expansive windows provided a beautiful view of the sea, and a lush garden complete with many fruit trees surrounded the house.

How do I know there were fruit trees? Because I was told how my mother and father met while climbing over each other's fences, playing robbers. My mother had been assigned as a "safety watcher" for her two brothers and my father, who were cutting lilacs and stealing apples from an unoccupied estate nearby: Mother was to give them a warning signal if anyone were to approach.

The Black Sea can be very rough and a breaker wall had been built to create a safer swimming area. However, a few people dared to swim out into the open water, my father among them. When he was sixteen the high waves of a sudden storm prevented a swimmer's return to the safety zone. Young Boris swam out to help the drowning man, supporting and guiding him the length of the wall to the shore. A crowd gathered, watching the two swimmers fight for their lives; some started taking bets on whether they would survive. One of the witnesses was an official of the Tzar, and after the swimmers' victory over the sea, he saw to it that my father, Boris, was presented with a medal for bravery—the first medal of what would become a collection of many in his impressive collection. The year was 1904.

In many families the wet-nurse employed during an infancy became a member of the family. Granny told me that Niania had been indispensable in taking care of the first-born Boris and in helping to manage the complicated routine of the household. Father told me that even after his marriage Niania would pour his tea from the samovar and stir sugar into it while advising him what to eat and what not to eat. The arrival of a second son, Gleb, and two years later the golden-haired Roman, created a real challenge for my grandmother—bringing up three sons.

Many stories come to mind as I try to recall the life before my arrival on the scene. One of the funnier incidents was that of my father, Boris, learning to walk. At first he had been holding on to some furniture or to a stick that was supported by someone. One day the stick was taken away while Boris was in the middle of the floor. He stood there uncertain what to do next; then, with determination, he took hold of the waist of his pantalettes with both of his little hands and walked his first independent steps. Father always remembered the voice of Niania saying, "Do not walk, do not run or you will fall." This became a family saying: Do not run or you will fall.

Sometime later, during my grandfather's long and final illness, the responsibility of raising the three boys fell entirely upon my grandmother. To make them "strong and fearless" she made them do things which few mothers would have had the nerve to do. The young mother would make my father run across railroad tracks as approaching trains were puffing out smoke and steam (she had previously judged the distance to make sure it would be safe even if young Boris should fall). She allowed the boys to climb trees so high that they made *her* dizzy. Once the boys wanted to climb on the roof of the house; she let them, sending a house-worker to stop them if any real danger arose. Once when Boris wounded a cat while using his father's gun to practice his marksmanship, Granny made him find the suffering animal and finish it off. There was no repeat of that incident.

One of the expressions Granny used to restrain the arguing boys—and later to be used on me—was: "You want to try everything? Without choosing? Well, you have not yet put your head into a garbage bin. Try it, why don't you?" Her advise on pornographic reading material: "If you eat something bad, you throw it up, but if you read or see filthy material it stays in your imagination and poisons your clean mind and thinking."

Her advice worked on my father and uncles. It certainly helped me, especially when we were surrounded by the treachery of the Revolution. Granny used to tell me: "Be above it. Walk past the ugliness. Do not get involved in anything that will make you ashamed. As long as your conscience is clear and you do not hurt anyone yourself, you can be proud of your own self-esteem. . . ."

The three sons were growing up. Since there was no institution for higher education in Odessa, it was time for a dramatic move; in 1908 Kiev was chosen. This was an important decision; it would be difficult for a widow and her three sons to give up their home and move to an unknown city. Most of the wealth was gone due to the extended illness of the husband-father. The sale of the house, however, earned enough to finance the move and to establish the family in Kiev, but what then?

3

The Sergievskys settled in Kiev—the city called the "Cradle of Russ," "Mother of Russia" or the "Pearl of Russia"; the place where the pagan Russ had first been christened in the 10th century. But it was difficult to find a big home or an apartment with a view of the sunset—necessities after the spaciousness of the Odessa shore.

The household was held together by the indestructible Niania, a faithful servant of many years. Due to her excellent education, Katherina was able to become a private coach, a teacher-helper. She prepared new students for examinations, and, with the aid of the accomplished mathematician Boris, she tutored backward students.

In no time the Sergievsky apartment became a center of youthful gatherings, a home-away-from-home for many. Some felt a part of the family; one youth, Andreii Kapsha, asked to be adopted into the family. He later became my godfather, and during the helpless, hungry years following the Revolution he sent us things from outside of Russia and generally helped in our survival.

The boys grew into youths. Problems changed, often multiplied, but love and duty were rules of the house. Whenever affairs of the heart—or other delicate decisions—had to be made, Mother was respected. Her advice, especially her rule that "Love between brothers is more important than the call of the flesh," solved many difficult situations.

In 1910, the Sergievskys' dream came true. It was possible at long last to move into their own home. Finances had improved; Katherina had more pupils, and the death of Vassily Sergievsky had not only diminished expenses, but provided an income from the government on account of his services as chief engineer to the Tzar. A house was also desirable because a child—to be son and grandson—was expected. That child was me.

The new home was not just a house *but a mansion* set back from a tree-lined street. On either side of the courtyard, as one entered the tall wrought-iron gates, were small buildings for the help (the coachmen, laundress, other servants and the *dvornik,* or caretaker) and a few tenants from the working class. The house itself, facing the courtyard, was a two-story building. The first floor contained the kitchen and cellar, where barrels of salted pickles, cabbage, potatoes, apples, and onions were kept. Three bedrooms and a pantry (containing another oven and a stove) faced the courtyard on the second floor, and three more rooms faced the garden to the rear. The central room, with its crystal chandelier, had French doors opening on to a forty-foot long porch lined with white columns. In the summer the porch was used for lunches and parties. The room to the left of this main room was another bedroom. The corner room, to the right, was the music room, and it had high double doors which were opened during the musicales.

The garden occupied a whole city block and was surrounded by a high wooden fence. A row of lilac bushes encircled the house, their branches reaching the windows of the music room, filling it with their lovely aroma. In the spring, the pear and apple trees mixed with the cherry blossoms to create a snow scene reminiscent of winter. Near the high fence was another row of lilacs, mixed with lacy white acacia. Paths wandered through beds of different flowers, and gooseberry, blackberry and raspberry bushes along the sides of the garden were favorite places for children, birds and small animals when the berries ripened.

*1909:*

Roman, the youngest brother, was still like a colt—all arms and legs. Only after his teens did he become a competition to his brothers with his good looks. The only one ever to exceed six feet tall, he was blond, with a sensitive face, full lips, blue eyes, and a carefree manner that made him the most uncomplicated member of the family.

Gleb, the second son, was a quieter personality—an artist. Music was his life. Some people thought he was better looking than Boris; in his own calm way, Gleb attracted attention at the grand piano, creating magic with his music.

Boris, the eldest, was usually the life of any party, charming the guests with his looks, love of life, and enchanting voice. He fell in love with a lovely young lady named Yadviga, who was often among the guests who used to attend the *vecherinkas*—the evening of talk, music, and singing at which tea was served with the ever-popular *pirojki*. Looking back on this—Boris's first passionate encounter with a woman—it is easy enough to see the pattern which their love would soon take: the inner storms, the unseen wounds which would fortunately dissolve with time, and the many things which remained unspoken but still created shadows on family relations.

Before graduation and receiving his diploma as an engineer, Boris had to acquire practical experience, to gain firsthand knowledge in different parts of the country. When Boris was leaving to spend several months in Odessa, Baku, Sevastopole, and other places, he asked his brother Gleb to keep the young fiancee, Yadviga, company. Gleb was asked to accompany her to concerts and parties so that she would not be lonely. But even before Boris left, the subtle charm, the deeper personality of Gleb, started to intrigue and fascinate the young woman.

The mother of the family, and gradually a few others, began to realize with uneasiness the possibility of drama in the near future.

Gleb did not encourage Yadviga; he was a gallant escort, but ever-conscious that he was with his brother's fiancee. Nevertheless, by the time Boris returned, Yadviga was hopelessly in love with Gleb.

After a few weeks of polite coolness and uneasy silence, Gleb left to visit a friend outside of Kiev. Boris had to go to Odessa; his mother wrote to the Bergau family in Odessa to try to cheer Boris when he visited them. The Bergaus had been neighbors of the Sergievskys; their sons and daughter Ella had been playmates of the Sergievsky boys during their childhood.

The "cheering up" of Boris led to his engagement and later marriage to Ella. I, their son, arrived upon the scene in August 1911.

# 4

Born in the past, nurtured in the present, our desires and thoughts reach into the future. Memories are the only real treasures our hearts possess.

Whenever the 23rd of November, my Saint's Day (name day), comes around, one of my earliest memories of life returns to me. Opening my eyes in the dark, either late in the evening or near morning, by the flickering glow of the icon's melted candle flame, I see a beautiful sled leaning against my bed. Then immediately, like the turning of a page, I remember my ecstatic ride outside, down a small hill from our garden gate through the open expanse of the front yard, stopped from continuing into the street outside by the wrought-iron fence and gate. The shining metal of the sled's frame, its blue leather upholstery, the red ball fringe, the cold snow, and the freedom of that fast ride downhill are in such sharp focus in this vivid recollection that it could have happened yesterday.

It must have happened on a special occasion, like one of Granny's name-day parties, in 1914 or 1915. Chrysanthemums, white and golden yellow, enormous in large vases, have been placed in the corners of the big dining room; festivities and smiles abound in the grand manner of the past; special *pirojki* and tortes (many-layered cakes) are part of a sumptuous supper for guests in evening dress; the air is filled with "grown-up" magic. One of my first memories is being awakened and brought out into just such a gathering for about fifteen minutes, to be petted, to taste some of the sweets, to be passed from one person to another. The naked shoulders of the ladies, huge chrysanthemums, dark evening attire or bright military uniforms, and the aroma of perfume—all created an indelible impression. I remember the frustration of being sent back to bed, trying not to fall asleep, listening to the laughter, the beautiful melodies of the piano and someone's voice singing.

The next memories are short and disconnected: My love for a small teddy bear that had to be with me at all times; holding up my father's heavy military *burka* (cape) as he was leaving for the front , and almost losing my balance on the chair; my first two friends, an Irish setter and a pointer. I remember curling up with them in their special place in the hallway, and following them everywhere. I was told later that, even before I could talk, there was a problem in satisfying my pantomime demand for a tail of my own. I was finally satisfied by an arrangement of one of my uncles' belts which was somehow attached to my shorts.

*1919:*
White snow, dry and brilliant, full moon high up in the sky, cold air frozen in its stillness. I remember my heart stopping, then racing to catch up, walking fast, with the small steps of an eight-year-old. A strange message, words memorized, trying to remember them, wondering what they meant. A gun held by my belt, pressed against my stomach. Not understanding but subconsciously feeling the importance of this tragic mission, repeating the words: ". . . if they find you—you know what to do. . . ." My grandmother

had made me memorize this message and given me the gun—both intended for my Uncle Roman, who as a White Russian had been forced into hiding by the advance of the Reds. My grandmother's words had been spoken to me with a steady voice, but a voice which also revealed pain and love.

These were the days when the last of the hiding White officers found near their families were taken away to be tortured and shot. Roman, a few days before, came back from the last stand of the White Army to see how we were getting along at home. The day before, the Red Army soldiers had come to search our house, but Roman was hiding in the library of a friend's home a few blocks away. The soldiers went there, too, but as if by miracle did not find Roman, who was standing in the window behind a heavy velvet curtain.

Knowing the cruelty of the interrogation and torture-to-the-death that followed, it would have been better for Roman to end it all by self-destruction if he were to be caught.

I remember rushing home, my mission accomplished, feeling an extra cold inside, looking about as if someone were following me; I had a sense of my shadow keeping me company among the high snow drifts and flat spots of snow on the way to the safety of my Granny.

*1919, Summer:*
The White Army was made up of men who were still faithful to the Tzar; many were in favor of moderate changes in the government, but they were against the idea of a complete revolutionary upheaval, such as that advocated by the extremists, the Red Army. As is usually the case with human nature in these matters, the Reds sought a way of life which was totally different from the old; their hostility, which grew out of years of suppression in the past, had been ignited by political agitators. All discipline and restraint were cast aside and in their place was brutality—a primitive, barbaric cruelty which became the standard of behavior throughout the long civil war which followed the Tzar's downfall in 1918. Brother fought against brother, and every day you heard hysterical accusations and ridiculous reports about the former "ruling class." The red-white-and-blue flag of old was changed to a red flag, symbolizing revolution—but also a symbol of the great amount of blood which was shed.

My Uncle Roman loved to sail and row on the Dnieper, the beautiful river that was the cradle of Christian Russia, where the first baptism was performed at the order of Kniaz Vladimir. A little chapel by the river's edge marks the spot where the subjects of the Kniaz Vladimir were rounded up and driven into the water to be blessed by a priest from Constantinople, the Greek-Orthodox stronghold of the Christian Church.

One day that summer of 1919—the last carefree day in my memory—Roman and I spent the day sailing across the Dnieper and sunbathing on the other shore where the flatlands created a perfect *pliage* for sunworshipers. Afterwards, on the way home as Roman and I approached our house, we saw a crowd of people at our gate. Suddenly, Maroussia, Roman's girlfriend, rushed from one of the gates a few houses before ours and took Roman by the arm, saying "Don't look back. Follow me." Slightly bewildered, I went on alone towards home.

The next thing I remember is one of the women of our household meeting me just before our gate, saying: "Your Grandmother is no more. . . ." A terrible noise escaped my throat, everything went around, spinning, and dived into violent emptiness. Later I was told that people heard my scream a block away. Coming out of my faint, I found myself inside our own house; but soldiers were everywhere, two of them with guns bending over me, asking where my Uncle Roman was. Where is the rest of the family? I still do not know where I found the presence of mind and the courage to lie, saying I was only with friends on the river. I pretended not to know about the rest of the family, that I had not seen them for some time. Strangers were all over the house, searching, carrying things out; many wagons were loaded with our possessions. Later on, people were heard bragging about how long it took them to take the riches away.

That night, I remember feeling lost and hungry. I slept on the doorstep of our house, after being refused food and shelter by neighbors and friends who were afraid to help me for fear they would be next on the list of the Red Army.

One of our maids had informed for the sum of 500 rubles that we were of "good" family and a White Army family.

The search and plundering continued the next day. Many proofs of our connection with the White Army were found. Behind the wood and coal storage area in the barn were found trunks with my father's and uncle's officers uniforms; guns and other military weapons were found under the barrels of salted cucumbers, tomatoes, and apples in the cellar. From the house itself, everything was "liquidated," including the silver, porcelain—even my clothes, a child's clothes.

I do not remember how the days of nightmare passed and how I survived. I do remember being questioned again and again; but the soldiers' anger at my silence was diverted by what they could steal from our house. Finally my Granny came back. She told me that she had been questioned and threatened. Somehow, someone intervened and a bargain was reached: She would not demand return of the "liquidated" possessions or request an investigation of open robbery, and in return she was allowed to go free.

Nonetheless, for many nights following, a sudden search would be conducted, unauthorized. During these days of tug-of-war, fighting continued underground and on the streets. All the shutters and doors were closed tight when the Red Army, Germans, Poles, and rebels were on the streets; but, as if by miracle, windows would open when the White Army would be retaking part of the city. They would find welcome and friendly smiles, and the little food we had saved from confiscation would appear.

One of those days, I remember a meal was set in our grand dining room with whatever could be offered. The distant sounds of guns were heard, and then a block away there was an explosion. I was told to hide under the heavy oak dining table. Moments later the house trembled, then a terrible crash. The roof of our house had been hit; the crystal chandelier crashed onto the table, covering everything with glass, plaster and broken dishes. Fortunately the bomb had actually exploded in the garden, hitting our favorite apple tree.

One of those nights when gunfire never seemed to cease comes to my memory. Granny woke me up, sending me to the gate of our yard to see if it was one of my uncles who was lying killed or wounded in the street outside. Granny was so weak she was unable to descend the two flights of stairs and cross the large yard to the wrought iron gate herself. I remember running back with a sigh of relief to tell her that it was someone unknown to us. A few hours later we heard the *telega,* an old wagon creaking its way down the street, picking up the bodies—but not before we had watched from our window as scavengers took the boots and coats, the watches and the jewelry from the victims. Many nights machine-gun fire with its ominous deadly staccato interrupted the heavy silence.

As the Civil War moved away from Kiev, the almost nightly raids and sudden searches without warrants became a part of the past. The dreadfully vivid memory of seeing a White officer with a nail driven into his forehead began to fade. The awful smell from the building where the White prisoners were buried alive in walled-in passages began to diminish.

Those of us left at home faced the new troubles of survival and the nerve-racking waiting for news of the dear ones.

Boris was the eldest son. The next in line, my uncle Gleb, was a mystery and object of admiration to me and to many others. He was very handsome, tall, even elegant, with eyes that would not reveal what was occupying his thoughts, but were at the same time intriguing. Many times a mood would shadow his noble brow, yet he was not really moody or sad; rather, it would be some exquisite melancholy or wandering musical melody that was casting its shadow on his calm countenance. The music was his world—a world he could share with others without being involved or exhausted by the sharing. He could create a spell. When Gleb was at the piano in his music room, the conversations in the other rooms of the house would gradually fade; people would be drawn into his room or the drawing room next to the music room. And somehow they would lose themselves in the melodies, relaxing in the emotional quality that charged the air.

In dress, Gleb was a dandy, but not a dandy of the current fashion. He created his own style. The flowing cape and low shoes with buckles of semiprecious stones gave him the appearance of a poet. He was always immaculately dressed, in well-cut but dark, almost somber, colors.

There were always flowers on the grand piano, an everpresent homage from his admirers. During the prosperous days in Kiev before the Revolution, the deep sound of the Blüthner (the best brand of piano at that time) could be heard at any time of day or night. His music never disturbed anyone because it was always subdued; only when there was a special performance, such as when he would play a whole composition, would there be a dramatic crescendo. Most of the time there would be a haunting melody, a passage of Chopin, or a new melody by Rachmaninoff (with whom Gleb had studied), wandering in and around the keys. His improvised playing on these occasions created a sense of light clouds in the wind; my grandmother said he played as if he never touched the keys. The shadow of one melody would replace another, and a familiar phrase of a known composition would unexpectedly be woven into the pattern of his music.

Years later, when Granny and I had finally escaped to Paris, some people while reminiscing said that "Gleb played like a divine being." Even well-known compositions acquired new meanings beneath his fingers; deeply felt melodies disturbed the imagination yet satisfied the spirit. Many were infatuated with Gleb, some in love with him. Few could separate their admiration for his music from an infatuation with his looks and personality. It is a well-known fact—though seldom realized by those afflicted with desire—that what is unattainable is even more desirable.

One of Gleb's admirers tried to make her appearance and her life "as beautiful as his music." Although it is impossible to translate a melody into a physical style, this woman would send flowers and dress herself in a sari-like creation decorated with flowers, thus costuming herself in what she thought to be an esthetic vision. Gleb found the whole thing too artificial and contrived, and told her so, instigating a painful disaster that was an embarrassment and annoyance to the whole family. This "Lady of the Flowers," as she was called by some friends and members of the family, finally overdid her theatricality. One musical soiree, attended by friends and specially invited guests, was interrupted by a messenger with a telegram to the effect that the Lady had committed suicide. The flowers that had arrived earlier in the day were a form of goodbye: White roses for Gleb, tuberoses for my mother Ella, and tea roses for Granny. Gleb continued his concert, remarking that it was just one of her hysterical scenes and that he was sure she was still very much alive.

He was right. The lady was discovered hiding in the garden to observe the effect of her telegram and her so-called death. This was too much for the family. She was asked not to visit them for a while. Poor soul, she had tried to make her life beautiful by artificial means, but only succeeded in making it more pathetic. She later attempted a "romance" with someone else, calling her new interest her "knight." But this failed too. Some time later the Lady actually did commit suicide, leaving a goodbye note to the family. A visit from the police requesting some details in the circumstances of her death was very unpleasant for the family.

There was a definite spiritual bond between Granny and Gleb. Somehow they understood each other without verbal communication. Granny often felt his moods—she had a special gift for unspoken understanding. One night, returning especially late, Gleb realized that he had forgotten his key to the fifteen-foot-high wrought-iron gate outside. Reluctant to ring the loud bell, he decided to climb over the gate. When, as was family custom, he went to say good night to Granny, she told him that she knew he had had trouble getting in, and then asked the astonished Gleb why he had looked into his wallet before climbing. He answered that he was checking to see if he had enough money for a hotel and—*Granny finished his sentence for him*— wondered if she would worry if he did spend the night out. The next morning at breakfast, as Granny and Gleb related this amazing bit of clairvoyance, she could not understand why, but she remembered someone somewhere lighting matches. Who? Where? My mother broke in; "Oh, it was me! I tried to light a candle to take care of the baby; he was crying." Granny could not have seen or heard, since the baby's room was on the other side of the house.

# 7

My Uncle Roman, the youngest of the three Sergievsky sons, was tall, blond, handsome. The complete opposite of his brother Gleb, Roman was always in disarray, with his shirttail out, wrinkled trousers, and wearing socks which didn't match. When Roman went out on a date, Granny had to "check him out" so that he would be "in order." Although he was six feet tall, he looked like a puppy that had not yet grown up—all arms and legs. The perfection of a well-dressed man was not his way, and yet there was a lot of charm in his carelessness, and bright friendliness in his smile.

My memories of Roman are few and fleeting. He taught me how not to be afraid of water; he took me in his sailboat to the other side of the Dnieper River, where I gradually learned to swim. From Roman I also learned to share my life by telling Granny what happened in my life—as he used to tell her about his—and about the problems which arose.

I remember once, when coming home from a party, Roman began to tell about the happenings at the party, but Granny interrupted, "How did you get there? There were five of you in the *drojki* (carriage); there was room for only four." So Roman had to tell what seating arrangement in the carriage had been made, how someone had to sit on someone else's knee. Granny, as I recall, was sorry for the poor horse, because the load was too heavy with so many people. This kind of continuing communication between them strengthened and reinforced the bond which united them over the years.

*Maslinitza*, the carnival-like festival week preceding Lent, was the time to get dressed up in different costumes, in the spirit of Mardi Gras. The young members of our family always took part in these festivities, visiting friends at their homes and receiving them in ours. I remember one season when my Uncle Roman surprised us, appearing in a ballerina-like outfit, complete with a wig of long blonde curls and a pink tutu. His fair complexion was the right color for such an outfit, but his six-foot size made it look ridiculous— and humorous, as it was meant to be.

The colorfully attired and high spirited visitors at *Maslinitza* created a kaleidoscopic panorama in my memory. In our entrance hall, as they bundled up in their capes and furs, there would be long discussions as to who was to go in whose sleds. The sleds were usually pulled by one or two horses, and huge blankets of bear skins would protect the youths from the bitter cold. As they drove from the courtyard, there would be a musical sound created by bells of different sizes attached to the horses' harnesses and the sleds.

When thinking of the past, memories of many events return, fitting like pieces of a jigsaw puzzle that constitutes the general design of the days gone by. Some of the pieces fit together; others are lost in yesterdays; at times isolated bright spots of color return, flashing with intensity.

My little brown velvet teddy bear—my own possession, my friend, companion, the first object of my affection and love, accompanying me on all my journeys and cuddling up to join me in the dream world of sleep. I felt that the teddy bear understood me.

I can still feel the sadness that shadowed my heart when I had to part with him upon leaving Russia—but by that time deeper sorrows had made this parting less important.

During the war years: Photographs—framed pictures of Boris, Gleb, and Roman, surrounded with fresh flowers—were the focus of our vigil. Not surprisingly, my father and uncles were to me at this time rather remote persons, partly because all the thoughts we had about them were filtered through my grandmother's deep concern. They were not as much my family, my flesh and blood, as they were people about whom I had heard a great deal, at a distance. I vividly remember hours spent with Granny looking at the photographs, wondering from which of these men would come the next bit of news or even a visit. We did not dare to express the anxious, frightening thought in the back of both of our minds: That we would receive, not news, but a message from someone else. That one of them had been wounded, or was missing. Or dead.

I remember my father, Boris, the eldest son, appearing in the doorway with a bandage about his head. He had received shrapnel, a fragment of an exploded bullet, just above his eye. The family doctor was called. I remember asking Father as he was lying on the divan waiting for the doctor to remove a bit of lead, "Is it hurting you?" And as it was being removed, there was not a sign or reaction from him. He just said, "Yes, a little." It was a lesson of will-power over pain: A brave soldier must not show fear or pain.

The sound of a plane overhead meant that it was Father, since his was the only plane that ever flew over our house and garden. It was usually a message; he has either to be home soon or was saying goodbye as he left for the front.

Our neighbor, Dr. Kotchoubey, and his wife, Alexandra, shared our garden; their house was on one side of our block, and her music room had windows overlooking the garden. During my father's visits home there would be small parties, singing. I would wake up and listen to the melodies of *Rigoletto* and *Traviata*. It was Father singing the operatic duets with Mme. Kotchoubey. I heard these melodies many times without knowing their names.

Dr. Kotchoubey was constantly away and the three handsome men, Boris, Roman, and Gleb, were tempting company for the future opera star. But Roman was always misbehaving. For example, he would start sneezing when a much-perfumed lady would pass the veranda. Gleb was too busy with his music. But Boris, a gallant officer who loved to sing, would oblige willingly and sing a duet or two.

The duets were followed by other meetings. In the evenings one could hear the melody of a then-popular romance, with a definite message in the lyric: "Sunset is beautiful across the river, the perfume of flowers fills the air; meet me, my dear, in the garden. . . ." Relations became more personal. As I write this, I still cannot understand why Dr. Kotchoubey used to give me chocolate candies. Was it because we two were left out—he by his wife and I by my father? I remember the Doctor telling Granny during the war (1914) that he was actually grateful to my father for "taking away" his wife. I remember, too, overhearing that Alexandra threw the doctor's wedding rings out of the train window on their honeymoon.

Grandmother had tried to call the romancing couple to reason. She had a talk with Mme. Alexandra, reminding her that Boris was a married man, that there was duty to the family in married life. But Mme. Alexandra's answer was: "Until one is thirty, life is ruled, experienced by the heart and senses; after thirty it is governed by brain and duty." Father was then twenty-three years old.

Ella, my mother, twenty years old, was naturally upset by this flirtation. She occasionally had to visit her parents in Odessa to get away from it all, taking me along, but she also loved her home in Kiev; the visits to her former home were short and not very happy.

My memories of these visits were mixed. Though I was only three, there are a few bright moments that I remember vividly: How I was spoiled by "O'Mama," my other grandmother, with all kinds of sweets! My Aunt Anna created a magic world of make-believe, appearing wrapped up in chiffon, dancing around a Christmas tree, leaving wonderful presents (including a "golden" crown) to make me believe that a fairy had visited.

Aunt Anna, a teacher of physical education in a private girls' school, was something of a dancer of the Isadora Duncan school. She was the first to ignite in me the fires of desire to dance and to take flights to imagination— the two activities which have been my guiding lights and consumed every other distraction that crossed the paths of my life.

I also remember, although faintly, the velvety charm of Mlle Marie. She was the "companion" of my mother's father, whom I called Grand-Papa, and his daughters. As mother of the family, it was O'Mama's duty to oversee the routine of the home. But when Grand-Papa ordered the carriage, O'Mama stayed at home; Mlle Marie accompanied Grand-Papa and the children whenever they went for a ride, to concerts or to the opera. This was accepted in those days. Originally Mlle Marie was the French governess; later she became a "member of the family," so to speak.

The Sergievsky household, like most households of the same social class, included many extra individuals. Besides the regular staff of servants, maids, cook, and a *dvornick* (a man who did the "hard labor" like taking care of the yard, the garbage, and providing wood for the fireplace), there was a teaching staff. This usually included a Mademoiselle, who was a French lady for French conversation and manners instruction, a German teacher for mathematics and discipline, and a visiting gentleman twice a week for English "speech" instruction.

But many things had changed by the time I was growing up, and at the beginning of the Revolution I was taken by Niania to a private French kindergarten where I was taken part of every day for over a year. Throughout the years of seclusion that were to follow, I received all my instruction from my Granny. My first "academic" schooling would not take place until I was admitted to a high school in the Panama Canal Zone many years later.

I remember very clearly the last time I saw my mother in Russia. I was three-and-a-half years old. Granny was very surprised years later when I described how Mother had been dressed: in a traveling suit with fur around her shoulders and a lovely feathered hat. I remember she bent down to kiss me goodbye. I must have realized that she was leaving the Sergievsky home. The strong emotion she must have felt made me conscious that it was not just a *dosvidania* (till we meet again) but a *real* goodbye, a farewell.

Many years later, when I was in my teens, Granny told me that because of the War, and because of the unhappy situation in her relationship with Father, Mother had decided to leave. She would not leave with me because she knew I would not be happy with her parents in Odessa, where I would be subject to a very straight German, almost military, upbringing. Years later, during one of my rare heart-to-heart talks with my father, he told me that if my mother had not left him in Kiev, he would never have divorced her. He said he really loved her, but in a family kind of way. Mother left when I was little more than three years old, and I would not see her again for nearly twenty years. For long stretches of time during that period nobody would know whether she was dead or alive.

My father left Kiev shortly afterward, in 1917 when I was six. During the first few months of his absence, he was somewhere in Poland, unknown to us, with the White Army, which was reorganizing with hopes for a victorious return. Mme. Alexandra followed Father, working as a practical nurse in the Red Cross.

There had been, before the Revolution, a lack of supplies and considerable inefficiency in the Tzarist army on the lower echelons; the upper class officers were generally taken care of, however. After the Revolution had begun, the White Army, with its ties to the past, met with considerable hostility. My Uncle Gleb felt that there was no respect for officers of the White Army, and he seemed to be able to foresee the ugliness which was to descend on the Russian land in the very near future. He left, and for years his fate was unknown to us.

The fight for survival dulled the anxious urgency of our knowing, but when Granny and I were finally free, and there was time for just thinking, remembering and wondering, Granny began her search for the missing Gleb. It was Paris in 1928. Among the ruins of many lives and fortunes, there were many people who had made their way to Paris, the capital of Russian refugees.

A cavalcade of information started to reach us, answers to the advertisements that Granny had placed in the Russian and Parisian papers. The replies were painfully varied in their contrasting information: some "had seen" Gleb recently in Marseille, others "had drinks with" him; they could go there and find him, given a certain amount of money for the trip. It did not take us long to realize that there are people who would take advantage of others' misfortunes to gain money. Finally real information came, from an officer who had been on the same submarine as Gleb.

When Gleb left Russia, we discovered, he asked to be transferred to a British submarine service, based near Sevastopol, on the Black Sea. It was during this assignment that he drowned, while returning to the base one night. It was not known whether he had fallen into the water, or if there had been foul play.

By 1917, my mother had been gone for several years, my father was fighting in the White Army, and Gleb disappeared. But my Uncle Roman left my Granny and me for a while, during this difficult period of adjustment to the chaotic changes in government. Roman managed to get work as an agricultural engineer in part of Russia which was still relatively free; that is to say the Red flag had not yet thrown its shadow on that part of the country. He would occasionally manage to send parcels of food to Granny and me, sending them through the peasants or others who visited friends and family who had remained in Kiev. I remember what happened to one of those packages: First, you can hardly imagine today the joy with which we received it. But, alas, the packages of food had traveled next to the kerosene and were soaked and full of fumes. It was impossible to eat the food, and when we put the treasured sugar into the tea, it smelled and tasted like lighting fluid.

Roman was also the last member of the family to be with Granny and me before the final disaster of the Revolution—and the emptiness which followed. The last days of his life are very real to me, forever etched in my heart and on my mind. I was with him during his final illness.

Roman showed up unexpectedly during the last hot days of summer in 1920. He was ill and he wished to see his mother and to stay with us, regardless of the risk which this might have involved. Upon the advice of one doctor, and a second opinion from another, Roman was wrapped in wet sheets every two hours in an attempt to bring his fever down. When Granny would collapse from exhaustion in her room, I would take over and stay by my uncle's bedside, trying to guess his needs while fanning away the flies. At times his fever would let up and he would relax, open his eyes, try to sit up, or start collecting the edge of the sheet, folding it in small pleats. The last few days he was stiff and almost lifeless because of the meningitis, and I frequently wiped his mouth with wet cotton in order to cool his parched lips, cleaning his mouth with wet cotton on a little stick. There was so much tar collected in his lungs from smoking that it was difficult for him to breathe.

Late one afternoon he suddenly relaxed and looked about as if to find where Granny was. I called, but before his mother could get to his side, Roman gave up his life with a deep, slow breath. It was a sad, small group that followed the horse-drawn cart, carrying the pine casket to the cemetery. Granny had one of her arms about my shoulders and someone else supported her on the other side.

By this time, all communications with the outside world had been cut off. The Iron Curtain had been brought down between Russia and the rest of the world. Soon it would be a national crime to communicate with a capitalist country, such as England or the United States. The Old Russia was no more—it had become the Soviet Union.

And as far as we knew, Granny and I were now alone in the world, which had collapsed around us. It was just the two of us; the years together during the difficult times ahead cemented our affections as well as our destinies. Only the realization that she was needed by me, her grandson, gave Granny the strength and will power to carry on.

During the winter of 1920-21, the cold was the worst of many hardships we had to endure. After the death of Roman, Granny and I were completely alone, real orphans of the Revolution—the "left-overs." We were also without heat, water, clothes or food; the few belongings we had were traded, bartered, and exchanged in the frozen wastes of the open marketplace.

I remember parting with my cherished collection of post cards for a few potatoes. Several beautiful, handpainted, gold-edged plates—among Granny's wedding presents—went for some loaves of coarse bread, a few carrots, some beets. I cried bitterly, with anger and resentment, when Granny's last possessions—the gold medallion and lovely watch presented her by the Tzar and Tzarina at her graduation—were traded for a sack of flour and potatoes. Granny's only comment was, "We must have food. It will last and feed us for a while."

Even going to the marketplace became a problem. By this time, at age nine-and-a-half, I had grown as tall as Granny, so I could use her coat. Since we shared this single coat, only one of us at a time could go out in the winter. She was becoming too weak to go far, and actually she did not know how to "bargain" with the marketplace crowd as I did. The additional problem of shoes was solved by wrapping the feet in any available paper—newspaper, if it could be found, and *valenki,* woolen boots, were pulled over our paper-bound feet.

A few times I had to persuade someone to come to our house to see some bric-a-brac that could be exchanged for food. At one point one of the *kulaks* (more-or-less successful peasant merchants) was persuaded to come to barter a few sacks of flour and potatoes for Gleb's grand piano. Though there was no one in the *kulak's* family who could play the Blüthner, he wanted to own it. Later Granny said that at least the memories of the music that had filled our home were still with us.

Life continued. My lessons had to be attended to, and some children of our friends, such as Irina, daughter of the opera singer Mme. Makarova, came to study with my Granny a few times a week. These were, like us, "left-over" people, who did not belong to the new regime and had not left Russia or escaped to other parts of the country that were still "free." In exchange for lessons, Granny received goods which helped us to survive. The parents of Granny's pupils would bring what they would share: a piece of ham (such luxury!), half a loaf of coarse bread, a few vegetables, a few slices of fat or bacon in which to fry potatoes, and on special occasions an egg or two.

Although we were getting a general education, we studied a great deal of Russian literature that was not allowed to be read because it gave too much information about the past life. Whenever I would complain that I was tired, Granny's answer would be, "Oh, you are tired? Well, a change of subject will take care of that." She believed that wasting time was a sin. Now I understand: She did not know how long she would last, and she wanted to educate me as much as possible before it was too late. My education was so intense that my first "official" schooling, in the Panama Canal Zone, was at the high school level. It must have been confusing to the authorities who asked about my pre-high school education when I answered that I had been tutored at home by my grandmother. The clerks in the U.S. Air Corps, and later at Columbia University, had a hard time figuring out what to put down on the forms regarding educational background. From French to Russian literature, arithmetic to geography, from reading to writing, and so on, the only thing I missed was the spelling practice that is taught in grade schools. I am forever grateful to my Granny for the varied and concentrated studies.

The visits of the "White Russian" children for studies were my only contact with the outside world, a hostile world, where a cruel new social existence was growing out of the collapsed world of our yesterdays. I had no companions with whom to play. The other children who might have been my childhood friends were all antagonistic to the upper-class, well-mannered, strange boy—who was becoming a stranger even to himself. The toilet and water supply were major problems that frozen winter. No water at all. No electricity. We were now occupying one room, formerly Granny's bedroom, in our own house. The other rooms had been requisitioned and government employees were living in them. In the summer, somehow, the water and toilets had worked, but when winter came everything froze. So, behind a screen in our one room was arranged a "throne," a chamber pot. After it was used, I had to carry the pot out to the far end of the yard to the outdoor toilet (a kind of outhouse). I invented an ingenious arrangement for camouflaging this errand with an old market basket.

Obtaining drinking water was much more difficult. Everyone had to walk to the marketplace many blocks away, where at certain hours a well—or rather the pipes feeding it—were thawed out with a small bonfire. I would get two buckets of water and struggle uphill towards home. It was not bad enough that it was cold, that my feet were wrapped in newspapers and rags, but I was also followed by hooligans, homeless orphaned youths who knew that I was different—a "White Russian." They would follow me almost to the gates of the house, then spit into the buckets. I would come to Granny in tears of frustration and fury. She would try to console me, saying that they didn't know any better, that I would just have to bear it. And so long as I didn't do anything like that myself, I would still have my pride, my self-respect, my honor. So I would go back to the well again, this time with a neighbor who provided some protection.

There was also a problem with washing. Although we had scarcely anything to eat, there were still a few knives and forks and a plate or two to be washed up afterwards. I remember arguing with Granny, saying we only needed to wash them once a day. I used to say that it wasn't dirt, it was *food*, and that we could use them again at night. But I had to clean and wash them after each meal anyway.

Once a week "wash-up-time" was another problem. Gone were the days when I used to go, as a special treat, to the lovely marble baths with my Uncle Roman. Now we had a little stove with one place on the top on which to boil or fry our food. It was a cast-iron, pot-bellied arrangement, with a long chimney which twisted several times and led out into a lovely, hand-painted enamel stove that was left from the former days. This beautiful but inoperable relic of a stove-heater occupied the entire corner of the room, all the way up to the ceiling. On "wash-up" day, while warming the room with the pot-bellied stove, a bucket of water would be warmed on top. Then in a round barrel-like wooden pail I would wash, sponge, and rinse. As I became conscious of my masculinity, shyness added to my problems. But Granny solved this by simply saying, "If someone sees it, it will not fall off."

Our illumination was, for many months, of the most primitive sort: a former sauce-pitcher filled with a kind of oil-wax fluid, with a wick made of heavy string or tightly rolled cotton. When lighted, this gave off enough light to live by. Two of these elemental lamps had to be used for reading or writing. Most of the time the reading and writing and studying was done before the daylight faded. Then, for a while, everyday misery was hidden in darkness and conversation took over. Memories of past luxuries and feasts would come back to revive our poverty-dulled imaginations. Stories of the past, tales of the days gone by, filled the evening hours and became more real than the present.

At the present I am sorry for the young—yes, for the older ones too. The constant drive and insistent intrusion of the ever-present television, loud music, fast activities, constant restlessness, rob our lives of the tender glow of memories and the awakening of our minds to new ideas, new dreams and, most importantly, of just communication with one another.

Gradually some of the people found places in the new government and were able to find work, earning the means to buy food, and starting to live again. So a few of our friends from the past began to visit and care for Granny and me. My Godmother, who lived near Kiev in Belaya Tzerkov, came one day bringing vegetables and dairy products from the farm. It was from her farm years before that milk had been obtained to nurse me (I was only a few months old) when our family physician had ordered that I be fed cow's milk, when my Mother contracted a breast infection.

I remember a visit to my Godmother's farm with special clarity. As I was approaching the *dacha* (summer house) I saw an elderly gentleman sitting on the stump of a fallen tree, leaning on his walking stick, his white hair snow-like, his eyes looking into the distance as if he were seeing into the past. He was the master of the estate, husband of my Godmother, reminiscing, with the silhouettes of tall slender white birches around him. His face was kind, sadly smiling, welcoming me, but in a distant sort of way, as if we were only partly there, the other part remaining in the past. He was completely coherent, but just not completely in the present; polite but distant. Meeting him was a strange experience for me and made an impression.

I have met a few people like that, physically in the present, but mentally elsewhere. They performed the duties of survival without accepting their present condition. They removed themselves from everyday life and slipped back into the refuge of the past. It was easier to survive the cruelties and hardships that way, remembering how it used to be. . . .

A few of our friends, who still hoped for the return of the White Army and the restoration of the Old Regime, had children my age. Although the children had to be educated, the parents were reluctant to send their offspring to the "Red" schools which were beginning to open. In these schools the teachers had to be "processed"—if they ever talked about, or alluded to, the past they were dismissed. One of our friends who was teaching in such a school lost her job because she thoughtlessly brought a colored egg for her lunch during Easter Week.

Once in a while, when things were a little better and there was something to cook, Granny had no idea of how one was to go about it. I had to ask neighbors for instructions. I remember once when I returned from a visit to a neighbor with information on how to fix potatoes. When Granny saw me putting the potatoes into water to boil them, she said, "And I thought you just steamed them!" All her life she had run an efficient household, but she had never done any cooking herself. Her health had always been fragile, and there had been servants to do the actual work. I gradually learned to cook by asking, each time when the problem came up, a kindly woman who lived in our yard how things should be done. Although these women were of the newly "liberated" class, they still had respect and pity for the "left-over" individuals of the past regime.

It dawned on me years later when I was sixteen that I had never been so hungry that the pain in my stomach made me unhappy. There were times, however, when I experienced pain from the so-called black bread we ate to add substance to the small amount of food that could be obtained. The bulk of the dough was made from the outside layer of tree bark.

Years later, as we were reminiscing in the comfort of our villa in Cartagena, Colombia, I asked Granny why she had spent so much time in bed most of the winter, even teaching her pupils from her bed, propped up with pillows supporting her back. She told me then that she was saving energy because she was so weak. This image of her troubled me, recurring in my mind for years. I did not realize until this conversation, many years later, that she had even occasionally refused to eat her dinner, saying that she did not feel like it, in order to let me eat her part. Only there, in South America, did I realize her sacrifice. As I thanked her with tears in my eyes, Granny said, "You needed food, you were growing up."

*40*

*Easter-time; Pride, Religion:*

As I remember, one Easter before the churches were closed, I went with a few friends and neighbors to Kiev's beautiful eleventh-century St. Sophia Cathedral; and then we went later to the St. Vladimir and St. Andrey churches, built on the high hill overlooking the picturesque River Dnieper. The Easter service is especially beautiful and dramatic because it is performed at midnight. Just before midnight, the priests lead the congregation, carrying lit candles, crosses, and icons, out of the darkened church. After circling the church three times, one of the priests comes to the closed door of the church and, after knocking, opens the door and with a joyful voice announces that Christ, the Savior, has risen. Everyone joins in the moving melody, "Christ has risen, with death he conquered death. . . ." Then everyone embraces and kisses, three times.

The memory of the candlelight in the immensity of the cathedral, the emotional surge that lifted everyone's spirits, and the number of people who still dared to come to the church, left deep impressions.

One Easter morning some of our neighbors—members of the New Regime to whom religion was a thing of the past—were, although unbelievers, having the traditional Easter feast of *paska* and *kulitch* on our veranda. (*Paska* is made with cottage or cream cheese, butter, candied fruit, vanilla, eggs, and a lot of sugar; *Kulitch* is twice-raised dough enriched with raisins, saffron, butter, and eggs.) I was only ten years old at the time and as I was passing by in the garden, these neighbors called me over to give me a plate full of these Easter goodies. When I brought the delicacies to our room, Granny would not touch them. I asked her why; we had not had such luxuries in a long time, and they looked so good. She reminded me that these "new people" had taken away everything we had had, that they in fact were living in the very house which had once belonged to us, and that they might kill her sons if or when these sons should return home. She could not bear to touch their food. I understood and respected her feelings and her pride. I took the Easter plate back to the veranda and with a sad smile thanked the people who had given it to me. Although they were angry, I believe they somehow understood.

I was criticized for not going to church regularly. Later the churches were closed anyway to become clubs and museums. Granny made me understand that God was everywhere and as long as I said the two prayers I had learned ("Our Father" and "Mother in Heaven") every morning upon waking and every evening before falling asleep, and as long as I did nothing to be ashamed of or to hurt other people, then I would be a good fellow and did not have to go to church for the sake of appearance.

41

Finally the almost nightly searches were no more. It was a relief to spend a night without a sudden banging at the door, rough soldiers rushing in, upsetting the little we had left, forbidding us to have an icon, remarking, "There is no God. Can you see him? Show me God." One of the reasons the searches ended was that we had nothing else for them to "liberate," to confiscate. We had managed to hide some money in various places, behind the wallpaper in the corners of the room and under the marble top of Granny's dresser, but it was of no value. We kept the money out of loyalty and sentiment, and with a faint hope that these beautiful bills, with the image of Catherine the Great and the faces of the Tzar and Tzarina, might someday regain their value.

During the years of uncertainty between 1921 and 1923, we were completely exiled from our home. Granny and I were moved, with just our clothes and a few books, to the front part of our complex—that is, to the front of the yard, where the townspeople and servants had lived in simpler buildings in the old days. I really did not understand the move, unless it was to break our spirits, to prove the Red Army's power, or to create "justice?" One of the most unpleasant of our troubles was the savage attack of bedbugs. The assault would begin after midnight; it was like part of a nightmare. I cannot imagine where they came from, but after killing dozens of them, the smell in our room was sickening. I do not remember how, but we managed to obtain a metal bed for Granny and an army cot for me, so we could burn the wooden furniture; it was the only way we could get rid of the unpleasant insects.

This move placed us in closer contact with everyday life and people; we could see and hear our neighbors' problems from our windows. There were three other so-called apartments on our floor, sharing a common staircase, so we were involved with these neighbors, whether through sympathy, rudeness, or (at the best) mere curiosity. Some of their lives touched ours, others provided only minute points of interest.

Later on in my life, when I was in high school in the Panama Canal Zone (which began in 1928) and in Stratford High School in Connecticut (1931-32), and during my studies at Columbia University in New York (1950-51), I used some episodes from this period in Russia as subjects for English composition. They are included here because they are true and help to illuminate the background of my youth. These short stories are true; the events in them occurred about 1920-1924.

The story of Lussia is about our next-door neighbor, who while she could still walk, would visit us to sit by our window (her room, which she shared with her father, had no window to the outside). The conversations overheard in the story I actually overheard; they shocked me and have remained in my memory because this was one of my first contacts with the cruelty of life.

## LUSSIA

Outside, the Easter night was calm and dark, proud with its importance. The sky was bright with stars. The air was fragrant with the timid promise of the early spring. In the cold dark room on the second floor of a tenement house a young girl was awake. Lussia knew she was to die; as she was resting between her spells of coughing and the fever that followed, she remembered.

She remembered the days before the Revolution. Those happy, carefree days, cloudless in their lack of worry, innocent in their everything-ready-routine-do-not-worry-enjoy-yourself way of life. She remembered how tender and sweet her dear mother used to be. She remembered how different and generous her father used to be.

Everything was changed now. Her mother had died a few months ago of tuberculosis. Her father, nowadays, was silent; he did not talk with her the way he used to. Then suddenly she remembered the conversations she overheard a few days ago, and she felt cold and strangely empty inside. At first, when she heard the voices, she could not believe that it was her father that was saying these words:

"Please, could you write the certificate today?"

"But how can I?" a voice answered. "Lussia is still alive."

"Well, you know," her father's voice pleaded, "she will leave us in a few hours or a day or two, then there is so much to do, so many things to take care of. If I get the certificate now, the coffin will be ready."

Somehow the trick of her feverish mind and the terrible realization, created an image. It was death, a shadow-like figure embracing with her father, whose face expressed a waiting expectation looking in her direction. Her father embracing death, it made her shudder. The realization that her father killed all the love in her heart and was now waiting for her death impatiently, filled her being with feverish loneliness. Giving in to feverish dizziness, Lussia fell asleep. Upon awakening some time later, another conversation came back to her mind. This time it was the gossiping of two women who lived next door. They were talking on the landing, opposite Lussia's room.

"Dr. Ivanoff told me the other day that Lussia could be saved."

"How?" interrupted the other woman.

"Well, you know how it is with the rations. Her father saved all the coupons of the rations, that old devil. If he had used them up to feed the poor girl, she would have been stronger. Or if he had taken her to the Crimea, south, it would save her from her mother's fate. He even told me yesterday that there will be more to eat, after Lussia dies."

"It is terrible what the Revolution has done to him," started the other voice, "and to think how important and rich he used to be."

In the dark corner, sitting in a chair, half asleep, the old man was waiting. He was thinking how, after Lussia's death, he will be able to get more food. Oh, yes, and after trading on the flea market with her clothes, he will be able to get a few really good meals. Strange, the realization that it was his own daughter who was dying never came to his mind.

Easter night was deepening, the wonderful hour of midnight was approaching, when in the churches—those still open—in Russia everyone would be singing "Christ has risen." The church bells still were ringing the sad monotone of the funeral, before changing to a joyful reverberating, ringing happy, old but forever new and wished-for message of the Resurrection.

Lussia, there in the shadow, felt light and at peace. She did not feel any resentment against her father anymore. Now, as the image of her mother became clear in her mind, she could almost feel her presence—Lussia gave up her struggle. As she was drifting away, a memory of the early spring flowers come to her vision—a momentary, wistful wish to reach and touch them passed into shadows. A sigh—and her soul, free, joined the sound of the ringing of the Easter Resurrection Bells.

There is a saying in Russia: Whoever dies on the Easter night, goes straight to heaven with all sins forgiven. We knew that Lussia's soul went to heaven, because she *never* sinned—Lussia was only seventeen.

Poor Lussia actually had some spring flowers near her at the finish. I remember managing to get some for her; she had kept wishing for them whenever we talked. Granny told me that when she had realized how seriously ill Lussia was, it had been her wish to die at Easter time. We were all sad for poor Lussia, but in a way were glad, because her suffering was over.

The next story, "Escape," is also a true story. Olga was a dear friend of ours; her mother had been a lady-in-waiting at the Court; Kolia was a friend of my uncle.

## ESCAPE

It was a time of terror, the year 1919, the year of killing and suicide, the year of tears and sorrow in Revolution-time Russia. The prisons were overcrowded, there was no more room for all the victims of cruelty and suspicion. Victims of the Revolution and counter-revolution were shot; even in the cemeteries there was no more place or time to bury them, so "common-graves" for many corpses were used. The horrible, uncomprehendable deluge of human meanness, heartlessness, and hypocrisy was reaching the high-tide-mark of destruction.

But, notwithstanding all this, in the young hearts of some people there was still hope, love, and devotion.

Olga was nineteen years old. She was a true example of a Russian beauty. Long, dark-brown, wavy hair; blue-grey eyes of a water-nymph, at times dreamy thinking about "him," her beloved Kolia; charming smile, merry melodious laughter. In her graceful figure there was something special, that she inherited from her noble parents, which made her still more charming and attractive. She had an exceptional talent in painting and drawing, as well as in playing the piano and singing.

It was morning, but Olga could not work—it was too beautiful outside. In the window of her studio, blooming branches of lilac and acacia could be seen and spring wind filled the room with their aroma. She started to imagine how tonight she will meet him, Kolia, by the river, at the end of the garden. He will tell her, while nightingales sing, what she will be so happy to hear: He will tell her again how he loves her. Her dreams were interrupted by a knock at the door.

"Oh! Olichka, darling, the most terrible thing happened! He . . . he . . . he is taken!"

"Who is taken? Where?"

"Kolia! They took him an hour ago; a whole bunch of them came with the guns to his house and arrested him."

Everything turned black, she felt strangely empty, only the words: ". . . he is taken . . . Who? . . . Kolia . . ." were ringing louder and louder in this emptiness; then everything became quiet and calm.

The first thought, when Olga regained her consciousness, was to save him, to do her best, even sacrifice herself, but to *save* Kolia.

Three weeks passed. The blooming branches faded and the hope in Olga's heart almost died. It was impossible even to find to what prison he was taken. All efforts were in vain. Her happiness was gone. She was almost sure now that "they" killed Kolia. She could not even know where his grave was, where she could go to be near him, bring flowers and her tears.

Suddenly one day she received a note: "In a few days Kolia will be shot." Olga knew why: He was accused of being an officer in the White Army of the Tzar and that was enough to kill the youth. At the end of the note was the name of the prison. Though she now knew where he was, there was no chance, either for ransom or escape. She could not see him, her darling Kolia; she could not caress his golden head, or admire his handsome face, look in his blue eyes. But Olga had wisdom in her pretty head, and love in her heart inspired her to a plan.

Olga began walking by the prison, looking into the yard, and once she and her girlfriend even managed to get into the long corridor, pretending to be curious visitors who had never seen a prison and would be interested to talk with a guard, even to flirt a little. On the first visit she managed to find out that the group that Kolia was with was to be transferred to another building. Her girlfriend knew the plan and was doing her best to help. On the next visit, Olga found out which of the soldiers was Kolia's guard.

On the next two visits, flirting with this guard successfully caused the poor soldier to fall almost in love with her. Finally, one day, Kolia appeared with his guard. Olga came near the soldier and started to talk with him while walking down the long corridor. Olga did not give, of course, any sign that she knew the prisoner, and with her flirtation occupied the guard's attention.

Her girlfriend, meanwhile, whispered to Kolia what he had to do. At the dark end of the corridor, just behind the corner, there was a door which led to the back of the prison and then to the forest. Olga accidently-on-purpose bumped on something and fell down. While the soldier helped her up, Kolia vanished. The soldier ran to the door and out, but could not find Kolia. Then he understood the trick, but it was too late. Olga was willing to be arrested, but the soldier happened to have a good heart and told her: "Stay away," ("*smoysia*," wash away) disappear, before what she had done became known. Later, after investigation, it was learned, the poor soldier was shot.

Two weeks later, a peasant girl and a peasant boy were walking in the forest, which was near the border of Poland and Russia. Weary, nervous and exhausted, they were approaching the border. Luckily there were no guards around, and they passed over the Line unnoticed.

The shadow of death was behind them—happiness was waiting in the future of Olga and Kolia.

They were among the few fortunate ones to escape.

Many other youths and soldiers, especially officers who had been in the service of the Tzar, were hunted out. Many of them were tortured by the Reds to make them inform on their friends, and then shot. Others were "buried alive" in empty buildings; they were herded into dead-end corridors, windowless cellars, and closets, and the openings then sealed over with brick, or nailed shut with boards. There were a few places near our house where the stench became so terrible that we walked blocks out of the way to escape the smell of this cruelty.

I remember once seeing an officer that I recognized as a friend of my uncle's carried out of one of these houses with a big nail driven into his forehead. When I got home I could not talk for a long time; I was in a state of shock. Only later, after hysterical crying, could I tell about it.

The next short story (written years after we fled Russia) is also true. I remember the man who was involved in this triangle of human relations. I remember him as being an unhappy individual, although he seemed to get what he wanted. Somehow, I have the feeling that if circumstances had been different, he would still be happily married and living with his wife.

### FROM THE BASEMENT TO THE THIRD FLOOR

They, the neighbors, were all surprised when Peter Zorin became involved with Masha. It was even more of a surprise because his wife was such a lovely woman. But as a few old gossip-wise women remarked: "As the silver-gray begins to shine upon the head, the devil starts monkey business between the ribs."

Nina and Peter Zorin lived in a nice community, adjacent to the Big House, the mansion with a garden in back, where Barinia and her family lived. The yard of the Big House was well kept. On either side of the yard there were a few one-story buildings occupied by the "help" of the "house" and common workers. The big gates of heavy wrought iron faced a tree-lined street. On each side of the gates there were three-story buildings—office workers and clerks rented small apartments or rooms there. It was considered of social importance or standing to live on the second floor—or even better the third floor. So, it was the ambition of many young girls to marry someone who lived above the street floor.

Peter Zorin was a nice, clean-looking fellow, a public notary. Nina, his wife, was romantic, sweet, rather pretty looking, the daughter of a lawyer. She married Peter "for love," somewhat below her station. It was love at first sight. They met in a public garden one Sunday afternoon. A band was playing; the concert created an atmosphere of gaiety. It was spring. Spring returned many times after the snow-filled winters. Peter and Nina lived comfortably—happily. When the seventh spring arrived with melting snow, the gossip-wise old women noticed that Nina was to have a baby, that she was in an "interesting condition."

That spring Masha, who lived in the basement, blossomed. Her body was like "fresh ripe cherries," tempting to look at and taste, for all the men. Her sparkling eyes and loud pleasant laughter was disturbingly, temptingly annoying. Men, seeing her, could not pass her by without noticing her youthful "ripeness."

"Peter Ivanovich, I brought you something to eat."

"Thank you, it is very kind of you Masha."

"And how is Nina Vassilievna? She has been in the hospital a few days now. Hasn't the baby arrived yet?"

"No. She is having a hard time."

Masha, looking with her star bright eyes at her idol, a dream of her ideal of a man. Peter noticing her freshness and readiness to be loved.

The world-wise old gossip women, sitting on the benches in the yard, shake their heads, realize and know more than the people who are about to be involved in the ageless, familiar triangle of the sexes.

The baby is born dead. Nina, advised by the doctor, leaves town to recuperate, somewhere in the country. The natural course of human behavior continues on its path. Peter and Masha give in to the temptation Destiny offers them.

"Peter Ivanovich," asks one of the gossip women, "Why are you looking down on the ground lately? Have you lost something?" Then, after a pause, almost in a whisper, "Could it be your conscience?"

On the benches in the yard, there is much to talk about.

"Did you see him last night, going to the basement?"

"Again?"

"Ya, he traded such a nice wife for a pretty skirt."

One evening Nina returns. Peter is not at home. Kind gossip women—neighbors—relate the latest. On the benches, in the yard, sympathetic whispers:

"Poor dear, she took it hard."

"Ya, but not a word, not a tear."

"Just turned and went upstairs."

Nina felt empty, just the way it was, when they told her about the baby—all empty; the pain and heartache will come later.

The gossip women were all excited:

"Nina Vasilievna is leaving."

"Ya, wonder where she is going?"

"With all that luggage, to her parents, where else would the poor dear go?"

Life's dream becomes a reality, Masha is moving upstairs, to the third floor.

Another true story of everyday life in the courtyard of our household.

## ROMANTIC?

There are many triangles in this world of human relations. Many of these triangles are equilateral, many are not. This triangle in question was very irregular.

He—the husband—was a yard sweeper named Pavel. He had some money, due to a few extra jobs, but told everyone that he had none. She, Sonia—the wife—was a beautiful example of a country flower. She was always smiling and laughing a healthy laugh.

Well, as an old Russian proverb states: "For color and taste there are no comrades."

The outsider, named Gregorie, was a male nurse but with only one leg. It was not known when? why? or what was the reason?—the heart of beauteous, healthy Sonia started to bloom with love for Gregorie, the student. Perhaps it started with pity—who knows? Gradually the husband, Pavel, learned from neighboring children that his wife, Sonia, invited the student Gregorie to dinner and fed him. Fed Gregorie with Pavel's hard-earned supplies of food!

Spring holidays were nearing, the Easter time, and unavoidably the drinking of vodka was reinforced. Many a time Gregorie would go as far as he could up the stairs, then collapse before his door, in the happy slumber of drunkenness. Then, what was hidden secretly inside of him would come up, and in his vodka-fumed sleep he would whisper and groan the name of his generous sweetheart, whom he named "Sosunia." When Gregorie was drinking alone it was safe, but, when one eve, he was drinking in the company of Sonia, it was asking for trouble. One unlucky evening, Sonia and Gregorie drank too much, somehow managed to get to Gregorie's room and there to fall asleep. Pavel, the wronged husband, waited for Sonia in vain. The drunken sleep took possession of his darling Sonia and that "one-legged devil," Gregorie. Pavel knew but did not want to accept it. Finally, in the early dawn of that unfortunate day for the unhappy triangle of human relations, Pavel went to the door where Gregorie lived.

It was the end for the "triangle" relation.

"I will kill her, this daughter of Satan, and I will send that one-legged devil down below to Hell, where he belongs!" stormed the enraged husband.

The listeners of the household added more oil to the flame of anger, adding theatrical flavor to the dramatic situation. While this fermenting was going on and the momentum of the attack was gathering, Sonia managed to escape the room and to hide in the attic.

By the time the door was attacked the "Barrinia," the lady who owned the house, arrived, summoned to prevent the killing. After some talk and persuasion, Pavel, the yard sweeper, consented not to kill anyone.

"I will beat the evil out of her, and that one-legged devil must leave this place immediately," raved the husband.

So, everything comes to pass. Though Sonia swore that she did not love Gregorie anymore, that it was just because she was drunk that she had sinned, Pavel did not trust her anymore. Whenever he went away, he locked her in the house, taking the keys with him. When he was home and Sonia had to go shopping, upon her return, poor Sonia had to knock on the door for a long time and call to be let in.

Neighbors were of different opinions: Some said "Poor Pavel, wronged husband!"

Others thought that unfortunate Gregorie lost his shelter and the one person who was nice to him. And Sonia was secretly admired by some others for living the "full life," having romance and now being punished for it.

"*Alors, c'est la vie,*" thought "Barrinia."

Meanwhile life was continuing. Even during the period of readjustment to the Red government, all the regular, everyday needs had to be met. One of these was the desire to acquire knowledge. Granny, although weak, managed to walk, with my help, the few blocks to a small square, where the semblance of a newspaper was posted daily on a bulletin board. A small crowd was always waiting to read the little bits of news that were allowed to be printed and read by the people. This was the only possible way to know a few of the events of our times, to learn of what was going on.

My need for education was being taken care of quite thoroughly at home by Granny, and the daylight hours were filled with studies. If any of the few friends, left from the past, overstayed their visits and interfered with my studies, Granny would with a charming smile bring attention to a sign near the table where I studied: "Time is valuable—Do not waste it." The visitors would soon depart. Of course it was considered a little unusual, even eccentric, but most people understood that Granny was trying to educate me as fully and as rapidly as possible.

At twilight, when reading became a strain to the eyes, Granny would talk to me in French. Mistakes would be corrected by conjugating the verbs or rearranging the sentences in different tenses. My favorite time was when I could persuade Granny to tell me about the past or narrate the stories of the operas or tell about the different theatrical performances she had seen, especially those of Sarah Bernhardt or Eleonora Duse.

"Necessity is the mother of invention." In one particular case, necessity forced us to adjust the terms of honesty to fit our needs. Even with a clear understanding that stealing was wrong, "stealing" pieces of our own fence in the middle of the night with which to keep warm and cook our meager supper was forgivable, and not considered a sin. So, under cover of darkness during the cold winter, I did manage to rip some boards from the fence at the far end of the garden, bringing them to our room and, with a borrowed hand saw, cutting them into small pieces for our little, iron, pot-bellied stove.

One of the ways to make these difficult years bearable was to try to forget by getting lost in the world of books, fantasy, and imagination. Granny managed to arrange for a continuing supply of books; some of them she read to me, others I read and even memorized.

Reading James Fenimore Cooper, with all the vivid descriptions, resulted in strange behavior on my part. I remember some of Granny's friends asking why I was hanging, obviously uncomfortably, across a chair. The answer—that I was being kidnapped by Indians—was not quite enough to convince them of my sanity. When I climbed "to the top of the mountain," wrapped in Granny's scarf, she would tell them that I was a cloud—this was the result of reading the poem about "The Mountain and The Cloud." The story had touched my heart: One evening a cloud had rested overnight on the top of a lonely mountain, and in the morning when the cloud sailed away, there were tears sparkling at the top.

At other times, Granny would be a captive on her bed, and the rest of the furniture would be piled on my couch, and no one was allowed to walk across the room—it was the sea. That was the period of Anderson's fairy tales. I was the water *russalkol,* a nymph, or the drowning prince at the bottom of Neptune's kingdom. Next materialized my interpretive dances from the *Sadko* and the illustrative mimes of *Schéhérazade.*

It was, I am sure, trying on the nerves of Granny and her few friends, but they were considerate and usually understanding, and I do believe glad for me that I could create a world of my own. I had no friends. Playing outside our rooms was out of the question. The outside world was hostile, cruel, and in ruins; many people were still resentful of the past and those who repre-sented that past, whether or not they had been responsible for that which had been unjust or wrong. So I grew up in my own make-believe kingdom of fantasy. Reality itself was like a bad dream: Learning how to cook, trans-forming curtains into shirts and pieces of carpet into ballet slippers, imagin-ing how a simple dish would taste if it were a banquet served for a special event.

There was once laughter at my expense: Many times I had heard how wonderful sliced oranges tasted in champagne, and when we somehow were enriched by the gift of the first orange I ever had, Granny told me that I could have it. I still remember the bitter taste as I bit into it. Never having seen one before, I thought it was to be eaten as if it were an apple. The manner in which I bit into it and the expression on my face amused everyone.

There was a saying during those days which best illustrates the conditions under which we had to live: "Until five o'clock the coat you are wearing is yours; after five it might be ours." It was spoken, supposedly, by someone who relieved you of your possessions as you were hurrying to the relative safety of your home. These "someones" were what we called *hooligans,* the homeless orphans of the civil war who had to survive however they could, including theft and terrorism. It was a case of those who hadn't anything taking from others who were fortunate enough to own something worth stealing.

During this period, we had to be adaptable, always. I remember how some of the clothing which had belonged to my uncles was cut down to fit me. Summer sandals were created for me out of pieces of wood. In the winter, we wrapped our feet in paper and pulled on a boot-like contraption called *valenki*. The *real* valenki were made of a very heavy feltlike woolen material about a quarter of an inch thick, but during the early 1920s we used any material that was handy.

The dancing shoes which I made were cut from an old curtain—which we were fortunate enough to own—the pattern largely a product of my imagination. We needed our drapes, of course, to keep out the cold drafts, but eventually the hem of this particular drape was sacrificed to make the top of my ballet slippers; a patch of old carpet from the corner of the room or underneath a piece of furniture became the soles. For a Russian-style blouse, I sewed together part of an old sheet, which had been cut up for me by a friendly lady in the neighborhood. After it was sewn together, I embellished it with a cross-stitch of Ukrainian design, applied to the sleeves and neck. To finish it off, a tassel from one of the draperies, and a cord for the belt. This outfit I wore when dancing at the Sunday folk-dance concerts in the park, where a small volunteer orchestra of balalaikas and accordions accompanied local people who gathered to sing and dance.

When newspapers began again to be published occasionally, Granny would read articles of interest to me. The most exciting was waiting and listening for the next episode of disaster to the victims of the "curse" of Tutankhamen of Egypt. The excavations were just being done, the riches uncovered. The unbelievable glory of the past fired my imagination, and kindled a desire to someday be there to see it in Egypt myself. Forty years of dreaming passed before this became a reality, but when I finally visited the Valley of the Kings and walked among the splendor of Karnak, descended and entered the tomb of Tutankhamen, I had the uncanny feeling that I had been there before, as if I were reincarnated; I am afraid, however, that this feeling was due to my Granny and our shared enthusiastic interest many years before.

*1920-1921-1922:*

Granny and I had been allowed only one room for our use; later the two daughters of the former governor of St. Petersburg lived in our house, creating excitement with their activity and talks about the ballet. Their father, Prince Bezabrazoff, had left with the White Army; his wife and daughters

51

found refuge in our house. We were lucky to have these friends occupying some of the rooms. Princess Bezabrazova became Madame Bezabrazoff, the teacher of languages. The daughters, thanks to an education that included ballet lessons, were admitted to the Kiev Opera corps de ballet, and I had the good fortune to be invited to some of the rehearsals. I would later "practice" wherever and whenever I could, imitating the steps I had seen. Finally Granny somehow arranged for me to take some lessons. These lessons were taken sporadically due to the weather and various other factors, such as the availability of transportation for me to and from the studio, class arrangements for special students, and rehearsals for the opera ballet. But I was stricken, as if by magic, by the beauty of it all. After my lessons, I spent hours alone trying to recreate the combinations of steps which I had been shown that day.

My complete infatuation and surrender to the magic spell of the ballet came with my seeing performances of *Rusalka,* the underwater ballet in which water nymphs (suspended by invisible wires) glided in a magic shadowplay. Shortly afterwards I was overcome by the splendor of the productions of *The Humpbacked Horse* and *The Seasons.* All the special effects, the illusions of floating in space, the gorgeous costumes and lush music entranced me, and to this day, half a century later, the memory of these performances still thrills me and remains a part of my life.

The last performance I was scheduled to see in Russia, of the opera *Demon,* was canceled, to my great disappointment. This was during the time of the fighting back and forth between the Reds and the Whites. When we arrived at the square facing the Kiev Opera House (which was a copy of L'Opéra in Paris), there were groups of Red soldiers circling the building. I believe this marked the final take-over of the Communist regime. The Opera remained closed until after we left Russia. My enthusiasm for study and love of the ballet, however, continued and matured through the following years.

The human soul is without limit. The heart is bottomless. No one knows the depth of love. If or when the opportunity to prove it comes along, in surprise one finds how strong and powerful, at times, are the emotions within one's heart. Love offers uncontrollable, immeasurable treasures. Yet is also as un-predictable and changeable as the April wind.

There are individuals who are like ships in the sea at night, like waves in the ocean, like trains on a long journey. They meet for an instant, and may be remembered with longing. And there are others, sad cases, beloved enemies who loved but love no more.

Still, there exist in this world, in which even stones are not lasting, in which even saints and angels do not speak the truth, there exist occasions of devo-tion without limits, tender, everlasting love:

> Some love with the mind—
>> they love sensibly.

> Some love with the heart—
>> they love with passion,
>> with every drop of blood
>> in their body.

> Some, but very few, love with the soul—
>> they loved unbrimmingly and
>> holy.

*Interlude:*
Perhaps due to a lack of experience or to my uncontrolled enthusiasm for new things, beginnings have usually been scenes of disaster for me. I still re-member with considerable embarrassment one of my first public perform-ances in Russia—a total disaster—as was my first American appearance, in New York City's huge Hippodrome many years later.

The "first" in Russia, when I was thirteen or fourteen, was a performance of *Bluebeard.* I was a dancer in a harem. After the actors finished their scene, they sat down on a couch. One of my friends watching from the wings realized that the long narrow carpet in front of the couch would be in my way as I started my dance. I was making the Oriental bow to start my dance (a low reverence, my hands and arms folded in front of me), when, helpfully, she decided to pull the carpet off stage. Beware of helpful fools! I found myself flat on my face. The end of the disappearing carpet, unfortunately, had been under my feet. The music for my dance had begun and although off-stage voices were whispering, "Get up and start your dance," I would not move. Finally, after even the audience had heard my stage whisper, "Close the curtain," it was understood that I was not going to get up. The curtain was swung down, and we started again. This time I danced, and danced well, displaying all the sparkling glamour of my Oriental costume.

In New York years later, at the Hippodrome, according to the wishes of our impresario, Salmaggi, the performance of *Aida* was to be enriched with live camels, semi-nude girls carried on golden platters, and so forth. My family were not ready to see me bare-assed, but that costume—or lack of a costume—was in keeping with the rest of the production. I wore what I was told to wear.

There was in the middle of the ballet a formation that gave credit to a pyramid; the men lifted the girls above their heads, creating a pyramid-like effect. The dancers wore a lot of body make-up, and only those slender strips of costume essential to cover what is not usually seen by the general public (not in those days, anyway). As I was slowly lowering my partner to the floor, her jeweled bra became entangled in the only article I wore which approximated clothing—a towel-like, narrow loin cloth. Underneath was only a posing strap. Fortunately, I handled this loss better than the time the rug was pulled out from under me. Picking the loin cloth off the floor, I wrapped it about my waist, holding it with one hand, and finished the ballet doing the Egyptian movements of the choreography with one arm.

Sundays were my only contact with the "outside world," the only times it was possible for me to be a part of the life of those days in Kiev. On Sundays there was dancing in the park, starting with the *horovod,* folk dances everybody knew. As the balalaikas and accordions and dancers warmed up to what they were doing, it became more competitive. Each of the dancers tried to jump higher than the last, or to do the *presiatka* (kicking the legs from the sitting position) longer and more times, than their fellow-dancers had done.

Just as the art of dance was later respected, and artists honored and even exempted from the military service in the Soviet Union, the love of singing and dancing made the barriers of political differences vanish for a while. These were neutral, non-political occasions, and the warmth and enthusiasm of the people who participated is still very vivid to me to this day—one among a very few pleasant memories from this period of my life.

# 11

*Letters:*

The next part of my narration will not be my own writing. After the death of my father in 1971, I found in his desk letters which he had saved—correspondence with his mother, who was my Granny—and now is the time to take a look into these documents written so long ago.

The letters, still in their original yellowing envelopes, with stamps of the early Soviet mail (1923-25), had been sent to Poland and were then forwarded to America. Rereading them now gives me a strange feeling of remoteness, as if I were reading about someone I knew once—a third person, another person, but certainly *not* me!

I should add here a note regarding my father's whereabouts. After working in Poland as a translator and instructor of physical education, he and Alexandra, like many other Russians, found themselves in Paris, the center of White Russian refugees. French, of course, had been spoken at the Tzar's Court, and the influence of things French had been felt on the upper classes in Russia for generations. Catherine the Great bought all the French artworks she could to grace the Hermitage, and Paris had long been regarded by Russians as a mecca of culture. The French styles of dress, furniture, and cuisine—not to mention that particular style of dancing which began in the French court, ballet—were all imported to Russia over the centuries. So it was, I imagine, quite natural that the White Russians should gather in Paris, having been forced to leave their homeland. My father had a very good singing voice, and Alexandra was a well-known opera singer, so they were soon able to earn their living by performing in Parisian nightclubs and restaurants. With the money they saved from these engagements, they were able to buy their passage to the New World—to the promised land of America.

My grandmother wrote to my father in a postcard which had been sent from Warsaw to Kiev, a distance of a few hundred miles:

   . . . The postcard travels faster, it took only two weeks.

Soon afterwards, she wrote to my father again:

> ... The boy, as you see, would be a great painter [drawings had been enclosed]
> ... it would be so good if it was possible for him to receive instructions from someone
> ... also he likes to sculpt, I will get some clay for him.
>    ... We received the food parcel: 49 pounds of flour, 15 pounds of sugar, 25 pounds of rice, 10 pounds of lard, and 20 cans of condensed milk. But only half of it was for us; the other half was taken by the government for distribution to the other needy.
>    ... I keep the boy under my wing. He could already earn some money selling candy and cigarettes. Many boys of his age sell them on the streets, but I do not want to subject him to this. His health, mental and physical, is more important ... the street boys are so unruly, some of the groups are becoming a nuisance to the older people. *(5/9/1923)*

By this time, Russia had become a land of "no religion." "Show me God," some people demanded, totally rejecting the centuries-old teachings of the Eastern church with all its rich traditions. Religion was said to "cloud the brains of the working class," and any obvious religious articles, such as icons, were frowned upon. Most of the churches were converted into clubs or gathering places for the "masses," or used as warehouses. Some were destroyed, out of vengeance. Only in recent years, as the Soviets have learned the importance of tourist dollars, have some of the old cathedrals with their priceless heritage in paintings, sculpture and architecture been restored and opened as museums.

The following letter shows something of my disregard for doing what was considered proper:

> Orest is very nervous and has constant headaches. I try to toughen him up, but he had grown so much, already he reaches my height . . . He keeps Roman's grave covered with flowers that are in constant bloom. The other day, when he came back from the cemetery, he told me that after he raised up from his knees, after the prayer, the few people who were nearby stared at him in surprise, because he was praying and crossing himself.

The relationship between my grandmother, and her son Boris's second wife—Alexandra Kotchoubey—included a wide range of varied emotions, and a strong sense of duty. Now that the upheaval of revolution had changed many lives and situations, it was time to try to mend the difference. My grandmother wrote to her son Boris:

> ... But Alexandra knows now that I understand, and see where your happiness is.
> ... No one could wish more happiness. . . . No one could wish more happiness than

a mother to her son, so these days I do wish you both complete happiness, and I hope that Alexandra does not hate me anymore. As they say, "from love to hate there is but a step," so maybe from hate to love is not so far?. . . . Nowadays it is most important that you are not alone in your new life, and that you are happy, is all that I care about. . . .

Just to give an idea as to the state of the economy in Russia, and the fantastic currency situation (we were all millionaires), here is an excerpt from a letter which Granny wrote:

. . . We received the five dollars from you through the Red Cross and from Ella [my mother] two pounds . . . The other day we bought a pound of [tea baloney] sausage for 40 million rubles; today it is more expensive—60 million. Our friend Moora finally bought herself a dress for 10 billion rubles; she could afford it because she has now a government job.

Now, about one of my first sorrows, written in August, 1923. I was twelve.

Dearest Papochka . . . you do not have to send greetings to my little kitten, because she is not in this world anymore. We bought smoked fish (we can afford it very seldom). We ate it all, but did give a little to the kitten. I left the bones to enjoy what little was left on them for later on though Granny told me to throw them away. I put them up on a shelf. The little cat jumped on the shelf and before I noticed swallowed a bone. She was sick for two days, then during the night she died. Granny was holding her body and I was caressing her head. I buried her in the garden. I cried for two days, even in my sleep I miss her.

Every morning Granny feels worse, after the night of not moving. I have to help her to sit up. I pull her by the shoulders and the head. After she sits up for a while, I help her to move to a chair, then I comb and braid her hair before putting it up for her. When she finally manages to go out she is sick for two days afterwards and a moan even escapes her when she has to move or raise her arms. . . .

I remember waking up at night a few times and seeing poor Granny walking back and forth in the room, holding her elbows with her hand, trying to massage them to ease the pain—she had severe attacks of rheumatism/arthritis.

. . . Before and after my birthday we received from Mother ten dollars, and also this amount from you, too . . . Granny and I went to the marketplace with 400 million rubles and spent it all. For Granny we bought some medicine, for me a few pieces of colored paper for my "wings" for my dance, a folder for drawing and painting, a watermelon, two pounds of pears and plums to treat our guests, and even some flowers for 50 million. Then we hired an *izvoschika* [carriage], which was rather cheap, for round trip to the cemetery for 50 million, and went to the monastery for the Duchess where the Pokrovskoe cemetery is, to visit the grave of Roman. I planted white daisies before; now we added some white asters and left a few more flowers. The rest of the flowers Granny told me to take home, she told me I could use some for my dancing with singing which I improvised. When we came back, Mme. Raevskaya arrived with a gift of salted cucumbers, so we had a feast with all that we had bought, then went to the apartment in the other building where there was still a piano. Mme. Raevskaya sang "The Nightingale" and a romance of Chopin; it was very beautiful. Then a few of us went back to our room and had the cocoa my godfather Andrey had sent to us from Zagreb, and the fruit. . . . Then I danced and tried to sing like a nightingale. . . . Your loving son. P.S. just now a letter arrived from you from Cherbourg. . . . When Granny was reading it tears were running down her cheeks . . . She kept saying: "Now Boris is leaving for America. . . . So far, far away . . . to the end of the world."

Granny wrote to Boris soon afterwards:

. . . My dearest son, remember the old Russian saying: "Measure seven times before cutting the material once" to avoid a mistake . . . America is so far away . . . let us wait awhile . . . perhaps we will be able to find Gleb . . . somewhere . . . it may change our plans and help you in taking care of us. . . . Orest has outgrown all his clothes; before winter comes I must manage somehow to buy him long pants. . . . The money Ella sent will help; instead of buying him a birthday present I will spend the money for his clothes.

. . . Do not hurry . . . there is still time . . . though there are dark clouds hanging over us . . . let's wait . . . your career is taking a turn for the best . . . in our thoughts we are together . . . love conquers the distance . . . your worry and concerns about us warms my heart . . . after your last letter I felt so secure . . . and started dreaming that someday my oldest son will shelter his mother and son, and we will be warm and secure together. . . .

With this letter there was a P.S. from me:

Dear and beloved father, Granny bought me some colors for my birthday for painting, and I color all the postcards you send us . . . our dear Papochka—Borichka, we love you more and more . . . embarrassing you, your loving son, Orest. Kiev—1923.

My Granny wrote:

. . . We are preparing for the winter . . . the boy himself installed the little wrought-iron stove in the middle of the room, then managed to put up the second window [a frame of glass to make protection from the cold more efficient], but we will not use the wood as yet for heating, except while cooking; there is still some wood left from last winter. Orest and I decided to wait awhile, until it gets really cold, about the first of November, before we start using wood to heat our room. . . .

. . . Your money order arrived . . . the joy of having money to buy the necessary things is combined with the happy feeling that it also means our Boris is well and safe . . . whenever your letter finally arrives, I kiss it with joy before opening and reading it. . . .

The other night I woke up crying; it was after a dream that was almost like reality. I heard a voice saying: "Ah the youth will never return" . . . then repeated with more sadness. I recognized the voice—it was Roman lamenting that he left us so young without accomplishing the things he wanted to do, and that he was separated from us now, reaching out from somewhere, tormented with sadness. . . . Burning sorrow pressed heavily on my heart, but then thoughts of you lightened my burden, because you are now my lighter air that brings life to my existence.

. . . We can wait, do not hurry, and it will be so expensive, our leaving here. . . . Let's wait until you get settled, then we will see how everything will turn out. If you were alone, I would have made all possible efforts, would worry and long to hurry to be with you to help take care of you, but you do have your wife with you, and it gives me a sense of security about you. Evidently she is your friend, too, because now you write, not "I" but "we"; it means a lot. You think that the boy is too "mystic," what he writes once in awhile—he is very sensitive, but seldom expresses his inner thoughts. Usually he is very bright and sociable, and his voice sings out, he talks louder than others, very often I have to quiet him down. He is never bored—if he gets tired of one thing, he starts with something else. Something that does give me trouble—his stubbornness, which he inherited from his German grandfather. One good thing is that it is not an angry stubbornness. He takes care of me with touching tenderness, and with childish adaptiveness became used to my sadness.

. . . You can understand and appreciate it, remembering your own childhood, how you felt and could almost foretell trouble, the trouble I tried to hide from you all, your father's illness, how I tried to keep your childhood bright and free of care. Remember how we went for the holidays to the Crimea, to greet the spring . . . upon return the arrival of the terrible, tragic telegram . . . seeing my face, guessing the message, you said: "Mamochka, I see you have great sorrow; know and remember I am your oldest son. I will be your friend and will help you all I can, always." All this I still remember; you were twelve years old. We lived then through difficult times . . . now it is almost the same, with Orest, and as before, I try to shield him from the sorrows of life . . . and though we live during difficult times, he has the "joy-of-life" in his outlook. He too offers me a shoulder to lean on. I bless you, my dear son, on your new journey and wish with all my heart success in your new life. Take care of your health, do not drink too much, especially because of your flying, save your energy whenever possible, sleep enough. There is no more responsible work or profession I think, than being an aviator. Once more I plead with you do not take chances for our sake; we will manage. God bless you. . . . with deep love . . . your Mama.

. . . reading newspapers, I foresee in the future dark clouds from different directions; it is possible that there will be even harder times. It is possible that the correspondence with the outside world will be stopped again. . . . Orest has headache-neurosis and the doctor says that his heart does not keep up with his fast growing up, also anemia. Orest will be a big man. If his heart gives him more trouble, I will take him to another doctor, a specialist. But our doctor says that the journey across the ocean will be quite safe. . . . The headaches are not as constant as they used to be. I had to adjust his studies not to overtire him. I had to buy him a sweater; he came home the other day crying because he was so cold. The material is so bad now days. I bought him socks; in two days there were holes in the toes. At the present food is easier to get than clothes or other things. I do worry though, that you sacrifice your own living to help us, but without your help, before, we almost perished.

. . . It is sad that I cannot arrange some lessons for Orest, like music. He is so inclined to the arts, but at the present there is no possibility of developing his talents. The other day a neighbor of ours stopped by the window, asking Orest to sing again; she had not heard him sing lately. Orest answered that he has no more voice. He has constant headaches—the doctor says there is not enough nourishment; Orest is growing so fast. When he is hungry there is only bread and butter to satisfy his hunger, but it is not enough.

The other day two musicians, well dressed, evidently from the Intelligencia, stopped by the window. One was playing the violin, the other the viola. Orest and I listened for quite awhile; they seemed to realize we were enjoying their playing. We gave them two eggs; as they left they took off their hats and bowed to us. The boy was almost crying, he reacted so much to their melodies. His favorite game of Kingdom has about 100 figures and many animals. The game consists of dances, singing, and travel, a kind of moving tableau. From painted figures, the game shifts to him personally, when he starts to move and dance himself. A piece of furniture, like a coat hanger, becomes in his imagination a different thing—a horse, a camel, an elephant, or a window, balcony, or at times a high rock of a mountainside. . . . what a son you have!

. . . At the present, Princess [now Mme.] Bezabrazova, with her two daughters, is living in the room next to ours. Her daughters study and perform often; they try to persuade us that Orest should study ballet and should make it his career. . . .

You asked me about some people; there were so many, many deaths. . . . In the apartment where we lived for almost a year, the whole family died of TB. The last one, daughter Lussia, died while we were there. The people who lived underneath us, the wife and her two sons, died of typhoid. In another apartment all five persons died. In our whole compound of apartments there is not one that does not have someone dead during the last two years. . . .

We now have a crusade to save the right to visit the cemetery. They allow only a few hours a week for a visit to the family graves. [Russian graves were usually the size of a coffin. The raised part, about two feet high, was used to plant flowers, the sides covered with ivy. It was the custom to plant flowers and change them as the bloom fades. In the winter pine branches were placed to cover the empty earth. At the head of the grave was a wooden cross, and if possible, a *lampadochka*, or candle was lit before an icon of a saint.] If the graves are not kept up, they even them with the ground; the area is then used for a vegetable patch.

Orestik made friends with two women, who visit the cemetery often. They are trying to get more people to keep the graves up, to plant flowers. The church of the Pokrovskoys cemetery has been changed into a club. We do hope to keep the grave of Roman undisturbed. . . .

. . . The other day the husband of the opera singer Makarov came to visit us. Their daughter Irina studied with me for a few years. He is earning his living now by creating toys, especially dolls. He offered to take Orest into apprenticeship, will pay him a little money too. Though it would be good for the boy to know some trade, I refused to sell Orest's time. I treasure time most of all; his education, for the future, is of the most importance. Every free hour we use up to pour the knowledge into his head. Though, poor boy, he has headaches often because of malnutrition. He memorizes anything with such difficulty, what he learned yesterday he forgets today. Still the most difficult period is passed. He sometimes complains as if "something like liquid moves about in the head," and he gets dizzy. Now thanks to your parcels and help our nourishment is improving and our health.

Then my postscript:

Papochka, we are very sad worrying about you, we have not heard from you for a very long while. I had a cold and did not go out for a long time. I was coughing very hard, especially at night. It was so cold in our room that some of my plants lost their leaves. Because of high humidity, Granny has been feeling very bad. Please write soon. Your tenderly remembering you, loving son, Orest. Cold is worse then hunger, Granny and I decided.

Dear Son, I do not now have a special religion—but I do have a very strong faith in the Afterlife, somewhere. . . .

Some of our friends come to see me, ask for advice or to share their doubts about the present life. They are surprised or admire my willpower or as they call my wisdom. I do believe that I have the sensitivity to understand their problems. Life taught me to have a bird's eye view of situations, which helps me to think more clearly about the present problems, give some advice. But I myself have difficulty fighting my weakened condition, only willpower gives me strength, for the sake of the poor boy, to keep going. I remember what utter despair Orest experienced when I was arrested. He cannot be left alone now. Until it is decided where we will be, after it will be possible to leave Russia—an idea comes to my mind, perhaps in Rumania, even in a village, we could stay until the visa permission comes through.

My mother, Ella, was trying to get permission to get Granny and me to Scotland, but without results. She could not even arrange for her own mother to visit her from Germany. Granny wrote to my father:

. . . When Orest heard there could be a possibility for just him to leave, he cried all

61

evening and told me that if he was sent away from me, he would run away from one of the stations and return to Kiev, just to be in the same city with me, even if just to see me or worry about me from a distance. Last night I tried calmly and carefully to bring up the subject that it might be possible for him to travel to you, his father, because the future here is so uncertain. Orest did not cry, but become moody, did not talk with me for the rest of the day. Before going to bed he said he will jump from the train and come back. . . .

. . . The Makarovs invited Orest for the Christmas tree celebration. It took them a long time to light the tree, it was rather late when they served the tea and sweets. Orest started to worry about me. Mr. Makarov, to calm him, came over to me to ask if he could stay later, but before he came back to his family, Orest had already bolted, and came running back to me. I persuaded the boy to go back to the party, to have the sweets, and Mr. Makarov promised to walk him home in the dark.

. . . He is very nervous and has headaches, and often in the night has *koshmars* [nightmares] about death and losing me. I have to wake him up and calm him down.

. . . The other night, during his evening prayer, I overheard his asking Roman, begging him to let his Granny stay with him.
It is not a healthy attachment, to such a degree, but no wonder, after all he has lived through. Hope everything will solve itself somehow in the future. . . .

These days we are better and we can wait and survive, especially now that we have the future to look forward to—to be with you. We dream about safety, to be with now the only son.

Your loving mother.

P.S. I was deeply touched by your last letter. I trust our mutual dream to be together will materialize.

Here is one of my own letters, added to one of Granny's; it is strange to see my own childish writing of fifty years ago.

. . . My dear, very much loved Papochka,
I want to narrate to you about my small mishap. A while back my godfather Andrey sent me a dollar in his letter. I, for some reason, did not want to part with it, and asked Granny not to sell it, but to keep it for a rainy day. The other day something was bothering me in my throat; I kept coughing. By the evening it was really hurting. Granny looked into my throat and saw a bone from a herring deep in my throat. We had had it for lunch. Though it was late, I begged our doctor to admit me, to take care of me. He took the bone out; I gave him the dollar from Godfather. That is how the saved dollar came in handy. My studies suffer a lot from all the troubles we have. My memory is not so good and my eyes are rather weak. Granny says it is because I am growing up so fast and we do not eat the right food. Granny is trying to give me a good education and develop my knowledge—she believes I will be an artist. I do love to sing, dance, and to invent all kinds of fantasies in my games. I am under Granny's

wing; I do not spend any time with any one, because the boys outdoors are so rude. They play games of killing, espionage, fighting all the time. When I go out it is only for some errands, but I am never bored at home.

Granny has a sign above our table: "Do not waste time with unnecessary conversation—Time is very valuable." She arranged the sign because so many people come by, they disturb my studying and distract me. Also Granny is so weak she gets tired easily. In the morning Granny is so stiff with her arthritis I have to help her to dress, to pull on her stockings. I am worried she is so much worse; she should have some treatment, but what can we do? We both worry about you too. You took up so many jobs to help us—it is not good for your health.

Your very loving son, Orest.

. . . The boy has a nice voice, he often sings in the evening. Suddenly there is applause outside the window, and someone asks him to continue his songs. Then he is doing something else now; he started to sculpt. He made a few things for our friends. Someone who understands sculpting told me he should study it. . . .

. . . Once more I am thinking: What a riddle is this world we live in, and our very existence. Our high ideals, attempts at reaching beyond our power. How insignificant is our ability to achieve our goal. How in our lives we have minutes of joy, but endless sorrow and suffering. The more conscious we are of our existence, the harder it is to live.

. . . Now about Orest. The last few months he is growing terribly fast, he is becoming tall. His voice begins to change. He is noisy, very emotional. On his upper lip there is a shadow, hardly noticeable, while down below, at the bottom of his stomach, there is a lot of fuzz, but still lower it is still blissfully calm . . . in his soul and otherwise he is childishly pure.

His sexual instinct is not awake yet. So far there have been no doubts or questions about male or female problems. He is completely calm and undisturbed. But I am thinking and getting ready to make clear what is necessary at the first questioning. He is still a dreamer. The only question that came up, he asked me if girls are born with the seed of the baby inside of them. He was satisfied with my sketchy answer: It happens only in the grown-up women.

. . . He is now preoccupied and very interested in the ballet and character dancing with one of our friends who is studying and performing. But we have a real problem with that because he started to have pains in his heart, so we had to cancel the lessons for awhile, because he has an enlarged heart and neurosis. Now it is worry again about his heart.

. . . I am troubled that we added the responsibility and an extra load on your back with all the help you are sending us, while you yourself are just beginning to get established, doing such a dangerous profession as flying. If we were there with you, Orest could have been of some help earning money somehow, but here at the present all I can do is preserve him for the future. Our friends call him "conserved youth" because he is so protected and is the last example of the past. . . .

. . . I have good news—Orest is feeling better. His heart troubles him seldom now days. Evidently the dangerous period is over. The headaches are occurring not as often. The doctor says that as soon as he will be stronger, now that we have better food, all will be well.

Then a postscript from me:

Unmeasurably beloved Papa,
    Lately I am painting and coloring postcards and am busy sculpturing. Dearest Father, if you only knew how much we love you you would be very happy. I am embracing you very strongly and wish you a very happy birthday.
Your loving son Orest. [1925]

    . . . The day of great importance is approaching—your birthday. The seventh of February, at 3:15 pm you were born. We both were very weak, but happiness was in my heart. Now your mother is very weak again, from life and troubles, but you are healthy and strong. I congratulate you on your birthday and wish you happiness. A memory of you comes to my mind—when you were just a little boy playing with your toys, how you would drop them and suddenly run to me with extended little arms saying: Mamochka how wonderful, I am so happy! Now you took up the most wonderful though brave and dangerous profession. . . . I want you to know that I am thinking and praying for you. . . .
Your loving Mother.

    . . . You said in the last letter: Damn money troubles—you are right, but it is so, almost always, during the lifetime. No money creates problems and disturbs peace of mind. I was hoping that my sons will live comfortably, but instead such years of hardship and suffering we all had to live through. But wealth is not the most important, it is not the greatest happiness, though for happiness money is helpful. Poverty is not the worse unhappiness. . . .

    . . . I do hope for your sake our wish to be together will come true, but just the wish is not enough—destiny, that is, circumstances, possibilities will decide that. . . .

    . . . About Orest, there is a serious worry, in any case he must be eventually with his father. In a year's time, that is the limit for when he must leave here. During this year I will do my utmost to do everything possible to teach him more, to prepare him for the inevitable separation and departure from here. . . .

    . . . At the present I am not sure I will be able to travel—or to last the whole journey. Therefore I started, slowly, to mention in conversation, as if in passing, the thoughts and doubts about the future and how inevitable are the separations with the loved ones . . . as lives move on.

    . . . With the death of Roman I lost the joy of life, but now I do have heartfelt warmth from you and I am resigned to whatever happens in the future for us all.
    . . . Now about the boy—to our great relief, so-called enemies moved away to

some other place, to another street. They were constantly pestering him whenever he was outdoors or walking. But there are still a few nasty youths left about. There are a few who come from down the street to play in our yard. One of them threw a stone at our neighbor as she was doing something outside on the veranda. There is one of them outstandingly nasty. Orest walks past them not looking at any of them, but the nasty one still annoys him.

The other day Orest went to the yard where the running water in which to wash the cooking pots and pans is. As he was washing I was at the window. This pest started teasing Orest, first with words, then by throwing the ball at him, then he came closer and struck him on the head. Orest screamed, "Leave me alone—I do not want to get involved with you," but the fellow hit him again. It was too much for Orest—he jumped up, started belting the pest with both fists. I just stood there by the window, trembling, I could not help the poor boy. But Orest beat up the nasty fellow so well that he ran away. Since then they leave Orest alone.

There was another incident last year, when Orest was driven to fighting; he tore the fellow's jacket to pieces. I had to pay for the jacket later, to finish the unpleasant issue.


. . . The other day I admired as Orest was dancing, inventing movements. He was specially dressed in some homemade costume made from some left-over pieces of material. He was interpreting clouds, wind, waves. He moved beautifully. He will be handsome; his chest and shoulders are wide, his calfs are shapely and strong, the arms, though thin, move with grace. He has good eyes and when interested in something they shine like stars. Though he is so grownup in size, he is still like a child. Small things can make him happy. He is different from other youths; people notice him with interest. One touching trait he has—he loves to sleep the way you used to sleep, putting his right arm back, lying on the right side. It makes me remember my oldest son, when he was a youth, you, his father.

. . . Remember I wrote you that soon I must clarify, explain the facts of life to the boy. He is still in a completely blessed innocent state of mind. But the time is here to have a talk, because of a happening the other day. We have a neighbor with a little bitch, Mimosa, a little white almost-a-poodle, mixed with a spitz. Orest came in with a preoccupied expression, told me that the neighbor asked him to chase away the boyfriends from Mimosa because she does not want her to have any puppies. Mimosa has a lot of company (?) lately. Orest asked why she thinks Mimosa will have puppies. My answer was, on the spur of the moment, how do I know what she thinks? I do believe it is the time to have that talk.

. . . So the other evening, when Orest was preparing tea, I told him to take a chair and sit by me, and that this time we will talk about the human flesh. I prepared a long program, but had to shorten it. I started it with the flowers, the female and male pollination. Then I asked him if he ever wondered how the animals multiplied, how living things repeated themselves—he said he did not think about it. I told him that it was the law of nature; that it was different with people. With humans it is different because they do not follow animal instinct, but have an emotional and personal attraction. When two people want to have a home, family, when they fall in love, the feelings are deep and intellectual, and they get involved emotionally and physically attracted. . . . Then I was going to continue with further explanations of possible complications, results of rash and just-the-flesh attraction, I saw the boy was silent, his

65

head was down. I asked, "Are you listening?" "Yes," he said, "but Granny dear, do not be angry, my eyes are closing and the tea is getting cold; thank you for telling me." Before going to bed that night, when he came to say good night—*spokoynoy nochii*—he told me, "Thank you for telling me all that, but I am glad it is before we go to bed, because while I sleep I will forget all those complicated, frightening things."

Now the frightening unknown became knowledge which will gradually settle in his mind, in his own way. He never talks about it and seems indifferent to anything concerning it. He is still in his dream world of fantasies. His defects are normal—laziness, stubbornness, but he has an obvious talent for the arts. Without a doubt in my mind, he will be an artist in some way. It is sad that now there is no possibility to develop it with proper lessons. Yesterday, again, he dressed up in some fantastic creations of his and told me, "Now I will perform the Dance of Life." Then he improvised some beautiful movements. . . .

. . . Dearest Son, you, "At last it is not long to wait, be patient; before long we will be together." Now it is easier to be patient with this knowledge.

All these letters I am translating were numbered, so that Granny and Father would know if any were lost, would know what information was missing.

. . . The loss of the letter is sad for me because when a letter is missing it is like not having a visit with you. (1925)

. . . My dear son—I am so happy that you are finally working in your specialty, doing what you love—flying. Life is so short, I am glad you are not wasting it by doing something else just to earn money. I do hope you are choosing your friends and companions. Please do not be angry that I give you motherly advice, but I want just to add, just in case, some ideas of precaution, not to have too many people about you who tire you and who would take too much of your time. I do worry about you not having enough rest or sleep. In your profession rest is so important. I know you are a wonderful instructor—I am happy you have flying pupils now; it must be satisfying, besides earning extra money. Not only because you are my son, but you do deserve the best with your knowledge, experience, and personality.

My mind is filled with thoughts; the human brain with its thoughts is the spirit, the soul of our existence. There is nothing equal to it in our physical experience. The past is kept and preserved in our memory. The question of our existence, our being in this life, is still an unsolved mystery. Our thoughts, emotions, memories live in this mysterious soul of ours.

The whole world is fighting, the earth is covered with blood and tears, and at the end becomes a cemetery. Here is the tragic riddle, if our life here is not a prelude to a different, better existence somewhere, then this life of ours is a sad unfortunate mistake. Though religion gives hope for the future life and the promise of the future being together for the loving souls, if it is really true, then the *koshmar* [nightmare] of separation would vanish. Otherwise the present life becomes nothing. Still, we two, my son, even at this distance, in spirit feel togetherness . . . by all that is holy, take care of yourself. . . .

. . . Now that your profession is being a pilot—in any plane, in any weather—I fear for you, worry so much more. A saying of Pascal comes to mind about the frailty of the human being: *"Il ne faut pas que l'univers entier s'arme pour l'ecraser—il suffit une qoutte d'eau pour le tuer."* [It is not necessary for the entire universe to arm itself to destroy itself—one drop of water is sufficient to kill it. ] But I do believe and hope in the other saying that creativity and inspiration will conquer—*"et même peut-être la mort."* I know you have these extra qualities to conquer all the troubles, and you will succeed because you are one of the few who are meant to be the master of his destiny.

I bless you, my only son, with love, Mother.

. . . Do you remember, there is an old doctor—Professor Yanovsky, a wonderful doctor and human being. He is very religious. About two years ago he had a fantastically wonderful experience, about which he does not talk, but a few persons know about it. We learned from another doctor who works with him.

One evening Dr. Yanovsky was tired after his visits. He asked his servant not to let in any more patients. Suddenly a young, pale girl came in, and pleaded with him to visit her mother. He wrote down the address; it was on the other side of Kiev. He took the carriage, arrived at the address, walked up the steps, rang the bell. The door was opened by an aged, pale, sick-looking woman. "Someone here called a doctor." "No," was the answer. But the address and the name were right. The old woman said that no one could have called, because her daughter had died an hour ago. When the doctor entered the room, he recognized the girl who had begged him to visit her mother. Dr. Yanovsky helped with the funeral and the mother. . . .

# 12

*Parcels:*
Some time during the year of 1923, a "breakthrough" happened. Thanks to President Hoover and helpful Americans—and later other countries as well—the "starving Russians" began getting supplies. Mail, letters, still did not reach us. First we received a food parcel from America; this was followed

by a package from England; then another from Yugoslavia. All three packages came to us within three months of one another. Each had a little message inside which said that the senders hoped the package would reach us. The package from America had been sent by Father, who wrote saying that this was the last time he would try to reach us, because for years there had been no reply. The second was from Mother, with a note saying that once more she was trying to find out if we were still alive. The third was from Andrey, my godfather in Yugoslavia, with the similar message. When we received these parcels, Granny had to sign for them, and could add one or two sentences to the receipt, which would be returned to the sender. Many weeks later, we finally received letters telling us how happy they were that we were still alive and that they had been about to lose hope of ever hearing from us again. It had been six years since we had had any news of one another. The people "outside" revolution-torn Russia thought us dead just as we had not had any idea where or who among our friends and family had survived in the outside world.

The first parcel contained essentials: sugar, coconut butter, white stuff in a few one-pound cans, rice, cocoa, several pounds of flour. After we signed the receipt, the package had to be divided. One half was supposedly given to another needy family, but most of the time it found its way on to the local black market to be sold or traded for high prices. I remember our looking at the "luxury" gifts of sugar and cocoa and not being sure what to keep and what to exchange for more basic foods or clothing. I do remember the first taste of cocoa mixed with sugar as I ate it by the spoonful. And I will never forget the entirely novel and wonderful taste of cooked rice combined with condensed milk. Each mouthful was an experience, a revelation; for two years we had been starving. Thanks to the American Relief Association we had been saved, and President Hoover became the savior of many a Russian. Due to political reasons the first break-through of supplies stopped; but later the help became regular, thank God.

The weeks preceding our final departure from Russia (now the Union of Soviet Socialist Republics), were full of uncertainty, hope, sadness, and even a little joy. We had to decide what to take with us, and what had to be left behind. Although there was hardly anything left from "the good old days," there were still a few possessions, perhaps worthless in the marketplace but full of sentimental value.

We experienced sudden fear when some of our friends—a young couple—who were lucky enough to receive permission to leave were arrested and "sent away" somewhere. In our minds we knew that they were being punished for their desire to escape. They were young, however, but

Granny and I were useless—only an old lady and her grandson. Granny kept me out of sight whenever official papers were to be obtained, referring to me as her "little" grandson. She was sure that if they saw me in person— saw how grown up I had become—they would prevent me from leaving.

# 13

1927-1928:

The final preparations—all the goodbyes and parting with our few dear possessions—are not very clear in my memory. Only a few instances remain clear; others are remembered as if in a haze-covered valley just before sunrise or after sunset.

The faces of a few friends, some with sad smiles, others with tears of hope for us, have remained in my memory. On the railway station platform as our train was pulling out, I remember a touching but ineffective gesture of extended arms, as if trying to hold back the movement of the train, a few seconds longer—running after the departing train to say *dosvidania* once more, or *prostchaii,* farewell.

As the train gathered speed, and dear old Kiev was rushing out of our lives, tears made it impossible for me to see. I remember Granny's voice: "Why are you crying? You only knew suffering there." While the dusk was beginning to cover the landscape, Granny was looking for the last time at the photographs of her sons in their uniforms, before tearing them up and throwing the pieces out of the window into the darkening space outside.

By the time we reached the border, near Brest-Litovsk, and were about to enter Poland, my nerves were shattered. I was crying bitterly, thinking that my Granny was heartless to behave as she was—dry-eyed, half lying in her seat without any visible emotional reaction. Only later did I realize how difficult it was for her to say goodby and at the same time to face an unknown future. Her desire was to be strong, long enough to accompany me to my father, her son, in faraway America.

Later in Cartagena, Colombia, South America, I heard Granny tell my father that her doctor in Russia had, just before we left, given her only six months to live.

The sunrays shining—
                  smiles of the past.
The shadows of passing clouds—
                      sorrows of the past.
The fog is all around—
                  doubts of the past.
Moonlight . . . silver glow—
                    dreams and wishes of the past.

# PART
# TWO

---

that came true

"Papa" Fokine, my teacher, 1932-1942.

Above: Maestro and Madame Fokine at Lewisohn Stadium, New York City. Left: Paul Haakon, Winona Bimboni, Patricia Bowman and Orest at Lewisohn Stadium. Below left: Paul and Patsy in *Les Sylphides*. Below middle: Orest and Virginia in *Schéhérazade*. Below right: Orest.

Opposite page:
Patricia Bowman and Paul Haakon in *Le Spectre de la Rose*.
Photos by Winona Bimboni.

Patricia Bowman in *Persian Angel* by Fokine. Photos by Maurice Seymour.

Opposite page:
Paul Haakon and Patricia Bowman in Schéhérazade.

Left: Mikhail Mordkin in Moscow.
Below left: Adolph Bolm, 1940.
Below: Mikhail Mordkin in New
York City.

Opposite page:
Paul Haakon, 1945.

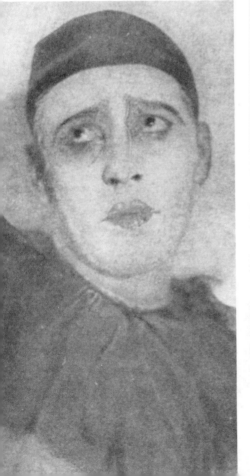

Above: Agnes deMille. Left: Bronsilava Nijinskaya, 1940.

Opposite page:
Above left: Angel Cansino, 1935. Painting by J. M. Lopez Mezquita. Above right: Helen Viola. Left: Mathilde Kschessinskaya, my teacher until 1963. Right: Edward Caton.

Left: Muriel Bentley and Rosa Feldman in *Boris Godunoff* at the Metropolitan Opera. Below: Ballet Theatre at Lewisohn Stadium. Below middle row: My car and Anton Dolin. Bottom: On the town at Times Square with Maria Karnilova, David Nillo, Nora Koreff and Donald Saddler.

Above: Lucia Chase. Above right: Richard Pleasant and Dolin, 1939-1940. Middle right: Jerome Robbins, David Nillo, Don Saddler and John Kriza. Lower right: John Kriza. Lower far right: Orest. Below: Orest, John Kriza and Jerome Robbins.

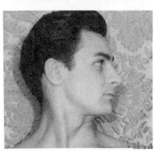

Left: Connecticut Symphony performance, 1940. Below: Orest in *Le Spectre de la Rose.* Below left: *After the Ball,* 1941. Bottom: Orest in Mexico, 1942.

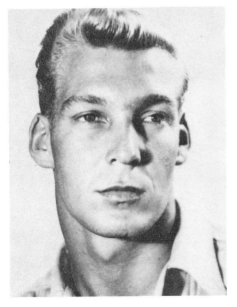

Top left: Orest in Air Corps, 1943. Above:
Bronner Shaul in the Southwest Pacific, 1943.
Above right: Bill Lord in the Air Corps. Right:
"Trade Wind" Robert Leigh in Hawaii, 1943.

Left: Paul Haakon. Photo by Maurice Seymour. Below: Paul with our plane, 1941-1942.

Opposite page:
Left: *Tartar Dance.* Photo by Empire Photographers. Center: *Gypsy Zamba.* Right: *Tango.* Photo by Grace Voss. Below left: *Persian Warrior.* Below right: *Hungarian Czardas.* Photo by Grace Voss.

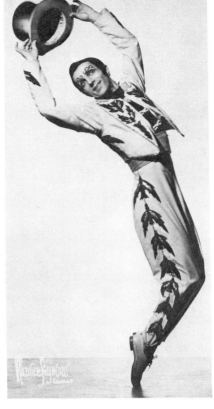

Above: Eugenia Delarova in *Gaite Parisienne*.
Right: Leonide Massine in *Gaite Parisienne*.
Below: Maria Tallchief in *Swan Lake*. Below
right: Alexandra Danilova and Frederic
Franklin in *Giselle*.

Opposite page:
Left: Photo in Original Ballet Russe souvenir
program. Right: *Farruca*. Below left: *Cape
Dance*. Below right: *Le Spectre de la Rose*.

Top: Ballet Theatre production of *Peter and the Wolf* at Center Theatre, 1940. Photo by André Kertész. Above: *Graduation Ball,* Original Ballet Russe, at the Metropolitan Opera.

Opposite page / Above left: Lucia Chase in *Carnival.* Photo by Oggiano. Above right: Patricia Bowman. Photo by Maurice Seymour. Left: Kirsten Valbor, 1940. Left: Don Saddler, 1940.

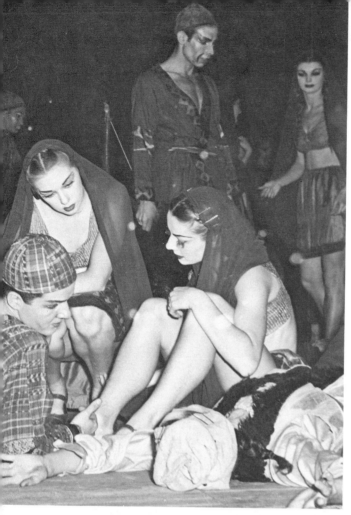

Left: *Prince Igor*. Below: Original Ballet Russe opening night at the Metropolitan Opera. Photo by Fred Fehl.

Opposite page: Above: Oleg Tupin and Kenneth MacKenzie in Lichine's *Cain and Abel*. Photo by Thomas J. Farkas. Below: *Eternal Struggle* by Igor Schwezoff. Photo by Ronny Jacques Studio.

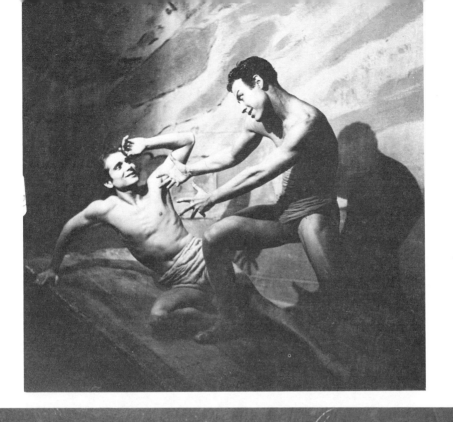

Left: *Les Presages* by Leonide Massine. Below: *Graduation Ball* by David Lichine. Photo by Fred Fehl. Bottom: Alicia Markova and Anton Dolin in *Giselle.* Photo by Fred Fehl.

Opposite page:
Above left: Leon Danielian, 1941. Above right: Dusty Warrell, 1941. Photo by Romaine. Left: Roman Jasinsky and Moussia Larkin. Photo by Maurice Seymour. Right: Natalie Clare and Oleg Tupin. Photo by Constantine.

Above left: Rosella Hightower in *Black Swan*.
Photo by Maurice Seymour. Above: Olga
Morosova in *Firebird*. Photo by Earle Forbes.
Left: Tatiana Stepanova in *Schéhérazade*. Photo
by Maurice Seymour. Below: Lorand Andahazy
in *Schéhérazade*.

Top left: Alicia Markova and Anton Dolin.
Top right: Lubov Tchernicheva in *Francesca da Rimini*. Above: Tamara Gregorieva. Right: Paul Petroff and Nana Gollner in *Swan Lake*. Photos by Maurice Seymour.

Top left: Michael Panaeff. Photo by Maurice Seymour. Top right: André Eglevsky. Photo by Constantine. Above left: Oleg Tupin. Photo by Maurice Seymour. Above right: George Zoritch.

Opposite page / Above left: Tamara Toumanova. Photo by Mme. S. Georges. Above right: Nana Gollner. Left: Irina Baronova. Right: Mia Slavenska.

99

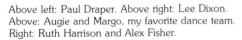

Above left: Paul Draper. Above right: Lee Dixon.
Above: Augie and Margo, my favorite dance team.
Right: Ruth Harrison and Alex Fisher.

Opposite page:
Above left: Ruth St. Denis. Above right: Doris
Humphrey. Far left: Ruth Page. Left: Katharine
Dunham.

Above left: Anna Ricarda. Photo by Bruno of Hollywood. Above: Tashamira. Photo by Teddy Piaz. Left: Kathryn Sergava. Photo courtesy of Warner Bros. Pictures. Below: Julia Barashkova at the Metropolitan Opera.

Above: Saul Bolasni, painter of my portrait.
Photo by Marcus Blechman. Above right:
Eleanore Boylen. Photo by Marcus Blechman.
Right: Winona Bimboni. Photo by
Conner-Geddes. Below: Patricia Bowman.
Photo by Murray Korman.

Above: Herbert Bliss. Right: Jimmy Jamieson.
Below: Vonn Irkust-Hamilton. Photo by
Maurice Seymour. Below right: Freddie
Franklin.

Opposite page:
Top left: Ralph Clanton. Top right: Steve
Brody. Photo by Robert McAfee. Lower left:
Jimmy Lamphier. Photo by Marcus Blechman.
Lower right: Bruce Davis.

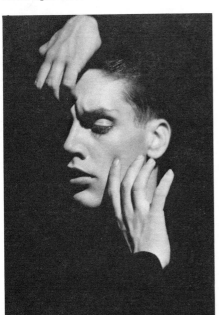

Top left: José Limón. Top right: Pauline Koner. Left: Maria Karnilova. Photo by Alfredo Valente. Above: Bruce King. Photo by Jack Mitchell.

Above: Alexandra Danilova. Photo by
Maurice Seymour. Right: Nana Gollner.
Below: Lubov Tchernicheva. Below right:
Yvette Chaviré. Photo by Seeberger.

Top: "Dusty," Mildred, Kenneth, on the train. Above left: "Miss Ruth" St. Denis. Above: "Natie" and Oleg in Rio de Janeiro. Left: Katia and Oleg, Ballet Russe in Montreal, 1941.

Opposite page:
Bernard Pfriem, an artist friend in Mexico.

# 14

The ride on the train began in daylight, and when we arrived at the Polish border several hours later, it was early evening. The trip had been a gloomy one, but now we had to wait even longer, until night came, when we could cross the border in train cars without lights on under the cover of darkness. The reason for the secrecy was that very few people were being "officially" allowed out of the U.S.S.R. at that time. Once safely across the Polish border, we entered a very different world—outside the Iron Curtain. I was stunned by the difference, by my impressions of life in the free world; but I hardly remember our first days there. There was the picturesque beauty of Warsaw, the busy streets full of life, and the well-dressed people, the white wing-like head-pieces of the Catholic nuns' habits bobbing in the busy crowd of pedestrians.

After Warsaw we were off to Berlin, where friends of my godfather Andrey arranged to meet us. It was not hard for them to spot us. Granny wore a lovely hat which dated back to the days before the Revolution but was still becoming, while I must have been a sad sight in my disoriented outfit, the only one we could obtain in Russia. The friends presented us with a bouquet of beautiful flowers; there were warm embraces, and friendly smiles, and we were taken to a *gemütlich* German home, where a feast had been prepared for us.

It was like a dream. Later that evening, Rudi, the youngest member of the family, took me for a sight-seeing trip of Berlin. This was for me an even more dream-like experience. In those days Berlin was full of life and music; bright lights illuminated the trees and houses. There were crowds of people, a great number of whom were dressed up, laughing, happy, and gay; it all made me dizzy with wonder, realizing what the world could be like. Among the many things which impressed me was the washing of streets morning and evening—and the spotlessness of it all which resulted.

Then, almost before we knew what was happening, we were off to Paris.

Paris in the spring—many songs have been sung, many words written, but none can really understand it unless they have themselves experienced this unique combination of events.

And I imagine that it must have been especially moving for refugees arriving from the hardships of post-revolutionary Russia to be in Paris, in April, in May. It was the first time since leaving Kiev that I felt at home; the harsh emptiness of having left Russia was beginning to be less painful.

And ever since then, whenever I arrive in Paris I feel that I am home. Even now, as I write this, after living in America for so many years and traveling all over the world, after admiring so many places and falling in love with the beauties of so many other cities and enchanting spots, I still love only Paris, where I have that feeling of restful calmness, of being home at last.

I remember Paris—the City of Light—in the rain, when fountains and lit-up monuments are reflected in gleaming pavements, creating a double image, disturbed at times by the spray of a passing car or a taxi. And I remember how enthralled I was that first spring with the beauty of the chestnut trees, even before I heard the song "Chestnuts in Blossom." Thank God, "The Last Time I Saw Paris" has been repeated many times in my life, always with gratitude that I am able to return—even if just for a visit—again to love and enjoy, to become a part of it.

Paris, majestic in its beauty, eternal but ever-changing, is not like New York, where the old respected buildings are torn down and replaced with tall, impersonal, modern, concrete, dark-glass coffins.

Paris respects its traditions, its grandeur, its glories, its signs of age stamped by the weather on its facades and the faces of its statues. London has left its old, blackened exteriors out of a sense of tradition, but London's is a silent respect for the old rather than a living pride in the past. Paris, be it young or old, embraces every day with the warm smile, from the grandeur of the Royal Palace to the paper-covered multi-colored *pensions* . . . through shady tree-lined avenues, the flower-covered Tuileries or Luxembourg Gardens, to the busy, populated, outdoor cafes, where people go to relax, to watch the passing cavalcade of humanity flowing past the chain of bistros and brasseries.

From that very first time in 1927 to my most recent trip in 1977, my love for Paris is constant—it is a half-century-old romance. Familiarity, memories of studying ballet there, the first impressions after leaving Russia, my ability to speak French, the loveliness and rich beauty of the Seine, the constant surprises as you walk, unexpected views, old statues, or hidden little gardens, tree-shaded squares where hospitable benches invite one to rest. All this makes me feel at home. The long vistas of the boulevards and wide spaces of the squares, like the Place de la Concorde, make it possible to see the sky and clouds, and to admire the stars at night (the street lighting is subdued, and most of the time shaded with trees). These are some of the reasons I love Paris.

But there was little time for enjoyment that first spring and summer. There was a shadow covering all our activities: The search for Gleb. The joy of liberation, the fact that we were free and on our way to a bright future—it was as if we had not yet fully realized these things. Constant anxiety, telephone calls, interviews with people who claimed to have known or seen Gleb occupied all our energy and thoughts. It was nerve-racking. The cruelty of some people, just to get a free meal or make some money out of the misery of others was a shock to us. Gradually we began to recognize the lies which some individuals told us.

After many weeks, someone who had really known and had been with Gleb finally solved the problem of uncertainty. Though it was a sad relief, it was better to know the truth—Gleb was dead.

I managed during this period to take some lessons from the wonderful teacher Olga Preobrajenskaya, a former prima ballerina of the Maryinsky Theatre; when I knew her, she was a little woman who inspired devotion, fear, admiration. She instilled in us a desire to do well, to love dancing always. Those who ever studied with her were very fortunate indeed.

Preobrajenskaya's ballet studio was located in an old building not far from the Place Pigalle. At this "Studio Walker," Preobrajenskaya was the great teacher, and pupils from everywhere came for lessons, especially the "new" generation of Russian émigrés. The petite Preobrajenskaya had an air of grandness and authority that made up for her small stature. I really did not realize the richness of her teaching until years later, when I returned to Paris as a dancer. My first lessons there are now hazy, somewhat confused with all the other impressions of my first stay in Paris. But when I returned a few years later, everything looked familiar—or so I thought—even if it did seem a bit older. The same pianist was present on both occasions, and Madame's method was to engage in a slight consultation about which melody would be best suited to play while she demonstrated a ballet combination. Later, when I visited the studio of another famous figure from Russian ballet, Mathilde Kchessinskaya, the difference in style and method between the two former ballerinas was immediately felt. Surrounding Kchessinskaya was the glamour of the past, like an aroma; this was especially true if you were fortunate enough to be invited to her home, Villa Molitor, where she even had managed to staff the house with servants from Russia who had left with her—faithful souls from the Old Days.

There were other ties with the Old Days during that sojourn to Paris, among them, the church. But this was not as pleasant as I had expected. In Russia, going to church had been a sincere religious act, not a social event. The memory of entering Russia's eleventh-century Sophia Cathedral, or any of numerous other cathedrals with which I became familiar, was that of a self-effacing experience. One had the feeling of being lost in the immensity of dark spaces, of tall columns, of being lost in shadows, and the secret presence of a divine spirit. The exterior of shining domes and multicolored decorations atop onion-shaped domes with gold crosses was a dramatic contrast with the darkness and simplicity of the interior.

Therefore, when Granny and I first visited a Russian church in Paris, we were shocked by the social activity going on. True, it was a natural place for refugees to meet, to find out the latest news about one another or to get information about available jobs or places to stay. But what unpleasantly surprised me was that the church had also become a place to gossip or compare worldly status in a whisper which could be heard above the prayers intoned by the priests or deacons at the altar.

By this time Father had settled in America and had become the chief test pilot for the Igor Sikorsky Corporation, based in Stratford, Connecticut. However, there was no way for Granny and me to enter the United States since the immigration quota had been filled; there would be a long wait. Because the quota for Russian émigrés had not been filled in Colombia, Father, through some connections, took a leave of absence from Sikorsky and accepted a job with Standard Oil as a pilot on their "life line" flights up the Magdalena River to Bogota. The headquarters were in Cartagena. At long last, after eleven years of separation, we received our visas to join my father, Granny's son.

Before we sailed, I was outfitted in Paris with my first "grown-up" clothes. All of a sudden I was a presentable young man; the chameleon-like change in my appearance was echoed in a similar change in personality—I felt like a grown-up, and my behavior, even my walk, took on a certain assurance.

This transformation resulted in a situation which we found amusing afterwards, but at that particular time was somewhat embarrassing. "Ladies of the evening," as is well known, are very abundant in Paris, and at that time the Gare du Nord, where our hotel was located, was a center of their activity. Seeing me walking by, they smiled; I smiled back, and they followed, offering "companionship." The first time this happened, I actually did not know what kind of companionship they were offering, or why they were so friendly. When I told Granny about it, she enlightened me, and told me to just keep walking. One night one of these *cocottes* took me by the elbow, and was most persuasive that I follow her. After my insistant *no*, and my telling her to leave me alone or I would call the *gendarme*, she gave me such a kick in my behind with her knee that I almost fell down.

Soon enough I learned to evade them, and if they were too close I told them I had no money: *"Je n'ai pas d'argent."* This statement usually cooled their attempts to follow me.

And now the time had arrived to say goodby to Paris—we were again to be uprooted. We had to get ready for the ocean journey. My ballet lessons and sight-seeing excursions were replaced with visits to ticket agencies; visas and money problems had to be settled.

Finally we were on the Paris-Bordeaux train. It was interesting to travel on an old-fashioned train with compartments that opened individually to the outside. We had to be rescued upon our arrival at the port of departure, because we did not know how to open the doors.

The first ocean-going port I had seen—the limitless expanse of water, countless ships of many nations, sizes and shapes—left an unforgettable impression. Then the three-funneled *Ile de France* welcomed us inside, with her grand red-velvet cabins and public rooms. But the first night we were rudely invaded by bedbugs. With profuse apologies, our cabins were changed, and after that we had only a few stragglers to keep us occasionally awake.

The journey south to the tropical islands of the Caribbean—with the magic landscape of St. Michelle and a long stop-over in Haiti—was like being in a dream. The loading and unloading was done manually in those days; the conveyor belt was unknown in those parts. I was completely hypnotized by the ebony backs of the porters shining in the sun, the colorful bandanas and full dresses of the women carrying baskets of fruit on top of their heads, the palm trees swaying in the breeze and the smells of the harbor, fragrant with spices and bags of coffee. Watching all of this from the top deck, I did not even go down for our afternoon meal, for fear of missing one moment of this fascinating, moving tableau.

# 15

*1927-1928:*

Finally, under the scorching, breathless glare of the midday sun, we docked at the historic port of Cartagena. The previous night we had arrived outside the harbor. The sparkling lights of the city, especially those from the line of villas along the shore, had been like diamonds—jewels shining through the tropical air on the black velvet sea. Father told us later that he had watched the lights of the anchored ships all night, wondering which would be ours.

Long ago, in the days of pirates, there had been a direct access to the harbor, but in order to secure their riches, the pirates filled in the entrance to the harbor. Rafael Sabatini used this harbor, with its castle-topped mountain, as the setting for his novel *Captain Blood.* We were told later that while the villas for the Standard Oil Company employees were being built on the filled land of the Boca Grande, countless skeletons and treasures had been found from pirate days.

As the ships neared the dock, through tears of excitement and emotion I recognized my father from the photographs I had seen; we had been separated eleven years, since I was six. He could not possibly recognize me now, except for the fact that I was standing with Granny. He could only guess that I was his son.

It was a tender, calm meeting. Before we knew it, we were off in the open car to the villa where, with a forced, cool politeness, we were welcomed by Alexandra, Father's wife. I was to call her *not* Alexandra Akimovna, *certainly* not Mother, but by the name Shoura, a Russian nickname for Alexandra.

This visit was the first time I experienced such luxury. Granny and I had adjacent rooms with a lovely bath; a large veranda-porch, covered with tropical ivy, faced the Caribbean. The sea was just across the road. A line of reefs made a barrier a short ways out, and the waves, breaking on coral and stone, serenaded us with sounds of a continuously restless sea. During bad weather or strong sea breeze, our windows and porch would be covered with spray and flecks of dancing foam.

I do not remember exactly the first adjustments to our new lives. It was all so new and different. Father was away a great deal, flying Standard Oil employees up the Magdalena River to the capital, Bogota. My studies started again; with a kind offer and the suggestion from Father, Shoura started teaching me English, and Granny continued her lessons in literature, French, and mathematics.

Cartagena had a very colorful and proud social circle of Castilian Hidalgo Spanish people; only a few "natives" were accepted. Even there, away from all the political and social influences, the caste system was strongly in evidence. In later years, I was glad to hear, the "caste habit" had almost disappeared.

Somehow, to be at the Sergievsky's—the pilot's villa—was like being on special, neutral ground. Our social soirees were a mixture of all nationalities, all kinds of personalities. I remember Father's mechanic, a small Scotch-Irish fellow, telling a risqué joke to a French countess; a Hungarian engineer courting a Spanish heiress, under the watchful eyes of a *duenna*, who sat fanning herself quickly; a handsome Viennese being wooed by a young American secretary.

Among the company of a few Russians and other Europeans, Alexandra found several people who could sing. This resulted in concerts, at which selections from operas were sung. Father was called upon to perform. During their stay in Paris before sailing to America, Alexandra and Father used to sing in the Russian cabaret/night clubs to earn extra money, and the singing at musical evenings in Russia had proven very useful. Now, to bring some cultural life and artistic interest to the rather provincial existence of the calm, lazy days and nights in Cartagena, musical evenings and events were welcome.

I was called upon to help with the make-shift scenery and costumes. There was a great deal to do and worry about, especially with Father, who was never one to enjoy dressing up in "silly" opera outfits. I remember many times having to use all my persuasive abilities to make Father change costumes. This was especially difficult when he had to sing two roles in the same opera, which he did in *Rigoletto* and *Traviata*. Father's voice had a good range. He could sing a love duet as Alfredo with Violetta, then break Violetta's heart in the next scene as Germont, the father. He sang the father, Rigoletto, with Gilda in one scene, and in the next was the amorous Duke. I remember holding up the curtain while making Father change his trousers on stage before letting him sing a different character. He occasionally had trouble remembering the lyrics, so at times I had to arrange prompt cards on the back of a chair somewhere on the stage, with the words to be sung, just in case.

Father and his wife became familiar characters in Cartagena, Father because he was a well-known test pilot working for an American oil company, and Alexandra because she was a well-known opera singer and gracious hostess who loved to give parties and entertain at musical soirees. When Father drove through the city streets or suburbs, police would catch up to him, after some pursuit, and beg him to remember that he was not in the air, but on the ground in the city of slow traffic and siesta-loving people. Somehow they were too polite to give him a traffic violation ticket.

# 16

*1928:*
Our household was very colorful, to say the least; our *hacienda* was practically a menagerie. At that time servants were paid very little; there were even servants for the servants. It was understood that the cook was to have help in the kitchen; she did not wash dishes, nor did she set the table. The cleaning girl was only responsible for the "front rooms." There was a cook for the "help," and another girl to do the laundry.

It was stylish at that time to have matching shoes and handbags of snake skin, so Father used to fly an assortment of snakes in from the jungle country, including several species of boa. These creatures were stored in a lightly built wire net structure in the back lot, and a few times Father had to be called to shoot a large snake which had managed to work its way partially out of the cage. Other big room-like cages were filled with an assortment of large monkeys and parrots of different shapes and colors. The smaller monkeys and lovely parakeets had the run of the house. Alexandra had two favorite monkeys named Mashka and Petka; although they were definitely of tropical origin, their names somehow fit them very well. The lovely fawn-deer called Bambi was a graceful creature, lovely to look at, but he misbehaved, becoming involved in mischievous pranks with Mashka. When no one was about, Mashka and Bambi would sneak into Alexandra's bedroom. In imitation I suppose of Madame at her vanity table, Mashka would soon be covered with lipstick and powder. She would then get into the dress closet and proceed to throw silk dresses down to Bambi, who would chew them up, pretending to be a goat. Mashka and Petka would often visit the villas in the next block where our friends lived. There were many calls for us to come to get them because they were hiding somewhere after doing some damage.

Our big porch was covered with ivy and climbing flowers, providing a home for the parakeets. I found out that if you cut part of the feathers from one wing of the birds they could not fly away. Some of them took over the inside of the house, each member of the family choosing a favorite. Granny's favorite, Cinderella, all in water-colored blues and jade greens, would follow her everywhere, and at the table Cinderella would be the first to taste whatever was on the plates. *Razbushaka* (troublemaker) was dark green with blue, and was also everywhere. As a result, he had a bad accident with a slamming door, and lost one of his legs. He looked a little like a pirate, limping as he rushed about with his feathers always in disorder. The smallest of the love birds was appropriately named Mionionne: She seldom left her favorite perch near Granny, on one of the many plants in the room. All together, there were about a dozen birds free about the house and in the vines surrounding the porch. In the early morning there was no way one could relax until some food was offered to our feathered colony.

For a brief visit we had an alligator in a big tub and a baby panther, but frightened screams from the monkey Mashka and bouncing retreats of Bambi the deer cut their stay short—they were given away.

The sight of natives passing from the village down the road, with their custom of bleeding animals before killing them for the market, eventually would result in my becoming a vegetarian. The poor animals were punched with a sharp, fork-like stick; although I am glad to know the method has been abolished, the memory is still very vivid.

The almost tropical climate in Cartagena made things very different for Granny and me, and our health dramatically improved. Things were done for us with tender care. I carried two buckets of sea water at a time to be warmed up to make a salt-water bath for dear Granny. This treatment, the sunny climate, and the doctor's care worked a miracle. Granny felt better and began to feel new life coming into her frail body. I had a whole drugstore of all kinds of medicines and helpful supplements to take with each meal and in between. My teeth, though large, were terribly lacking in calcium, my blood was too thin, and my entire system was undernourished; that was the reason for my headaches. The doctors were trying to help me catch up with all the many essential nutrients that my system had for so long been denied in my growing-up years in Russia.

The main reason that my father was in South America had been accomplished, now that Granny and I were safely established. The next step was to arrange for me to enter some "official place of education" and for Father to return to the States to continue his work with the Sikorsky Aviation Corporation, testing new models of improved planes, and also getting permission for us finally to join him in his home in Stratford, Connecticut. But Father had to remain in South America to train the pilot who would replace him on the trips. It was a very tricky job to fly in such variable weather, with its sudden tropical storms, and different stops at very different altitudes. The new pilot also had to be taught in detail the many stops en route up the river, some of them very out-of-the-way places.

Jealousy, again, started to complicate Granny's life and mine. Alexandra could not share Boris's love and affection, especially with his mother and son by a previous marriage. So, when Father was away, Alexandra became a different person. Now there was no longer any "free time" to instruct me in English. Even though she knew that Granny could not eat fish in oil and without lemon, invariably the dish on the dinner table would be swimming in oil, and there would be no lemon available, even though lemons grew on the trees outside the dining room window. Granny and I were too proud to make an issue of it, and we did not want to disturb Father when he was home, tired from his flights. But he found out about Alexandra's resentment of us from other people, with the result that we were supplied with our own "native" cook, who fixed us what we wanted, how we wanted it.

One day we received a letter from my mother, who was now living in Edinburgh, Scotland. It created excitement in interesting ways. I was filled with joy at the prospect of seeing my mother; there was genuine gladness on Granny's part, because Mother would be able to come to see me. She had won, she wrote, the Irish Sweepstakes, which, though small, enabled her to afford the journey to South America. A different emotion gripped Alexandra. She tried to persuade the police and local immigration authorities to prohibit Ella, my mother, from getting off the ship, on the grounds that she was coming to ruin the marriage! All these emotional disturbances created even more tension and suspense around my mother's arrival. She had always, for some reason, been secretive about her life; we still wrote to her as Mrs. Sergievsky.

As the day of the arrival approached, Father found out that the ship she was sailing on was to dock in Barranquilla, a port quite a distance away. He arranged to use the plane to meet her, and Father and I flew to Barranquilla. Upon our arrival we could see, even from the air, that the ship was not there. After landing, we found out that the ship had come early that morning and had already left. So we started to search the hotels. Finally, in the third hotel, we found that there were some passengers from the ship, but not Sergievsky, only a Mrs. Hogg and her daughter. We decided to ask the lady if Mother had been on the same ship.

As we were walking through the lobby of the hotel, I a little ahead of Father, I heard an exclamation: "Boris!" Then, my father, "Ella!" As I turned, I saw a girl with blond hair about eleven staring at me, and then at Father, who was embracing a lady. Almost simultaneously, Father said, "This is Orest," and Ella, my mother, said, "This is my daughter Colette." It was like a scene from a movie, very dramatic, almost too theatrical for real life.

Just before the arrival of my mother, it had finally been decided, after some consideration of my joining the Catholic school in Cartagena, that I would go to the Panama Canal Zone. Through some connection, because of working for the Standard Oil Company, Father had received permission for me to study there for a while.

It was just as well; the tension in our family was not very pleasant. Since Mother and Colette had to stay somewhere else, the family's remaining together was something of a problem.

# 17

We sailed for Panama. Mother and Colette stayed a week with us there before sailing back to Scotland. While Granny was finding out how, where, and when I could begin my "formal" education, lessons at home continued. I was trying to learn English—while everyone around me spoke Spanish, Russian, or French. At last, a multi-lingual entrance examination was to take place. I was to be tested with the help of two people: A mathematics teacher, who was a Russian translator living in the Canal Zone, and a very understanding English teacher who spoke French.

Since I had had no "formal" education up to this point, there was the additional problem of deciding which year of school I should enter. After another consultation which included another teacher, the decision was made to put me in the freshman class, primarily because of my lack of command of the English language. In other subjects I was placed on a sophomore or junior level. To this day I still have trouble spelling in English, probably because I missed the usually rigorous training in spelling which most people get in grade school.

In the Canal Zone High School I was fortunate to study under a most fascinating woman, Martha Emmons, who helped me tremendously. She was not only a sensitive human being, but a born teacher, as well, capable of inspiring real interest in her students. She recreated the past with the vividness of the present, bringing to life events and people of the days gone by.

I had a hard time with my English—but so did my English teachers. It was very difficult to grade my writing; I would sometimes get two marks. I would often get D for sentence structure, and A or B for the subject matter and development of ideas in my compositions. A few times a "wish" was added to the marks—wishing that I would learn to put the horses in front of the carriage, not the other way around.

I was very fortunate to be in the Canal Zone High School because the teachers there were especially good. Due to the location of the school in a section inhabited by Americans, the best teachers were hired; it was a showcase school designed to demonstrate to Panamanians and to South Americans the American way of teaching. Most of the teachers had a background of college teaching before having been signed to instruct in the Canal Zone.

In 1929, Granny's wish, which had also been one of my dreams, was realized: Piano lessons were arranged for me. Perhaps it was part of an unspoken desire to bring the past into the present; but when I was very young, the love of music had provided a constant background for our lives in Russia, due at least in part to Uncle Gleb's influence. So now, far away in the Canal Zone, Granny wanted to give me the chance to enrich and enjoy my life with music.

At first, we obtained permission for me to use an old upright piano in a nearby Boy Scout camp for practice in the afternoons, when the camp was not in use. So my lessons started, and every day I spent two or three hours practicing in the heat of the afternoon. Months later, when my progress was sufficiently good, Granny arranged to buy an old piano from one of the Canal Zone employees who was being recalled to the United States. We also received permission from our landlady to have the piano on our porch, since there was no room in the house in which we were staying. (Through Father's connections with the Standard Oil Company, permission had been given for us to stay inside the Zone itself, where only government employees had the right to live. We were also allowed to buy essentials and food in the government commissary, a department store of American supplies.)

The hacienda-like high school was built on a small hill at the end of a lovely street lined with royal palms and hibiscus. The windows of the building were facing the canal where the ships from the Pacific were entering the first set of locks, or the ships from the Atlantic were leaving, after their journey through the locks. I often marveled at the arrangement of lifting and lowering ships through different levels of water. The Atlantic side of the Canal was the Caribbean, with its port of Colon, while we were staying on the Pacific side at Balboa. Many times, while in school, I was pleasantly distracted from my studies by a fantastic moving tableau: A vision of a ship or a streamer slowly moving among the trees and houses of the Zone. The flags of different nations fluttered in the wind and took my mind off studying, and my imagination helped me to sail away to other lands, temporarily satisfying to some small degree a growing desire to travel, to see the world—at my own leisurely pace. I would not be able to travel at my pace for many years to come.

One of the most memorable events during the two years of our stay in the Zone was our unexpected, forced, but dream-like visit to Tobago Island. One weekend we had decided to take a boatride to an island, the loveliness of which everyone had been talking about. It was a paradise, just what one dreams about—or sees in movies. Granny and I were so enchanted that we did not realize how far or how long we had strolled, and it took so long to return to the pier that the boat which brought us over had already left. Using a lot of pantomime and the little Spanish we knew, Granny and I discovered that there would be no transportation for two days! Again, with the same limited means of communication, we succeeded in getting a room for our stay, until the boat returned to take us back to the Panamanian mainland.

Tobago, a little Pacific island about an hour's sail from Panama, was a miniature Hawaii. On it were cultivated the most fragrant and most delicious golden pineapples I have ever tasted. The beauty of the island was untouched, unspoiled as yet by the ever-destroying influence of our so-called civilization.

The evening of our arrival, as if by special request, we were lucky to witness a local pageant. It was some kind of native ceremonial masquerade dance that must have originated in pagan times. Drums and other primitive instruments were used to create a strange accompaniment for dancers dressed in strange costumes decorated with straw and feathers. Years later I used the memory of their movements and mood for one of my concert dances.

Granny and I were a bit wistful as we left the island; we knew that we would never again witness anything so naive and picturesque.

Although most of the Panamanian natives were rather poor, the Carnival just before the beginning of Lent is resplendent in the richness and imagination of costumes and floats. For months everyone saves money and devotes countless free hours to creating his colorful costume, many of which sparkled with rhinestones and sequins. I created a costume inspired by the Arabian *A Thousand and One Nights*. The happy results of my efforts was that I was chosen to sit atop one of the floats and to receive the admiration and applause of the crowds as the procession moved down the main street during the last night of festivities.

For the second year of our stay in the Canal Zone, I prepared a different costume for each day of the Carnival, but to my tearful disappointment I was not to enjoy the pleasure of wearing them. I contracted a bad case of mumps. I remember how I felt, listening to the revelry, the music and songs mixed with laughter. My heart broke: In my youthful innocence I thought I would never be the same. Granny, in her wisdom, consoled me by saying that there would be other opportunities to wear my costumes and that life had many disappointments in the future for me which were greater than this event.

My memory of the stay in the Canal Zone is rather dim, although it was a time full of sun, flowers, and hot days. There were few eventful "happenings" which made any lasting impressions. All the days were filled with study, piano practice, going to the store to buy food, or taking a taxi to the Panama City market for our supply of fruit, such as pineapples, mangoes, and bananas. On one such occasion, Granny and I set out to buy some rum for a party. It was still Prohibition in the Zone, and we had to "smuggle" the liquor back in under the seat of our taxi on the ride home. On one side of the border was Panama City and on the other, the Canal Zone; although the ride was just a few blocks, Granny whispered to me, half jokingly: "Imagine me, an old lady, and you, a young student, arrested for smuggling liquor!"

On the weekends we often attended the movie in the employee's theater, where I fell under the spell of Greta Garbo. Her charismatic personality became my ideal, and my admiration has lasted a lifetime. Years later, 200 photographs of Garbo decorated the walls of my studio in Connecticut, and I still have 500 photos in various albums in which I preserve the image of that great lady. There is one photo, my favorite, which still hangs in my room.

During the three-year stay in the tropical climate of South America and Panama, I missed the snow and cold climate, with its aroma of pine trees, the colorful change of leaves in the autumn, and the tender greens of early spring. But the beauty of the hibiscus flowers, the graceful swaying of palm trees, the drama of tropical sunsets and the sudden deluge of tropical rains almost made up for the change of seasons that was missing from our lives. I remember trying to find a tree to take the place of the traditional pine or fir tree for Christmas decoration, but my search was a failure. The tree I finally decided to use wilted as soon as I finished decorating it.

Before I realized it, permission was granted for us to enter the United States. Again Granny and I were uprooted and had to get ready to travel north to the Promised Land.

# 18

Father had made all the arrangements for our trip to America. I do not remember any emotional goodbyes or sad partings from the Canal Zone; our stay had been too short and I had been too busy learning and studying to make any close ties. There were a few friends from the high school with whom I continued to correspond. One of them, Vincent Reynolds, who played trombone in the orchestra, had been very nice to me and used to invite me to his house. In later years, he visited me in Stratford on his visits to the States. Another friend, Jack Chase, also visited me in the States, and years later married my dance partner, Dorothy Hall, a soloist with the Fokine Ballet.

My memory of the journey north is bright with the excitement of seeing the Statue of Liberty through tears of emotion, and I can still feel the beating of my heart, worrying that we would have to stay on Ellis Island a long time. We had heard so many stories of long days of processing and waiting—but our worries were unfounded. Even before we neared the dock, Granny and I were paged, and one of the steamer's officers came to get us. We were met in the main lounge of the ship by an immigration official and a special officer from the ship's company who had a permit for us to by-pass the visit to Ellis Island. Thanks to Father's position as an aviator, and his connections, and because he had paid the security money necessary for our entrance into the United States, we were permitted to disembark without the usual delay and formalities.

We drove through New York City and I remember one of the first things that attracted my attention. Later, I asked my father about it: "Why is everyone running about? Why are they in such a hurry?" The skyscrapers amazed me, but I had expected them because I had seen them on the postcards that Father had sent to us when we were still in Russia. Another thing amazed me and amused our friends when later on I asked about it: "Who is turning on and off all those lights? They must get very tired!" I actually thought that someone was sitting somewhere near the electric neon lights, pulling the strings, manually controlling their blinking and twinkling. I especially remember being impressed by the lights of Broadway, the Latin Quarter marquee, and the huge lighted sign advertising Rudy Vallee. Before we knew it, we were speeding through New York to the west, then north up Riverside Drive on our way to Stratford, Connecticut.

Stratford in 1931 was a sleepy, lovely, residential community. There was, however, a great deal of activity and noise in the area where the Igor Sikorsky Aviation Corporation was building and testing newly developed airplanes. The community of engineers and workers—mostly made up of emigrated Russians—and their families added a new touch of color to the calm gray of the everyday life. The Russian church, with its Easter celebration services, the charity concerts with artists from New York, gypsy songs, and visits by famous personalities and nobility all involved the local people and brought a new vitality to the community.

Granny and I arrived on California Street in Stratford and were settled on the first floor of a three-story house. The second floor was occupied by Father and his wife, Alexandra. The third floor was for guests.

At first, everything was politeness: Our days and evenings were filled with parties in our honor, at which we met members of the Russian colony and a few American friends. But an undercurrent of something that was not quite right started to be felt as the days went by. I was busy adjusting and going to interviews at the Stratford High School, where I was being transferred from Balboa High in the Canal Zone. I was finally admitted into the junior year, to continue my formal education.

Among my new acquaintances I was lucky to have met the Comers family, in which all six sisters were gifted and charming and most helpful to me in my love of dancing. Irene, the eldest, had a ballet school; Dorothy helped me with lessons to improve my knowledge of American ways; the youngest, Virginia, was studying in New York with the great master of dance, Michel Fokine. I had heard of Maestro Fokine for years, and now I had actually met someone who studied with him! I could hardly believe my good fortune. Finally I was going to be able to study with professionals, and the years which were to follow would be happy ones of traveling back and forth to New York with Virginia to study—and finally to perform in Fokine's ballets.

So, among all these activities and new discoveries, my life became very busy. It took months for me to realize that the Sergievsky family was on the verge of another emotional upheaval.

Father was busy with testing newly developed seaplanes. Alexandra, who sang professionally, was involved with concerts, many parties, and guests from New York City. I was adjusting to the new high school, and the more demanding schedule of studies. Before I realized it, Granny and I were on "our own" with separate household problems—the maid, cook, and cleaning woman were suddenly too busy "upstairs" to help Granny and me. I began cooking the way I had in Russia—just for Granny and me.

*1932:*

One wonderful addition to my life at this time was Zara, my dog, a police Alsatian, with silver-fox coloring and orchid-colored ears. She was a beauty and very smart. Years later, a charming friend of ours, Mme. Maria Kurenko, used to say, "Zara can understand everything; she is like a human. The only thing she cannot do is speak."

Among my social activities were the duties to participate in some way or other in affairs arranged by the Russian church in Stratford. A few times a year a concert was given for the benefit of the church, for the fund to build a real "Russian-looking" structure.

In the beginning, services had been held in a house which had been converted into a church. Our priest was the wonderfully sincere, selfless Father Antonuk. Matushka, his wife, was full of life—a vivacious, talented singer who enjoyed all the duties of being a priest's wife, and of giving all her effort and time to the community.

The year I arrived they were blessed with a daughter, Olga, and I was asked to be one of the godfathers.

Whenever there was a concert, or *vecherinka* (an evening of song and dance), I took part in the entertainment, along with the local talent of Stratford. Matushka usually sang since she had a wonderful voice. I would arrange a moving tableau, such as "Persian Market" or "Song of India." Once Tania Sikorsky, the daughter of the inventor Igor, and I danced together in the gypsy dances "Dark Eyes" and "Two Guitars" as a floor-show, while the audience sat around at tables consuming Russian food and drinking tea with the ever-popular *pirojki.*

One of these social events I will never forget, because it involved me in three different ways. It was to be for me the highlight of many seasons to come. The Grand Duchess Marie and her escorts Prince and Princess Tchavchavadze were to be our guests. Count Tolstoy, son of the great author, was to be there as well. Granny coached me on how to address the

Grand Duchess, but when the time came to say all the proper titles address-
ing her, I fumbled terribly. The Duchess helped me out by telling me to skip
the titles, to just say hello and to kiss her hand. At the reception later, I was
the "page-boy," standing next to her and holding the bouquet of flowers
that had been presented to her. It was hot and I was thirsty, so I drank a few
drinks, one following the other in rapid succession, and proceeded to pass
out. The drinks were "orange blossoms" (vodka, orange juice, egg whites,
and sugar). Ever since that occasion, I have had an aversion to that drink.

Later, I did not do much better with another guest, Prince Tchavchavadze, though for years my "accident" remained a family joke. During
their stay in our house, Prince Tchavchavadze used the bathroom next to
my room. My dog, Zara, had her own brown soap to fight fleas. To my horror, I discovered that I had forgotten to exchange the dog's soap for regular
soap after I washed Zara one afternoon. Embarrassed and worried, I told
Granny that the Prince had used the dog's flea soap. Prince Tchavchavadze
remarked with a twinkle in his eye at dinner that evening that he would no
longer have to worry about having fleas. Later that night I was amazed again
by how human and regular royalty can be. The Grand Duchess Marie
amused our after-dinner party with very risqué anecdotes and some sexy
poems by the famous poet Pushkin, who had apparently used his talent on
occasions just for fun, to compose poetry not exactly suitable for drawing
room recitation.

After that weekend, my idea that high-class persons and royalty are above
the human and everyday behavior definitely changed. I learned that they
had humor. I was disillusioned, at first, but soon recovered and enjoyed their
human qualities and weaknesses, admiring their ability to be grand when it
was necessary and later to behave like everyone else.

*1931-1932; High School Friends, Parties, Treasure-hunts:*
On a few "free" evenings, which were scarce, I arranged parties in our
house (the first floor only)—but they were never ordinary parties, like
everyone else's. In my part of the house they had to be special events. I had
to give a party, every once and a while. Because I was a new face, the
son of a famous pilot, not to mention my becoming a dancer, I was
something of a curiosity. A lot of invitations were coming my way and it was
only natural for me to return the courtesy. Besides, I wanted Granny to meet
the people I was associating with during my hours away from home. Years
later, when I was dancing at the Metropolitan Opera House, I used to come
home with a group of my friends, the dancers, to have a midnight snack at
our apartment in New York. And, if Granny was already in bed, before long

there would be one or two of my friends in her room, sitting on the edge of her bed talking with her, some of them asking for advice or telling her their troubles. Somehow, Granny understood everyone, and an age difference did not exist.

One of my friends, though already graduated, was Freddy Smithson, a wonderful pianist who accompanied many of our Russian affairs, playing for singers and dancers. What became a favorite game for everyone was one that I suggested: Freddy would play a few musical phrases and we had to guess who among us—there would be perhaps ten people—he was imitating. At times he was really uncanny. One could almost "see" the person described by this music—how he walked or what he looked like.

For a while treasure hunts became a popular fad. My parties created problems, and twice the police interfered. I would dream up, without realizing it, things that were illegal to get. One morning after a party, there was a backyard full of flat tires. Some of them had been "lifted" from nearby car repair stations. The rest room signs had to be returned, and direction signs and street name plates had to be reinstated in the places where they originally belonged. One lady was very upset—dear old eccentric Miss Herrick had been troubled to give a few of her red hairs. She called up to say that she was going to be bald if she accommodated all the requests, and there were very unpleasant telephone calls from the library and railroad station because they were missing out-of-town telephone books. We also received an annoyed telephone call from some lady who thought it was a sacrilege for young people to be in the cemetery at night with flashlights. We had been searching for the oldest tombstone inscription in the church cemetery.

I recall a few of my high school friends very clearly, although our lives turned out so differently and our paths seldom crossed after I left Stratford. A few personalities and faces are even now bright in my memory, and I wonder what happened to them:

Florence Walker was my favorite, even before she was named the "Most Popular Girl" of the 1932 graduating class. There was something very pleasant and sweet about her, and the way she dressed and behaved gave her a very classy appearance. She and her parents lived on one of the main streets in a lovely house facing a wide divider with a nice statue in the middle. All of this together made me think and feel that she was an ideal American girl. Being romantic, I admired her and what she represented; besides she was very nice to me without making a fuss, and she did not laugh when my imperfect English caused others to snicker or make fun of me. I remember having a fight with someone at one of the socials because the young man had been drinking and annoying Florence. I became a knight-of-old, protecting her. It was a surprise to many, including myself, how I became enraged and pushed the man away, sending him across the room. I later found out that my "Dream Girl" married our football hero, and I hope they lived happily ever after.

I also remember Col. and Mrs. Clinton and their daughter, Molly. They were more or less the "society" of our Stratford. It was always a pleasure to visit them because it was all so correct and in such good taste. Though some young ones laughed at Molly's desire to give classes in deportment, I thought it was a very good idea. And I felt that many other young girls could use "lessons in grace and good social manners." Molly spent a great deal of time in Washington, and was very impressed with the way social people were behaving.

My two other favorites were the sisters Eileen and Jean Kelt. They were very different in both looks and personality. Eileen was serious and studious, and later married either a doctor or a priest (I have forgotten which) and moved somewhere far away to "do good" for people. Jean was always full of fun, and getting herself into trouble, but I loved her bright smile, good looks, and "live today" attitude. For some reason, I remember fixing her a special corsage for one of the big events which crowded our high school days.

I do not remember having any male friends. Somehow, I must have been too strange for them, being a few years older and being a dancer, traveling to New York City all the time. The only young man that I remember being a friend of mine was Myles Reilly. I had met his father in the Canal Zone. Myles went with me once to New York to see a new bridge—the George Washington—and could not wait to get back to Stratford.

My graduation *summa cum laude* from the Stratford High School in 1932 surprised even me.

The last few months of school were not as busy; there was even more time left for parties and fun. I still remember a few of the events with sentimental pleasure—the innocent amusements, the treasure hunts, musicals, parties.

At the graduation prom, I created unusual excitement and attracted many glances of disapproving admiration. My "date" was a lovely lady, dressed in white skin-clinging satin, "the very latest" in evening gowns—not an organdy, girlish, sweet-sixteen outfit. I had persuaded the charming Larochka Koodroff, the wife of a friend of the family, to be my guest, and being a good sport she had agreed.

After my high school graduation, I enrolled according to Father's wishes in the Engineering Institute and started to work part-time at the Sikorsky Aviation Corporation, starting as all dutiful sons are supposed to do, at the bottom. First I was a riveter on the leading edge of the wing of the big Sikorsky S-40, the world's largest amphibian plane.

Being a dancer, I was better coordinated than just about any worker, and was able to climb inside the rib cage of the wing and get into the uncomfortable twisted position inside the leading edge. I still have an aftereffect of working there. As soon as I finished riveting, another worker would follow with a spray gun, painting with an ill-smelling antirust solution. The sensitive membranes in my nose and sinuses were affected, and I became a victim of hay fever, and am still allergic to any fumes.

Working on the wings of planes that my father was to test caused another problem; I was especially careful, and a nuisance to other workers, asking them to recheck and inspect their work.

Evenings were spent fighting with mathematical problems, trying to get familiar with the much-hated logarithms, while my emotions, mind, and frustrated love of dance created an invisible but much-felt barrier between reality and the future. One thing I could not be stopped from now was doing what I wanted on the weekends. Thank God for Granny's understanding and moral support. All the money I earned—later supplemented by contributions from Granny—helped send me off Saturdays and Sundays to magical New York, to the haven which was the ballet studio of "Papa" Fokine. Group lessons were followed by my private lessons, and then private coaching to learn the dances from Fokine's ballets, or to rehearse for concerts or benefit shows.

# 19

Every weekend I went for two days of lessons in New York. In addition to private and group lessons with Maestro "Papa" Fokine, there were extra lessons with Mikhail Mordkin. It was a happy time of learning, absorbing like a sponge all the wonderful sayings, corrections, and new steps of ballet technique.

Fokine enriched our knowledge of dance by giving us steps from his own ballets or by trying to give us new ideas for new works which he planned to choreograph in the future. Mikhail Mordkin would have fun shocking us in class with his over-exaggerated eccentricities, just to make us lose our self-consciousness, to free us to express our emotions, to make us develop our personalities. Both of these great teachers believed that dance requires the personality be controlled by a technique which is hidden, in no way obvious to the viewer; the dancer should dance his best, yet the audience should be unaware of the effort required to perform the difficult steps of the dance.

The famous ballerina Mathilde Kchessinskaya, years later, said that from the very first *plié* at the *barre,* one should begin to prepare for the performance. This great lady of ballet advised us to mix, from the very beginning, the ever-necessary exercise at the *barre* with *port de bras,* the movement of the arms, thus breaking the monotony of countless *pliés* and *tendus* with graceful arm movements, creating harmony, and coordinating the whole body into one continuous graceful line.

These days, when teaching a class, I pass on this method. It is too bad that, so many times, I have had to repeat this statement, after seeing that a class is not doing its best. "You are wasting your money and my time, because you are not doing as well as you can," I have to say on these occasions. Only a few of the dancers may understand and take my advice, after thinking it over and applying to their dancing what I am trying to pass on from my rich past.

From Fokine: "Caress the air with your arms as you do the *ports de bras,"* or, in *Le Spectre de la Rose,* the first arm movements of the Spectre, as he appears on the windowsill, create an embrace—not a continuous movement of the arms "like the winding of spaghetti on a fork." This embracing movement changes into the gentle sending of the rose perfume to intoxicate the young girl—not just waving the arms. Another gem comes from Mordkin: "Reach to the stars and pick up strawberries." This statement was used to make the dancer reach up and bend down during the *valse pas* (waltz step) up-and-down *balancé.* Another wonderful suggestion from Fokine is an ever-useful reminder that while doing *ports de bras* you should think and extend from your inner self to the space beyond. In Fokine's words: "Do not show the walls of the room. Show the horizon beyond. Do not stop at the ceiling, but reach for the sky."

Writing this, a sad thought comes to my mind, of how the fragrance of the subtle emotional choreography is being replaced by mere acrobatic technique. The saddest example is the *Dying Swan* by Fokine. The very first steps—a bending on the knee—the dancer's body leans from side to side in an effort to fly, then a *relevé* with an odd arm movement symbolizing the effort to fly. This is now done acrobatically. A snake-like arm movement is used, and the sad supplication has become a slow pleading. What was once an effective lifting of the head has been replaced with fast turns, the arms moving rapidly up and down. And the last helpless lifting of the arms and the final tremble of the wrist is non-existent in the present, so-called "original" version. Too bad. Too sad.

The emotional struggles, the exhausting physical work at the Sikorsky factory, and the equally exhausting workouts at my ballet classes, plus the housework at home, finally took their toll. I was on the verge of a nervous breakdown.

For two years this continued. Physically exhausted from work at the factory, I would come home to take care of household chores, then go off to classes at the University of Bridgeport. Then I attended to my studies at home, all the while counting the days and hours until I could escape to *my* reality—the ballet studios of New York.

The problems of our family life also added to the turmoil. By 1934 Father had moved to the first floor to be with me and Granny. He then realized that I was having to do all the housework, because the maid/cook was too busy upstairs with Alexandra's second floor to spend any time on our floor. Any time we tried to ask her to give us an hour or two after she finished upstairs, there was always something else to do—preparations for a party or some other alibi. In other words, we were left without help. Eventually the problem was solved. Father arranged for someone else to come for a few hours a day to help us do the chores.

Youth can adapt to changes; so it was with me. The ways of South America, then the high school in Panama, were replaced by the calm life of Stratford. It was all so different from distant Russia. This variety was actually helpful and my natural ability to adjust to new places and people was instrumental in developing my personality. The hardships of living through the Revolution made me appreciate the good things in life and not just take them for granted as so many people do. I also developed a certain stamina and will power to achieve, to work with determination for what I wanted or needed. But the discipline taught me by my Granny made me obey my father, trying to be what he wanted me to be. However, a combination of things—my will power, my irresistible desire to dance, and the subconscious knowledge that I had talent—all worked in my imagination, and my dreams created pictures of the future which gave me hope and strength to rebel and fight for becoming what I knew I was meant to be.

But my future was not so easily solved. Granny was in favor of letting me try to succeed at what I wanted to do and be. Many a time I overheard Father and Granny arguing about me. The discord, the seemingly hopeless future, made me unhappy. Due to all the circumstances of our lives, years of separation had created barriers between me and my father. We did not have a common language—no understanding of each other. Being a military man, a brave aviator and war hero, he had developed a dashing personality and his background was one of discipline and bravery. My world was of a different kind—one built on the courage to survive and the discipline to overcome obstacles.

As I have thought many times later in life, I was glad Father had not suffered the tragedy and ugliness of civil war, the undignified surrender of the land, property, and, most of the time, ideals. His departure with the White Army was a grand exit, and although he later faced the difficult adaptation to a new life in Europe and then in America, to the very last Father practiced the Grand Old Way of Life.

I admired Father for being a war hero, for all the medals he had received for his bravery and outstanding achievements in aviation. He broke many records during his test flights—eighteen in the fifteen years of his test-flying career—and I admired him for this, too. Genuine achievement—all of it. Almost everyone fell under the spell of his charm; everyone admired his singing and his success with the ladies. The men admired my father's horseback riding, his daredevil escapes from difficult situations, and his ability to speak six languages.

But an understanding father he was not. I was always having to prove myself to him. Thinking back, most of this may have been good for me, but it also greatly slowed my getting to my own achievements. Father was a generous man: I could have had almost anything I wanted—except to be a dancer. So the fight for my survival as an individual continued until his death. We were never really close friends, sad to say, though through the years we learned to love one another, at a distance. His military upbringing did not allow for sentimentality, shows of emotion, or even affection. Only during a few moments of tragedy, which touched us both, did we experience a deep love and understanding for one another.

The conflict between father and son is, I imagine, eternal. In our case, both of us had high standards, very individual needs, and both of us had backgrounds of spiritual strength and high ideals; each possessed the will power and honest belief in ourselves which had been instilled in us by our mother/grandmother.

After one of numerous arguments over my going to the ballet studio in New York, I finally broke down in hysterics and left my father's home—on a cold, snow-filled night. I did come back later because of Granny, but by then I was so sick that they had to call a doctor. After consultation with a second doctor, it was decided to let me be myself for a while. For me, this was a breakthrough, an escape into a new life. The year was 1933.

*1975:*

Confidentially speaking—some thoughts written during my cruise in 1975. I feel that it is time to talk about my inner self—my point of view, opinions, thoughts of what happened to me "inside" as a result of the cavalcade of events and situations which influenced my personality, my own self.

Thinking back, I am most grateful that I learned to control, and later to completely exile from my system, the ugliness of jealousy. Jealousy is, to me, the worst of all emotions. It can poison the mind, spoil relationships, and it slowly destroys even the strongest of characters.

Envy, on the other hand, can be either good or bad. At times, envy can create a new push inside the human machinery, guiding unknown forces to an unexpected achievement. Envy, like hate, gives a certain action to inside feelings, coloring our behavior. In my case, I give credit and thanks for my upbringing to my Granny, who taught me to be honest with myself and with others. She taught me to find out, to know, whether I have a clean conscience, to have the courage to face facts about myself without "ifs" or "buts." In the beginning I was envious of my handsome uncles; I overheard, ". . . too bad Orest is not as good-looking as his father or his uncles." It hurt, in the beginning. Later on in life I found that envy gave me a little push to work harder to the very best of my ability, to achieve the things I was envying. Many times, by working hard because I wanted to better myself, I got a part or a place in the ballet. The desire to do so drove me to accomplish the best I could possibly achieve. Being honest with myself, I did not reach for that which was clearly impossible—to dance or try for parts which required a beautiful physique, handsome face, long legs, and a nature-given appearance of beauty. When jealousy began to bother me, I found out just how ugly, useless, how utterly hopeless and destructive it was. As a result, I taught myself to admire what I had been jealous of, if it was worth admiration.

As life has progressed with all its ups and downs, I have many times been rewarded for my will power and being able to recognize my own jealousy. As a result of this self-honesty, my life has become much richer, embellished with so many things. I made a point of making friends, if at all possible, with the people of whom I was jealous or admired for their looks, talent, or abilities. What I could not have, I managed to be near; what I could not possess, I admired, like priceless works of art that one could visit in the museums. If it was not possible to be with someone I admired, I went to see them at their theater performances, or sent them notes or gifts of admiration.

Eventually my own self developed enough character and strength to be sufficient. As the years went by I found that I was more fortunate in this respect than most of my admired idols of the past or present. I also found that many of the beautiful people lead very sad and lonely existences when their glamorous days are over, when sparkling technique and charm have become things of the past. After the years in which they could cultivate and enrich themselves have gone, so have their admirers and passing friendships.

Even as I wrote this in 1975, my present situation came to mind: There was much unpleasantness where I had been teaching lately; after giving up my own studio, I was almost sure that I could not continue teaching there for long. This studio was being called "The Snake Pit" by many ex-teachers. It is too bad, but it was true. Instead of healthy competition, creating friendly relations, there was never a smile or greeting. The place was sentimentally nostalgic for me because it brought back memories of Mikhail Mordkin's classes and rehearsals: *The Goldfish,* the young talent of Viola Essen, Leon Danielian, the charm of Leon Varkas. Instead, it was filled with jealousy, misunderstanding, gossip. Only the modern classes were somehow above it—due, I am certain, to teachers who were good-natured and sure of themselves. The ballet department had become a disaster; it only came alive when the owner made his periodic appearances: And he had great *savoir faire* and personality.

I now realize why so many studios do not have a good faculty, good dancers, good material with which to work, to teach to improve. Jealousy is the answer. Only in the studios connected with performing companies is there any concentration of good dancers working in hopes of getting a job. Yet even these studios are usually run by only one or two "name" teachers; other good or experienced teachers are not welcome—too much competition. Yes, jealousy is a very destructive element.

In the winter of 1934 my ill health interrupted my studies at the Engineering Institute of Bridgeport, which I had been attending at my father's insistence since 1932. Later, it was arranged to continue my studies at the Massachusetts Institute of Technology. But this did not stop me from going to extra dance classes in New York, thanks to Granny's help with extra dollars from the household money.

My dreams were finally becoming reality as I felt myself becoming accustomed to the aspects of performing: The intoxicating applause, yes, but also the knowledge of how to perform and establish rapport with your audience, of responding to that audience's expectations; the heady assurance of what my body could now do, and the challenge of infusing the steps which I had learned with my own personality; and, of course, translating all of this into the image of the kind of dancer I had dreamt so long of becoming.

One's assurance and stage presence improves with experience. The benefit performances for the Russian church had been a good foundation for the next step: the President's Ball for the benefit of the March of Dimes. The Pas de Deux from *Les Sylphides,* which we had learned in New York with Maestro Fokine, was the highlight of this program. Virginia Comer and I danced it in the huge ballroom in the Armory in Stratford. Then followed the exciting celebration of Stratford's tercentenary.

In the big park behind the Sterling House, the pageant was staged. The event of the white man's arrival was to be illustrated in an Indian camp scene, and I was chosen to do a war dance as an Indian chief, with big leaps over the fire. The next day I read a complimentary write-up in the Bridgeport Post from a critic, saying that a real Indian dance had been convincingly performed by a Russian. For some time I was teased that it took a Russian to make a good Indian.

A few years later, after I had become a professional dancer, Virginia Comer, my partner, and I were asked to dance with the Bridgeport Symphony Orchestra at a concert in the park in Bridgeport. I felt that I had "arrived," because while waiting to go on to dance our Viennese Waltz, we found out that the house was sold out and a thousand people had been turned away. I did realize, however, that the name of my famous father and the fact that Virginia's sister Irene had a successful ballet school in Bridgeport probably had a lot to do with our big success.

Meanwhile, in New York there was a possibility of dancing professionally: The Art of Musical Russia were rehearsing Rimsky-Korsakov's *The Legend of the Invisible City of Kitezh,* to be given in the Mecca Temple (now City Center); the Fokine Ballet was organizing for summer performances at the Lewisohn Stadium; and the first "pop" concerts were to take place in Carnegie Hall, with the orchestra under the conductorship of Ernest Schelling. Oh, if I could only live in New York, I knew I could dance in these events. Granny braced herself to persuade Father to let me try my luck, even backing her suggestions with the offer of staying with me in the big city during the rehearsals and performances.

Without our even knowing it, destiny was on my side; a major change was about to happen in our lives.

# 21

Granny and I sensed that something was happening, not only because of Father's absence on the days when he was not away on flights, but also a few unfinished statements and his generally better frame of mind made us wonder what was going on. For months there had been talk of divorce, the difficulties of property settlement, and what would happen to Granny and me. But it always came to a dead end; no agreement could be reached.

Then one day, just before I left for New York, Granny told me that she was going to have an important visitor, and that she wanted me to help her decide which dress to wear. Upon my asking who was paying her a visit, she said that she did not know, that it was someone Father had asked her to meet. When I returned later that day, Granny told me that the visitor was a lovely, gentle lady named Gertrude, who wanted to meet the mother of Boris Sergievsky, and to receive an approval to marry him.

After many exhausting days of search, I finally found a hotel on 73rd Street, the Commander Hotel, only half a block away from Riverside Drive and the town house in which Fokine reigned supreme. Our new quarters were approved by Granny and Father for a "temporary" stay. Granny and I settled in along with my Alsatian police dog named Zara, who in a few days presented us with nine puppies: Three weeks later we had to find a place for the offspring. Because Zara was such a beauty and the puppies so adorable, and thanks to the glamour of the ballet world, we managed to persuade a kennel on 72nd Street to put them in the shop window. For the next month there were always spectators watching Zara and her family. The dogs were even mentioned in a newspaper story, and one of the puppies was lucky enough to be adopted by Betty Eisner (later Betty Bruce) and her mother.

Father's divorce from Alexandra Kotchoubey-Sergievsky created a lot of publicity, including a full-page tabloid cartoon, based on old press and publicity stills, which featured an opera singer floating down by parachute to Reno. Father's marriage to Gertrude was performed quietly on New Year's eve, 1935.

*1975:*
*This is actually being written at sea in the 1970s, but somehow it fits right now, filling in the written passages of my narrative, expressing the mood and state of my mind at present:*

The sun has just set, the sparkling lights of the shoreline slowly dissolve in the mist of distance. Emptiness, loneliness, like a gentle fog, is drifting into my being . . . a sad but welcome peaceful rest, my own self drifts back to the people left on the shore. . . .

*1935:*
I feel that the past, from my birth in 1911 until 1935, had been like a solid shoreline. Even with all the troubles and traveling, the past and the future were connected. My life had been shared, and that part of my life spent together with Granny had been what I would know of family life. Now the time arrived when the house which had been divided emotionally now became a house divided physically, as well. Granny and I were to live independently. Father entered a completely different new life, with new people and new surroundings. Without my realizing it, I finally became an independent person, myself, my own *I*. It took a few more years for me to realize this, because Granny was helping me with the final touches, polishing me to become a complete individual.

New York, that glamorous and exciting city, called the Capital of the World by so many. New York, to me, was the ballet studio of "Papa" Fokine and the theaters in which to dance. They are what mattered most. This time there were no sad goodbyes or heart-felt partings. The calm serenity of Stratford had been just a stepping place from which to enter the world of dance. Being able to dance was my foremost wish. I was possessed, nothing mattered, my only interest was in lessons, rehearsals, learning new movements, memorizing new steps, improving technique.

In those days men dancers were in demand; not too many men dared to dance because of the narrow and idiotic American prejudice against male dancers. Being European, I actually did not realize for some time that I had chosen to enter what was almost a profession of outcasts. Now, as I write this four decades later, people realize how difficult it is, and how hard a dancer has to work, what dedication is needed to be a professional, and the male dancer is beginning to receive the credit he is due.

As I relate in more-or-less chronological order the events of my life during my dancing career, a flock of different instances are crowding in like moths about a candle. Many faces and personalities shoulder one another into view, so I will give in and mention just a few as they appear on the screen of my memory. Later things will all fall into the correct place and time, a dancing mosaic of my life.

I had the good fortune of working with Mme. Bronislava Nijinska, dancer, choreographer, and sister to the world's most famous male dancer, Vaslav Nijinsky. The first occasion was in 1939–40 with Ballet Theatre, when Nijinska was setting *La Fille Mal Gardée*. (Later, I would work with her again in 1947 with the Ballet Russe when she was creating *Pictures at an Exhibition*.) On the first occasion, she asked me where I had first begun to study dance. My answer: "In Kiev, when I was eight or nine." "Where in Kiev?" she asked with growing interest. "I do not remember who the teacher was," I replied, "but I do remember that the studio was on the top of the hill called *Stolipinskaya Ulitza.*" It was as much a surprise to me as it had been a revelation to her when she stated, "Then it was me you were studying with, because I had the studio there, at that time!" I wondered how I could have forgotten my beginnings with such a famous teacher, but it had been twenty years before and my naiveté at the time had been overwhelming. In Russia we had known little about the famous Nijinsky, or about his famous sister.

In 1918–19, during the Revolution, the family of the ex-governor of St. Petersburg had been assigned to live in our house. He had two daughters, with whom I became quite friendly. They were both dancers with the Kiev Opera House company, and they invited me to take lessons and rehearse there. They had seen me dance, and must have suspected that I had an undeveloped ability for dancing; and this early experience with a professional company crystallized my love for the art which was my whole life.

Because my love of dance has been a part of me as long as I can remember myself, so long as I could dance, study, and rehearse I was happy. An ambition to achieve a great career was not a driving force; just to be where I could perform or dance in as many ballets as possible, this had always been my desire. I was surprised many times when in ballet companies so many dancers did not want to perform in every ballet. They must have thought me slightly "nuts" to keep asking for extra parts, even spots in some not-too-important works. These days, I am grateful for having acted on my enthusiasm, because whenever I choreograph or teach, I have a background of ideas, knowledge, and inspiration to use as I need. I also have the satisfaction of knowing that my efforts—memorizing roles, dances, variations—during my last years of performing with ballet companies enriched my ability to pass many valuable things on to the other generations of dancers. Instead of resting, gossiping, or just being in the dressing rooms, I spent much of my free time memorizing passages of ballets I particularly liked.

One of the bright memories that comes to light is of the time I danced slow Oriental movements on a big platform on a slowly moving truck during the carnival festival in Panama. I was in a dazzling costume that took me weeks to "realize." It was an exciting week and having been a part of that hysteria remains bright in my memory.

Later in Stratford, there were many benefits from which I learned about the intoxicating pleasure of applause. In my interpretation of "Song of India," I wore a sea-water green costume with veils and danced in front of a girl who represented a seabird with huge wings. The dance illustrated the famous song about an Indian legend. As the singer was telling the story, I tried to create the feeling of sea water with my scarves and cape-like veils. The sea and the waves were reaching toward the half-woman, half-bird creature, danced by my partner. The steps used included big jumps, *tours jetés,* and fast spins, which I used to create a whirlpool effect. The bird-like creature had a beautiful headpiece, like an old-fashioned Russian *kokoshnik,* and instead of arms she had sparkling wings. The rest of her body was covered with a dark cloth, which became a part of the stand on which she was perched. On a rock, nearby, a very good tenor sang the song, and a local violinist supported the beautiful melody. On the same program I danced an innocent pas de deux with a girl, Galia, to the music of Shubert's *Serenade.* The finale of the evening remains vividly etched in my memory, for it was my first attempt at group choreography—and I was working with mostly non-professionals. Notwithstanding their shyness and inexperience, the dancers' effort was successful, partly because of my choice of material, in which mistakes would not be too obvious. It was a moving tableau called *Persian Market*—a procession-like scene. I was the snake charmer, while different Oriental characters passed me by in stylized dance movements.

Then, when Granny and I moved to New York and I learned some pas de deux in my private lessons with "Papa" Fokine, I danced in private concerts. Finally, my professional performances began. One of the first was the unforgettable experience of working with the Art of Musical Russia company in the opera *Kitezh,* in which Ivan Ivantzev was singing the tenor role. It was performed at the Mecca Temple—now City Center. Then there were the

Popular Symphony Concerts in Carnegie Hall, where we danced on Saturday afternoons. Vecheslav Svoboda was the choreographer and we did some very exciting demi-character dances.

My first accident happened during one of these performances. While doing the *pozunok* (a dance step in which the dancer almost sits on the floor, traveling either in a circle or across the stage while the legs do circles on the floor), I hit my knee on the conductor's platform, which had been hidden behind a curtain on the side of the stage. I thought, "I will never dance again!" Later in life I learned that with dancers miracles do happen; where there is a will there is a way; dancers break the rules of "never again" many a time.

Summer performances with the Fokine Ballet at the Jones Beach Stadium and with the Shubert Brothers operettas at Randalls Island were quite exciting experiences and a lot of fun. Especially spectacular were the two performances in which the location added to the success. At Jones Beach, the *Sorcerer's Apprentice* was performed on a floating stage (we performed there before today's concrete edifice had been constructed). The orchestra was also on the barge-like contraption. We went to our dressing rooms and the stage by walking across a pontoon-like bridge. So when the apprentice, Eugene Loring, succeeded in the magic of bringing water and with it seaweeds (the dancers, in costume), the effect brought enthusiastic applause from the audience. This ballet was very effective in that particular setting; the "magic" effects, the exaggerated movements of the magician, the broom's coming to life, the corps de ballet girls dancing in water colors, and finally the men's entrances as seaweeds added up to a spectacle to be remembered. We were told that it really *looked* as if we, the weeds, were coming out of the water. At the end, Paul Haakon, as the broom, danced his effective dance in which he swept the water here and there; in our final exit, as seaweeds, we disappeared again, as if into the water.

At the Lewisohn Stadium, the full moon directly over the stage was a perfect setting for the performance of *Schéhérazade;* only the loudness of the planes overhead broke the spell.

At Randalls Island, the performance of *Prince Igor* also looked as if it had been placed in the right setting, with the fields all about. There we also danced the Shubert operettas. Between the acts, as a special attraction, the Fokine Ballet performed one ballet. We danced in the *Fire Fly* with the beautiful singer Luba Malina, whose lovely voice enchanted the audience, and with Robert Shaeffer as the charming Student Prince. It was in *Fire Fly* that we had to dance a number I hated, though it was a big success with the audience—the *Glow Worm.* Before the second act, as a special attraction, we danced on the lawn between the orchestra and the audience. All the lights were extinguished and each dancer was dressed with wings of china silk and a headpiece equipped with little electric lights, which were attached to batteries in our belts by long wires. We danced with the lights flickering on and off. We did get good hands for this trick, but I felt very silly—big me— doing an Isadora Duncan-style dance with veils and lit with twinkling electric bulbs. In the same operetta, we had to dance as a group of street urchins. Vitale Fokine, who was one of the choreographers, decided to up-date the scene, and told us to do a bump and grind as we were leaving the stage. I was mortified.

These performances at the Stadium were a great success, with sold out signs, standing room only, and hundreds turned away. Maestro Smallens conducted, and the best artists, even the stars, were pupils of "Papa" Fokine: Patricia Bowman, Paul Haakon, Betty Eisner (later Betty Bruce of Broadway), Winona Bimboni, George Chaffée, Edna Veralle, Dorothy Hall, Nora Koreff (later Nora Kaye), Gemze de Lappe, and Jerome Robbins.

I still do not know how Patricia Bowman and Paul Haakon did it, dancing *Les Sylphides, Spectre de la Rose* and finishing with *Schéhérazade* or *Prince Igor* all in one evening—with solos in-between especially choreographed for them by "Papa" Fokine, pieces like *Tennis* or the *Persian Angel* created for Patricia (*Tennis,* danced outdoors, was always a show-stopper), and Paul Haakon dancing the character piece *Igroujki* with Winona Bimboni. On these evenings, he performed *Spectre* with triple tours.

Thinking back, in those days we *danced;* these days most of the dancers *perform.* Technique is the great rule. Performers today dance *at* one another; they do not dance together. Abstract behavior is the style. Most of the time, even in the pas de deux, the partners walk about, jump, turn with amazing technique, then as if by chance, get together to accomplish a lift or a promenade; doing a pose or look past each other, with no personal contact or personality in evidence. The sexual poses and contacts are performed, but completely without human feeling. No wonder only a few dancers can perform the classics and create the believable interpretations which the roles require. The magic between the partners as of old is today almost nonexistent: Mordkin and Pavlova, Alicia Markova and Anton Dolin, Igor Youskevitch and Alicia Alonso, Alexandra Danilova and Frederic Franklin, Tatiana Stepanova and Oleg Tupine, Nana Gollner and Paul Petrov, Tatiana Riabouchinska and David Lichine, Rudolf Nureyev and Margot Fonteyn, Natalia Makarova and Mikhail Baryshnikov. These artists have the magic of communication, of rapport with each other. The charisma of a partner looking at his lady must get across to the audience, and give the individuals in the auditorium the feeling—even a wish—that someone would look at *them* that way. The illusion of love many times is more desirable and effective than a real, earthly contact—that is what I am trying to tell, to say to my readers and my pupils, that reality without a touch of poetry and individuality is emptiness.

The summer concert performances were followed by other new experiences for me—performing in the ballets of popular operas produced by the Salmaggi and the San Carlo opera companies. The Salmaggi was, in those days, a little like the New York City Opera is today. It was run on a small budget; with a lot of inventiveness, it covered a multitude of sins. There were many very good singers in that company, singers who became known and were eventually stolen or adopted by the Metropolitan Opera company. While San Carlo was a traveling company, Salmaggi used stadiums in the summer and the Brooklyn Academy of Music in the winter.

The San Carlo had, to their advantage, two people who were always able to turn out good ballet routines, Lydia Arlova and Lucien Prideaux. Student dancers, such as I was at the time, were hired on a free-lance basis; we were happy to rehearse and dance just for the opportunity to dance. For a while, we were a small group which included Nora Koreff, Muriel Bentley, Boris Butleroff, and me. We were all pupils of Fokine and we could, with a very few rehearsals, give a "passable" performance.

The woman who worked with us when we performed for Salmaggi was a fascinating individual. Mme. Phillips would arrive from Philadelphia in a suit, rehearse us, many times letting us use some of our own steps or choreography, order us to try on the costumes, and then disappear to get the money that was due us. Money taken in at the box office was then put in the "safe place"—at the center of her bra, from which we were paid as soon as the ballet number was finished. A bitter experience had taught her to get the money *before* the show went on. Several times we were allowed to watch a transformation: Taking off the skirt of her suit, Mme. Phillips would unpin the lower part of her blouse and, *voila!* she was in an evening gown. A new twist to her hair, a touch of fresh lipstick, and she would be ready for an official reception. Salmaggi was really lucky to have had Mme. Phillips to function as our manager and choreographer.

It was different with Mme. Orlova and her partner, Mr. Prideaux. The rehearsals were rather long, as they tried to get the best out of the various gypsies (as dancers on Broadway were known then). I remember once, during an adagio, one fellow, who had bluffed his way in with his looks, let his partner fall instead of helping and catching her. The poor girl broke her hip. The dancer admitted, too late, that he had never done adagio before.

We did manage to do a passable *Carmen* and *Aida* at the Brooklyn Academy and at the New York City Center Theater. The finale was almost inevitable; fast piqué turns (turns in a circle) by Mr. Prideaux and many fouettés in the center by Mme. Orlova. Whenever I remember those days, I regard those two pioneers with admiration. They worked hard, believed in getting the best from the dancing gypsies they had to work with. Most of us did try our best, and it was a good preparation for the future.

"Papa" Fokine was too great a choreographer and teacher to be jealous of other teachers. The only thing that upset him was when authorized artists or companies presented a ballet of his and to save money did not ask the Maestro to "brush it up," to rehearse the new artists that he had not personally worked with in the roles. That is why the charm and tender fragrance of *Spectre de la Rose,* the sadness of the *Swan,* and the delicacy of *Les Sylphides* lost their original quality, even during his time. Maestro, of course, approved of his pupils studying other kinds of dancing. Betty Bruce studied tap and Spanish dance; she had become too tall for ballet, so it was the right move for her to go into musical comedy.

Fokine sent me to study with Angel Cansino and the Spanish-Irish gypsy, Helen Veola, a wonderful teacher and a warm-hearted person. At. Mme. Veola's little studio there were soirees, evenings when friends were invited to sit on the cushions about the studio to watch our almost-learned dances, this way preparing us for performing our selected numbers for concerts or different charities later on. This small studio, on 59th Street between Madison and Park Avenues, was an incubator for many dancers who would be big names later on in the dance world. Valia Valentinoff, later Paul Valentine, became a principal dancer with the Fokine Ballet, then went on to Broadway and eventually to Hollywood. I remember Erick Hawkins being shy in class. José Greco, the world-renowned Spanish dancer, was, even in those early days, a dynamic personality.

After being hypnotized by the new splendor and flowing beauty of the Hindu dancing of Uday Shankar, I just had to study this new dance form. One of his dancers was giving lessons in the old Isadora Duncan studio on 59th at Lexington. His name was Bupesh Guha, and he was a very sincere teacher. I learned the flowing arms, the horizontal head movement, the stamping of the feet with bells on my ankles, but when it came to the really serious part of the Hindu dance technique I gave up. I was too impatient. The guru and the now-popular yoga were unknown at that time, so when I had to sit cross-legged, concentrating on my navel to make my mind "blank," my business sense was calculating how much it was costing me for "just sitting down." My impatience soon won and I gave up the complicated art.

As is usually the case, dancers run from one studio to another, and I too fell under the feverish spell. A Spanish dance teacher, Mr. Baucaire, who had a large following, was a very mild-mannered man, completely different from Angelo Cansino and Mme. Veola. Mr. Baucaire's mannerisms were not so much elegant as showy, with emphasis on the snapping of fingers, twisting of the wrists, arching of the back, and an almost effeminate elegance which was neither to my taste nor compatible with my style.

The next and last step in improving my Spanish dance was studying with Juan Martinez, a real Spanish gypsy. A fascinating-looking man, he was not actually handsome, but gave one the impression that he had been sculpted from Spanish clay, very earthy and somber. Yet when he danced, he became handsome. He taught me, or at least helped me, to have the "Spanish feeling of inside fire," a calmness outside and an explosive temper on the verge of eruption inside.

All these Spanish numbers which I had learned just had to be performed. The acquired knowledge became a part of my own technique and had helped develop my performing personality. The performing outlet was very easily obtained. In New York at that time were numerous Russian "Musical Evenings," also many charities and benefit affairs in which entertainment was a part of the evening's activities. Thanks to my grandmother's help, my supply of costumes was no problem, and my love of dance made me a very busy performer. Later on, these performances were an invaluable foundation for my professional career. I made night club and special variety appearances for money through different managers in almost every hotel and ballroom in and around New York from 1936 to 1950.

I must get back to the real foundation of it all, Number 4 Riverside Drive, the Fokine Mansion. It was a five-story town house between 72nd and 73rd Streets, and was, as were the Princess Mathilde Kchessinskaya's studio and the Villa Molitor in Paris, a mecca for serious students of ballet. To me,

Fokine's home/studio was a castle in which dreams came true. At Number 4 Riverside Drive there was a marble spiral staircase in the center of the house. To the left, as one entered, was a very impressive library, with dark mahogany furniture and large paintings of Vera Fokine, Fokine's wife, mostly painted by the Maestro himself. To the right was a reception room, seldom used, but intimidating in the splendor of its paintings and its air of the Old Country. On each landing portraits greeted one—a self-portrait of "Papa" Fokine, followed by portraits of Mme. Fokine in a red mantle, glamorous and beautiful.

On the second floor a grand piano was strategically placed between the music studio/study room and the grand ballroom. The grand ballroom was the "big studio" with fireplaces at either end. The grand piano was on the landing; the huge double doors were wide open, and numerous tall windows faced Riverside Drive. In those days, double-decker buses were very much in style and riders on the top deck could look in. Many times we "performed" for them when a bus would stop for a red light. It was nice to see interested faces almost on eye-level with the studio.

From the second floor landing, the staircase led up to the third, where hung a large painting by the maestro of *Les Sylphides,* depicting the corps de ballet during the Prelude and the beginning of the man's Mazurka. Down this staircase Mme. Fokine often made lovely, theatrical appearances during the morning or early afternoon classes, inevitably dressed in a lovely pastel peach or vieux-rose negligee with a small train touched with lace, her long black hair hanging down her back or tied up in a becoming bandana. She would descend slowly, responding with a half-smile to our admiring looks and hushed whispers. She would pose; she might watch for a little while the combination we were dancing; she might say a word or two to the pianist, Miss Agnes Kune (a pianist of very long standing, and accompanist for the rehearsals), and then continue on her way.

Part of the third floor was taboo; it was the private apartment of the Fokines. A small elevator, just for the family and a chosen few, was a lovely, usable antique. The third floor had two studios where the *barres* were used for the warm-up before descending to the big studio for the center work and the real dancing. Fokine called the upstairs studios the "kitchen"—that is, where you prepared your body, warmed it up for the "feast" of dancing. Still higher, the fourth floor held the dressing rooms and shower area; the view down the marble stairwell was dizzying from the fourth floor. The small studio on the third floor is where I had my first private lessons, where the son of "Papa" Fokine, Vitale, used to give me the *barre* and the painful stretches, many times under the suggestion of Maestro himself. Later on, especially when "Papa" was away, I took lessons from Vitale Fokine, a warm, friendly, gypsy-like fellow.

To many of us, this was a temple for the Art of Dance; we feared, but deeply loved, our teacher/choreographer. We were reprimanded; we were embarrassed or destroyed if we did not do our best; we were shamed if anyone forgot to get rid of his chewing gum. "How can you dance and chew at the same time?" Fokine would admonish. "Besides it looks so unaesthetic!"

Technique and correct positioning were to be worked out during the barre. While in the center, there could not be an obvious preparation to do a "trick." The dancing had to appear effortless, and the quality of line could not be sacrificed for a tour de force. This is the obvious difference between the style of dancing then and now, the difference between the harmonious pure line and continuous flow of movement of the old Maryinsky (now the Kirov) Ballet and the sensational acrobatics of the Bolshoi Ballet in our own times. Both the Kirov and Bolshoi companies have the much-admired "free Russian style," but the first represents harmony and the second a mere sensational technique. I do not agree with the present American style of body training; the American desire for the "most," the "highest," and so forth. The subtle feeling, the romantic lightness and effortlessness of the classic line is, most of the time, sacrificed to the highest arabesque, the most "turned-out, second position" acrobatic contortions. The most uncomfortable positions in the so-called sexy adagios lack the tender touch of simple human emotion and the lovely line of the body. Perhaps I am to be only a voice in the wilderness, crying for the awakening of some sensitive soul, trying to remind dancers of another kind of dancing, in the hopes that someday we will escape the present-day machine-like technique. I would love to bring back the lovely-to-look-at coordinated port de bras and the romantic human relationship between the dancing partners. I hope it is not just a dream.

Fokine expected us to do our best. He took this for granted. Repeated mistakes were reprimanded; an unesthetic line of the body was frowned upon; not remembering a combination was almost a sin; and almost never was there a compliment for a pupil. If some step or combination were done well, we were graced with a smile that made one happy and proud. My highest compliment was given to me when I was learning Spectre de la Rose during a private lesson. I was terribly nervous, too anxious. Fokine knew I could do better, so he stopped the lesson and asked me to come with him to the study, to sit down; there we had a talk. He asked me why I was so nervous. I told him I was in awe of him, and of learning Spectre, which had been danced by Nijinsky. He told me of a few incidents that had occurred during Nijinsky's rehearsals, then finished by telling me that if I had not been good

147

enough to dance it he would not have given me this great dance in the private lesson. Another compliment was given to me in front of many people during the rehearsal in 1939 of *Carnaval* with Ballet Theatre. We were working on the finale of the ballet, a circle of rather fast steps. It was a not-too-difficult but rather tricky (*chassé, pas de bourrée*) combination. Somehow, too many people were having trouble learning it. Maestro stopped everyone and said, "Let my pupil show it to you." I was so proud, and with a lump in my throat (it is a good thing I did not have to talk), I demonstrated. Thank God, I knew it well because we had danced *Carnaval* during the summer concerts at the stadiums. It was a big compliment when, during a lesson, Fokine asked one of us to demonstrate a combination or a passage from one of the ballets. You were envied and called "the chosen one" for that day.

As it always happens in this world, nothing lasts forever. Number 4 Riverside Drive had to go. The Fokines bought a house somewhere in Westchester, and the studio was moved to the Roerich Museum uptown on 103rd Street at Riverside Drive. Granny and I moved also. We had a lovely three-room apartment with a balcony on the nineteenth floor, with a breath-taking view of the Hudson River and downtown. To this day, whenever I pass the place where Number 4 used to be I have a twinge near my heart, and I look away from the skyscraper apartment house. Even the river is not seen anymore in that part, the concrete West Side Highway now cuts out the view. At the new Riverside Drive address uptown the lessons continued. I was very happy when "Papa" Fokine would come up to our apartment in between lessons. On hot summer days when he worked too hard—such as when he gave lessons to Lily Pons—he sometimes changed his clothes at Granny's and my apartment.

Maestro was teaching Lily Pons the dance and movements for the opera *Le Coq d'Or,* in which she was to sing the Queen of Shemakhan. My lessons were either just before or just after. I remember Mr. Andre Kostelanetz escorting the lovely French diva to her classes. I never dreamed that only two years later I would be on the same stage with her, and even get into some trouble because of her. This happened during *Lakme.* I was so entranced with Pons' appearance when she came down the steps of the temple after our ballet number that I forgot to get up and leave the stage, so I remained sitting in a Hindu pose during the entire "Bell Song." No wonder I was spellbound; Mlle Pons had a lovely figure, was very petite. In those days, most of the divas were of considerably respectable size, to say the least; but *here* was a vision out of the Arabian nights. The costume was made from mother-of-pearl sequins, with a glittering bra, and the short skirt, with only the merest suggestion of a transparent veil at the midriff, showing the naked waist of a ballerina.

During this period the dance war was on. Ballet and modern dance were in a great battle, each desiring recognition. The free dance of Isadora Duncan had become popular, along with the dancing of Ruth St. Denis and Ted Shawn, who had achieved considerable recognition for their talent and teaching. The arguments which appeared in print were very strong; Mary Wigman and Michel Fokine had some kind of big argument. Granny at that time was involved with some literary people. The very talented and well-recognized (at least by the refugee Russians) Lydia Feveisky was our friend, and Granny had helped her to publish her book of poetry. Now Granny was asked to translate an article by Mary Wigman from the German for Maestro Fokine, and then, with help from someone else, "Papa" Fokine's response was translated into English. It was quite an international transaction. All this activity gave me the chance to get to know my idol better and to learn more about Maestro, not only as a teacher and choreographic genius, but as a real person.

During all this activity Mother and Collette, my half-sister, came to New York for a visit. That is when I first visited the Statue of Liberty, the Empire State Building, and many other places which are never seen by most people who live in New York.

At the same time, my father helped Mme. Anderson-Ivantzova open the studio which later became one of the most respected and popular studios in New York City. I remember inviting Patricia Bowman and a few other friends for Mme. Anderson's first lessons. This gave a strong beginning to the success of her studio, although later we were to have a civil war with Madame. She did not, it seems, approve of the lyric arms of the Fokine style, so if I did my own arms at the *barre* or in a combination, I was called a "Russian disaster." But still, once a week, Mme. Anderson came to our home to have her favorite *cotelettes* and a social visit with Granny. She gave me, as well as her other pupils, a strong back, good discipline, and clean beats. "Papa" Fokine had never paid too much attention to exact techniques. One had to dance and be able to execute his combinations to be accepted by the Maestro. But he did not like to spend more time than necessary at the *barre*, which he felt was just to warm up the muscles for center work. The main idea was to dance, and as you danced you improved your technique. It was not so important how many turns were executed, but rather, how the line looked, the finish, the style. The pupils of Fokine had a special quality. The arms were very important. The movement started from the heart. There had to be the idea that the arms started the movement as a continuation of the inner self.

Many years later, while I was teaching at a convention in Portland, Oregon, a lady came to me and started talking about Fokine. She told me that she had known right away that I had been Fokine's pupil. This also happened a few times in other places. Even now, whenever ex-pupils of Fokine meet, one feels an invisible bond, usually sharing a wistful sigh or a favorite memory in understanding of each other.

Enclosed in one of the saddest letters I ever received far away in the South Pacific during the second World War, were the newspaper clippings and letters from Patricia Bowman and some other friends, notifying me of Michel Fokine's death in 1943. The great period of his universal choreographic creation was finished.

Every time I begin to wish that I were younger, I change my mind. If I were younger by a few years, I would not remember the way Russia used to be; I would not have an idea of how grand our way of life had been. And I would not have had the benefit of working, studying and dancing with Fokine. I would not have the treasure of knowledge that I obtained and experienced from being close to Fokine, and later to Olga Preobrajenskaya, and would not have known the grandeur of Mathilde Kchessinskaya. For all that, it is worth being old now, and remembering this rich past makes it easier to live through today.

# 23

1935 to 1938 were the "preparation" years. I was dancing, performing in many places and in all kinds of styles, and I was working with different choreographers and teachers. The Fokine Ballet was a company with a classical base, but it was always flavored and colored with demi-caractère work: Schéhérazade, the Oriental fantasy, required a flowing movement, in contrast with the vigorous, almost primitive, wild dances of the exciting Prince Igor. This might be followed by the romantic, elegant quality of Carnaval. My experience with the Salmaggi and San Carlo opera companies taught me how to deal with, and to find a place to perform among immovable singers. I learned to dance and to be looked upon as an unavoidable nuisance by the singers, who could not or would not move. They were *opera;* we, the dancers, were just the trimming. Too bad that the same point of view still continues into our present day. All those concerts and performances were valuable experience for me, but they occurred on chance-like, unpredictable occasions. And they lasted only a few weekends in the summer for a few performances at the Hippodrome, or City Center, the Mecca Temple, or the Brooklyn Academy. It was not, as they say, "steady employment."

Finally word got around that a big audition was to take place for a whole season's contract, with regular all-day rehearsals and performances almost every night. This was a very desirable contract. Although the pay was not great, the prestige and glamour of being in the Metropolitan Opera Ballet Company gave it a very prestigious status. The audition was not a series of short eliminations, like most auditions. Many dancers applied—a few hundred, I believe. A few dozen were told to come back later, for a long, nerve-racking period of learning steps and different styles of dancing for different operas. The elimination continued for weeks until a select few were finally signed up. This was a cruel period of suspense, of never knowing if you were going to be asked or not to come back the next day for more rehearsal.

Our choreographer was Dimitri Romanoff, who came from La Scala via the South American Opera Company. The "power behind the throne" at the Met in those days came from two ladies: Miss Curtis, the ballet mistress, and her indispensable, ever-present, ever-busy Miss Harding. Once in a while, the handsome director of the Met, Mr. Edward Johnson, made an appearance. I was grateful for my previous experience in opera as well as in Spanish dance, because it helped me tremendously to understand the styles of the steps and the proper behavior for various "period" settings. I also believe that my being a Russian helped; Maestro Romanoff hardly knew any English.

Thinking back now, I realize how selfishly involved I was in my love and desire of dance. I did not notice that Granny was gradually becoming very weak, and that she was losing interest in life. We had a Russian lady who visited us for a few hours each day to help with the preparation of food. She gradually took over a great deal of what had to be done for Granny, because I was absent for many hours at a time. One day Granny made a remark in conversation with someone: "Well, my job is finished. Orestik is on his own now. He has a contract with the Metropolitan Opera Company, and he has become a professional dancer. He has realized his dream to be a dancer." A kind, sad smile, and her whole attitude suddenly stabbed like a knife into my heart. I realized that she had given up the struggle to keep going. She felt that her job was finished.

The everyday life of rehearsals, lessons at the Met, costume fittings, the excitement of dress rehearsals, and the opening night of the 1938 season—with *Otello* starring Giovanni Martinelli—now filled my days and nights with new interest and meaning.

One night, after coming home late, the shock of reality again sobered me up when Granny asked me, "Why didn't you come up for such a long time? I heard you talking downstairs." I realized that she could not have heard me. I told her so, that the apartment was on the nineteenth floor and that she could not have heard me. I explained that I came home so late because the German opera was so long. (In those days the dancers were used in every opera whenever the action required our support. We had to stay in one position in *Lohengrin* and in *Tristan und Isolde* for half an hour at a time, as soldiers or attendants.) The Russian lady who was still with Granny whispered to me that Granny had fever, and that the doctor had visited her and that she was under sedation. After that night Granny never got up again.

But for a while she was better. One day a big event occurred. Granny asked that her hair be done up. She was comfortably propped up with pillows, and she put on her best wrapper with lace. Father and his wife, Gertrude, came to visit us with their three-month-old daughter, Kira. It was a touching scene as Kira was put at the foot of her grandmother's bed where she was admired by everybody. It was the last bright moment of our lives together. The weeks that followed were filled with sad worry, hectic rushing from home to the Opera House and back home again, where a nurse or a doctor would tell me that everything was ". . . about the same; no change."

The irrevocable tragedy of death has its own drama, a feeling of shock, most of the time a deep sorrow. There is also in the back of the mind the knowledge that someday it must happen to you. The unknown hereafter is frightening unless religion is dominant in the make-up of the person who is left behind. In my case, the sense of loss overpowered the fear, even the sadness. The sorrow was so deep that there were no tears. For twenty years of my life, Granny and I had been inseparable, living most of our lives in the same room, suffering the hunger and humiliation of revolution and civil war, surviving and learning to live again. Now we were separated physically.

That night, coming home, as soon as I came in I knew by the faces of those present that the end was near. But the doctor told us that he could not predict anything: Granny was in a coma. It was decided that if there were no change by the next morning, he would call for an ambulance and take her to a hospital. So everyone left; only a nurse who had been taking care of Granny for a long time stayed on. Exhausted, I fell asleep. Sometime after midnight I was awakened. Granny's breathing was very uneven. I was holding her up in my arms, lifting her a little to help her to breathe more easily. Before the doctor arrived in the early morning, Granny's spirit had left her. I insisted on dressing her in her favorite gray silk dress with white lace framing her face; for the last time I fixed her hair.

Then the funeral procedure took over. I really do not remember the details. The next and last time I saw Granny was in the Russian church, with flowers surrounding her. Somebody told me that during the singing of "Eternal Memory," the prayer for the soul, I swayed and fainted. All that I remember is following the funeral cortege to the Ferncliff Cemetery near Ardsley, N.Y. and feeling completely empty. Even when the last prayer was said and the curtain was closed at the crematorium door, I felt nothing but emptiness—wondering where her spirit was. A few days later we chose a niche in the mausoleum, where a vase containing her ashes was to be left. Through the years I did not like the impersonal coldness of that place, so a few years ago I bought a plot on the top of a hill in the same cemetery, into which I transferred Granny's ashes, and where I will have my final resting place. A Russian priest blessed the spot. There is now a plot with an inscribed plaque, which I did not order, waiting for me—the inscription reads: "Katherine Sergievsky 1868-1939" and just below it "Orest Sergievsky 1911-     " That empty space is waiting to be filled. When my friends visit the cemetery with me they are uneasy, but I do not mind. At least this place is "paid for."

A day after the funeral, still in a daze, I made myself go to the Opera House. I do not know how I managed to get through the performance, or the next few days, but some realization of life made me conscious that everyday existence was going along its way.

What brought me back to life was a new chance to dance—my caring about the result of another audition. Many dancers had auditioned and were talking about it, so I decided to try my luck. The Metropolitan Opera had just a few more weeks to perform before the summer layoff. Like the Met audition, this new audition was conducted as a series of rehearsals. Dancers who could dance the steps and understand the style of the choreography were told to return for the next rehearsal. It was a madhouse, but all of a sudden I came to life. I still remember the joy of movement, the excitement of the steps, and the dynamic personality of the choreographer—the first time since I left Michel Fokine that dance movement had contained so much stimulation and meaning. The year was 1939, the choreographer was Leonide Massine, and the ballet we were working on was *Capriccio Espagnol.*

Thanks to my study of Spanish dance, the steps were easy to perform and remember, and at the second rehearsal Massine even noticed and complimented me on how I was executing the steps. At the end of the first week's rehearsal, I was asked to join the Ballet Russe de Monte Carlo. I was one of the few lucky dancers to make it into the same company as Alexandra Danilova, Frederic Franklin and many other glamorous stars. This might have been the height of any dancer's ambition in that day. I was told by Massine to go to the office to sign the contract. He wanted me in the company.

But it was not to be. I would soon face my first contact with the intrigue of company politics.

At that time my father was very much in the news. There were stories about his adventures as a test pilot, as a leading figure in the emigré world of the White Russians, as Commander of the American Legion of the Russian Veterans of the Wars, as a member of the Tolstoy Foundation for the help of Russian refugees, and, along with his wife Gertrude, a patron of the arts, including (unknown to me) the Ballet Russe de Monte Carlo. All this proved to be an obstacle for my career, making it difficult for me to be "independent," to obtain a job on my own merits, to receive the recognition which I deserved for my dancing.

When I arrived at the Ballet Russe office and the contract was being prepared, I gave my name as, simply, Orest—just Orest, because I used it as my stage name. I was told that they had to have the full name on the official contract, that if I wished I could use only "Orest" on the programs. Finally, when I was asked to enter the inner sanctum in order to sign the contract, the Russian-born Sergei Denham, director of the company, changed his attitude immediately on learning my family connections. I was asked to sit down, and he told me that he was happy that I was to be in the company. He said that he had watched the rehearsal and that I was too good a dancer to be just in the corps de ballet, that I should be a soloist and that a new contract would be drawn up. Upon my insistence that I would be happy just to be in the company, the answer was the same.

I left the office without signing the contract, with a bitter feeling of disappointment. My pride was stronger than my desire to be in the company. Father, it seems, had agreed to "donate" an extra thousand dollars. I suppose my refusal to go back and sign the contract, and my statement that I wanted to get jobs on my own ability, was admired, but it was a hard pill for me to swallow. For many years I had harbored a resentment and hurt in my heart against such practices. But I now realize that many careers are helped by "oiling" the management, and though it does not diminish the talent or dim the personality, the self-respect and self-assurance does suffer from this "help."

154

But almost immediately after that a new audition was in the news, and the bright sun of Ballet Theatre was about to illuminate my life and the stages of the world.

# 24

*1937-1938:*
My memories of the old Metropolitan Opera House are rich and colorful, full of never-to-be-forgotten performances of the great artists. This is not just romantic nostalgia on my part; I happened to be lucky enough to have been there when all the fabulous singers sang, when saving costs on performer's fees was not a prime factor in determining the cast for a night's performance. Kirsten Flagstad, Lauritz Melchior, and Elizabeth Rethberg were the Wagnerian stars, and Nino Martini, Helen Jepson, Lily Pons, Giovanni Martinelli, Lawrence Tibbett, and the romantic hero Ezio Pinza were cast in the popular operas. The dramatic singing and acting of Thorborg in *Electra* (Pauly made guest appearances), the glamour of Grace Moore in *Louise,* the intensity of Marjorie Lawrence in *Salome,* and the dramatic acting and singing of René Maison made these performances a theatrical experience far beyond mere listening pleasure. Risë Stevens made her memorable debut, Licia Albanese came into her own tender characterizations, and the charming loveliness of Bidu Sayao captured so many life-long admirers.

In the ballet we had many top stars and the competition was great, making the performances even more interesting. The "comeback" of Felia Doubrovska, formerly leading ballerina with Diaghilev's Ballets Russes, was a main event, and her performance in *Orpheus* in the Elysian Fields ballet was a dream. (Recently, at a gala reception at Lincoln Center, the gracious lady introduced me as her former partner to some society admirers who were paying their respects to her. She recalled in particular our days at the Met and how I lifted her in *arabesque.*) The youthful glamour of Ruth Chanova from the Russian Ballet, and the excitement of Maria Gambarelli, with her unique technique and name—all these personalities were wonderful to watch and to dance with. It was really exciting when all three of these ballerinas—Felia Doubrovska, Ruth Chanova, Maria Gambarelli—

performed in the same ballet, as happened with *Lakme* and *Gioconda*. I remember helping Doubrovska add a little extra sparkle to her costume for the *Gioconda*, persuading her to do so because I knew that Chanova and Gambarelli had already done so to their costumes, which had been supplied by the Met.

Grant Muradoff and George Chaffée were our principal male dancers, and as it happened that season, most of the dancers were tall girls and rather medium-sized boys. I was lucky to be one of the few taller boys, and so was chosen to partner Doubrovska in the ballet for *Thaïs*.

Due to "star-gazing" and being stage-struck in general, I made a few faux pas during performances. Sometimes I was entranced by the artists and simply forgot to leave the stage when the other dancers left. At other times I could not leave due to mishaps. In *La Traviata* I was so enchanted with Nino Martini, looking like a cinema matinee idol, and with the loveliness of Helen Jepson that I had to be called off the stage by theatrical whispers as the singers began their love duets. During one performance of *Tannhäuser,* I was a dancer in the Venusberg section of the first act and then, in the third, came back dressed as a monk, for which I wore a long robe. As we, the monks, carried on the bier of the dead Elizabeth, my long robe caught in the stand on which we placed the coffin. I could not straighten up, so I knelt down and pretended to pray while the next aria was sung, and managed to escape during the scene change which followed. During another performance of *Tannhäuser* I had to be helped off the stage because of a collision. The Venusberg ballet was choreographed in such a way that we were to be seen in different poses in the caves of the grotto, but to get to those specific places we had to run from one side of the stage to the other in almost total darkness. While crossing the stage, another dancer and I collided, knocking the breath out of our chests, and we had to be helped offstage by other dancers.

Another, now amusing, happening occurred during the Hades ballet in *Orpheus.* We were arranged in "suffering" groups about the stage. As the curtain opened, and Orpheo appeared at the top of a staircase about to descend into Hell, the steam pipes started to exhale steam. Our costumes, consisting of a few rags covering our bodies, were not enough protection. I had to do a little choreography of my own to avoid the steam.

When *Aida* was being rehearsed, we tried our new costumes only to discover that the material was very stiff oilcloth and had a mind of its own. When we executed our angular "Egyptian" profile movements, the costumes remained up as we raised a leg, rather than falling into folds as they were supposed to, giving a rather sexy effect. At the rehearsal I asked the choreographer who the fool was who had designed the costumes. I could not understand why some of the dancers were making signs behind his back, until I heard Romanoff's answer: "The fool who designed these costumes is me."

Recently (1976) as I was listening to and watching the Met's production of *Die Meistersinger*, I could not help remembering another performance of long ago in which I was on stage during the street fight scene. I do believe our performance thirty-five years ago was more realistic, probably due to our misconduct. I also believe that the general lighting of the older production was better than the spotlighting which is so overdone these days. When we were on stage, long ago, the night scene was done almost in the dark, the small lighted windows of the set creating enough illumination to see the activity on the "street." Our misbehaving was very effective because we were allowed to improvise. We had only been told where we had to be at what time of the action during the pillow fight. During that particular performance, either by chance or on purpose, one or two of the pillows happened to split. The effect was spectacular; a snowfall of feathers was added to the flying pillows, encouraging applause from the audience and more realistic tumbling around on our part—therefore a very lifelike performance. Afterwards, we were severely reprimanded for overdoing it, but no one confessed that it was not an accident.

I have particularly bright memories of an after-performance supper given by Kirsten Flagstad at the Old Met, in celebration of her twenty-fifth anniversary on the stage. It was a wonderful party. Everyone connected with the opera had been invited. The great singers and divas could be seen sitting next to stage hands and mechanics at one table; work clothes were intermingled with lovely evening gowns. It was such a friendly and fun evening, enjoyed by everyone.

I remember how friendly some of the stars were, and the interest they took in the affairs of the dancers. For instance, Lawrence Tibbett represented the dancers at the union meetings, and he finally succeeded in obtaining better working conditions and more pay for us. We no longer had to "super" when there was no dancing on stage. In other words, we would no longer have to stand as part of the scenery holding spears during the long acts of the German operas such as *Lohengrin* and *Tristan*. I also remember Tibbett almost missing his entrance in *Rigoletto*. He had been in the wings learning a ballet step from us before the second act!

Rehearsals were great fun when Grace Moore was in *Louise*. Even her entrances were of movie-star quality. First, her lady dresser would announce that Miss Moore was on her way; then Miss Moore would make her entrance, depositing her furs with an elegant flair.

There was always some misbehaving during the long operas. Muriel Bentley, who was, like most dancers, not very well endowed in the bust, would appear on the balcony of a set padded in the right place with a turkish towel, breaking up the singers and dancers. Muriel was a good sport and always kept her sense of humor. When most of us were unhappy about some unpleasant happening, she would imitate someone, and we would all break up with laughter. She continued to do so years later at the Ballet Theatre rehearsals.

Another well-remembered personality is Mme. Savage. She was an irreplaceable "character actress," although she was later replaced rather effectively by her daughter. It was a real pleasure watching Mme. Savage do her little scenes and stage business in different operas, adding flavor and style to the action on stage. I can still see her busy doing bits with a bird cage, and remember her very responsive reactions to what was being sung on stage. Similar to her was Julia Barashkova. Although a dancer in the corps de ballet, she always took special care to be in the right mood to add something of her own to the little parts she had to do. She was as careful of her costume and make-up as if she were the star soloist on the stage.

I often meet the charming Bea, and Dorothy, another dancer from those days, at ballet performances, and we reminisce about the "good old days." Lillian Moore had been in the company. She was always very conscientious about everything she performed; later she proved how much she had learned by teaching others. Also, meeting Paul Sweeney, another dancer from the Met, once in a while gives us a chance to laugh and remember the past. Together, we relive some pleasant memories.

I remember the exciting, "history-making" romance of the season. In the ballroom scene Pinza sought out Doris, one of the ballet dancers; several times she tried to hide behind me because Elizabeth Rethberg was watching Pinza's growing interest in Doris. But he would, nevertheless, bring Doris out to start his aria about the "lovely hand" in Don Giovanni. I believe the final touch to Pinza's decision came when Doris was dancing as Jepson's shadow in Thaïs. Soon afterwards, Doris became Mrs. Pinza.

Another memory that comes to mind is the overpowering performance and interpretation of Boris Godunov by Ezio Pinza. The old production was so much more Russian than the one we now see, which reminds me of the Great Wall of China, instead of old Russia, with all those icons. One of the dancers, Von Irkust-Hamilton, intrigued me. He was a very good dancer, with a polish that none of us had as yet acquired. I kept asking him why he looked so familiar to me. Finally he, Von Irkust-Hamilton, told me that he had danced in a few New York concerts under the sponsorship of the impresario Sol Hurok. I had seen his concert some time before; after the first part I had bought a more expensive ticket so I could see the performance better. He was a very talented dancer, with a style reminiscent of Harald Kreutzberg. I was fortunate to become one of his friends.

During that season, one of Von's friends arrived in New York and tried to "make it." I made some suggestions and helped to arrange some introductions to help the newcomer, Jimmy, to get to the right places. Within a few short years, Jimmy was in the Ballet Russe de Monte Carlo and he became one of New York's most popular guests, entertaining everyone with his witty impersonations. Finally he became one of the most successful performers and choreographers on TV, with the delightful Imogene Coca and Sid Caesar on "The Show of Shows." Jimmy's last name, Starbuck.

One personality that comes to mind is Katharine Dunham, who was at that time a new star with a promising career in her future. I still remember how all of us applauded while watching her audition at the Met (she was auditioning to dance in *Aida* and some special ballets). We could not believe that she was not signed to be in the company. As years went by, Katharine Dunham became a big success, and I always enjoyed her concerts. Even during the War, when I was stationed in Kentucky, she graciously invited and entertained me. The final note in her success story—in my opinion a great triumph—was the fact that the best *Aida* ever choreographed at the Met was by Dunham. The dances were so right, the whole pageantry of different dances in the triumphal scene was so visually exciting, that one felt it was authentically Egyptian. (The blind, stupid "progress" of today has resulted in a version of *Aida* at the Met which is an insult to anyone's intelligence. The staging, à la German opera, includes a view of the Nile through an arched bridge—and the arch had not even been invented in those days. The temple dance is done like a contemporary American Indian eagle dance at a school recital, and I cannot for the life of me understand the karate-like exercise of two boys in place of a group number to the familiar triumphal music!)

In the old Met's *Aida* we had to use body make-up, which was terracotta in color in the Egyptian style. Our dressing rooms were on the very top floor, a few steps up from the big rehearsal studio where we had our morning pre-rehearsal class. Washing off the body paint after the ballet was a very primitive process. We had no union protection then and would not demand the "plush" facilities of today. So, after a performance, we all headed toward the wash basins—there were only a few of them in the corner of the studio. There we had to sponge off, helping each other to get the body paint off our backs. It was primitive, but camaraderie helped us to overlook the discomfort. It was cold up there in the winter, but we all survived, and now some of the hardships are remembered with romantic forgiveness.

Perhaps my looking back, thinking and describing all this, seems to have been colored by the flattering light of "surprise pink" spots, but that had been my first year at the Old Met, the first of ten years of my feeling "at home" there. After that season-and-a-half, it was to become my home with ballet companies every spring and winter season, most notably with the Original Ballet Russe.

# 25

In 1975, as we were entering New York's City Center, Patricia Bowman and I were reminiscing about the old Center Theatre (which once stood on Sixth Avenue & 48th Street) where we had both performed. As we took our seats in City Center, we turned the first page of our programs and both had a shock. The years were swept from under us. I had a feeling of "What was I doing, sitting here? I should be on the stage!" But this feeling lasted only for a few seconds; Patricia began to cry. The first pages of an old program had been reproduced for this, American Ballet Theatre's thirty-fifth anniversary gala, and we read on the pages before us: "The Toast of Vienna . . . Patricia Bowman in *The Voices of Spring* and Immigrant Dying One of the Living. . . . Orest Sergievsky. . . . *The Great American Goof.*" As the celebration of the ABT anniversary continued, and some of the personalities from the past appeared on the stage, memories of the first season and the very beginning of Ballet Theatre came into focus.

How well I remember the excitement and suspense of the long days of auditions, the countless rehearsals, and adjustments to the different personalities of numerous choreographers, each with his individual variety of steps and combinations for creating his ballets. As I understand it, the dancers selected to sign contracts were those chosen by the majority of the choreographers. The foundation of Ballet Theatre had been laid in the late 1930s by Mikhail Mordkin and his pupil Lucia Chase. Among the pupils in Mordkin's studio were the future stars Viola Essen and Leon Danielian, at that time in their teens. The other dancers included the talented Nina Stroganova, Vladimir Dokoudovsky, and Karl Karnokovski. Other dancers, such as Leon Varkas, were added for each New York season of the Mordkin Ballet, to partner the guest ballerina Patricia Bowman.

The success of the ballets and the new dancers in Mordkin's company was so great that a new and larger company was soon to be erected upon the foundation of this success. With the financial help of Lucia Chase, and the help of all the choreographers corralled under the guidance of Richard Pleasant, a never-before "happening" was taking place. After the birth pains of auditions and nerve-racking decisions, the early classes with Agnes de Mille finally got under way (Adolph Bolm handled the men's classes) on Madison Avenue at 59th Street, just opposite the School of American Ballet. We could see Balanchine's dancers working out across the street. The personality duels and juggling rehearsal hours among numerous choreographers were big problems, not only for the directors but for us, the dancers, as well.

For over three months the choreographers re-staged old ballets and created new ones. We, the dancers, rushed from one studio to another, or just collapsed, waiting for the next choreographer to come in to teach us new steps or to work over the already learned passages, perfecting them. From Fokine's romantic *Chopiniana* or *Carnaval* we would be thrown into the realistic *Great American Goof* with Eugene Loring creating a satire on the present-day ways. Or we would have to move in a comic style to the ideas of Adolph Bolm in the fairy tale *Peter and the Wolf*. Then would come an exciting rehearsal with José Fernandez, taking us to Spain with the music and the different way of dancing—and even walking—for his *Goyescas*. The most exhausting rehearsals occurred under Mordkin and Bronislava Nijinska. Tempers flew and the requests were commands—unlike working with "Papa" Fokine.

Somehow, with Fokine we did our best out of respect for him—because he expected his dancers, especially his pupils, to remember and to do their best. Mordkin and Nijinska had a lot of temperament and were nervous and somewhat eccentric in their manner of rehearsing. But these traits made the rehearsals more alive, although at times more difficult. *La Fille Mal Gardée* exhausted me because we had a fast and furious show-stopper, *The Dance of the Gypsies*. Nijinska chose Leon Danielian, Vladimir Dokoudovsky, and me to dance with Miriam Golden; it was a good thing we finished the dance by throwing ourselves on the floor, since we were exhausted at the end.

Mordkin's *The Voices of Spring* was fun to learn and dance, because the music of Strauss just made you want to dance. Mordkin's choreography made you enjoy his interpretation of the music and the characters who were personified. No wonder it was among the most successful ballets of those early seasons. It was a perfect vehicle for Patricia Bowman, who created the role of the flirtatious Toast of Vienna, with Dmitri Romanoff, Yurek Shabelevski, Peter Michael, and finally Edward Caton falling under her spell. This ballet—a bouquet of personalities—brought the best dancing from other characters interpreted by Nina Stroganova, Karen Conrad, Leon Danielian, Karl Karnokovski, and Vladimir Dokoudovsky. In the supporting cast were several future celebrities: Dolores Goodman, Maria Karnilova, Kirsten Valbor, David Nillo, Don Saddler, and my partner in the opening scene, Ann Wilson. It was fun to work with these people.

As the rehearsals progressed, the excitement and the anticipation of the opening date became more intense, and the costume fittings more hysterical. The costumes for *Swan Lake* were made of real velvet and soft leather; the *Goyescas* costumes were executed by the magical Karinska. The embroidery was applied using live mannequins—us. I remember not daring to move, just emitting a low-voiced "ouch" or "ly" or "lyii" as the pin or needle penetrated my skin. One dared not protest, one had to suffer for the Art's sake—this was the command of the great lady Karinska as she punched me with one of her many decorations hanging from one of her gold chains. I must say it was worth the suffering; the costumes were a dream.

The costumes we had to wear for the *Ballet Mécanique* were even more painful. They were knitted tights with a silverish metal-like stuff woven into the material so that when we moved it scratched us. The ballet had been created by Adolph Bolm, reconstructed from the Hollywood movie he had originally choreographed. Of those early seasons of Ballet Theatre, this was one of the hardest ballets to perform because we had to execute the movements with big silver balls, bouncing them from one platform to another as three elevators moved up and down. The effect created was of machinery at work, with the dancers as part of the machine. The make-up even further dehumanized us, covering our faces half silver, half black, or gray. The precision of the ballet was compared by the critics to the famous Rockettes of the Radio City Music Hall across the street.

The rehearsal of *La Fille Mal Gardée* was finished on the stage less than an hour before its premiere performance. In our beautiful dressing rooms we had loudspeakers so we could hear what was going on onstage. During a costume change, we heard a terrible crash. As I ran downstairs I thought someone must have been hurt, but I saw Patricia Bowman continuing her dance, with one of the painted backdrops lying on the stage. It had just missed her as it fell.

I will never forget the first performance on January 11, 1940 of *The Great American Goof*. I have never been shy or afraid on the stage. I love to perform too much, but *The Goof* was another thing. We had to speak the lines of the Saroyan script. What I had to say was coincidentally almost the story of my life—and my family was sitting in the audience. As I entered the dark stage, a spotlight hit me, but I could see the whole audience of almost 3,000 people. I opened my mouth but nothing came out. I continued my dance movement, hearing people helpfully whispering my lines from the wings. Finally, after a few bars of music which seemed an eternity I managed to find my voice. I know I projected my lines well because after the performance some of my friends repeated my lines to me, even though they had been sitting in the balcony. I believe it was the only time I ever had stagefright. It was due to the fact that I had to speak.

Years later when I had to perform in *Tovarich* as part of the Columbia University Drama School graduation program, I was still nervous speaking on the stage. This is due to my accent, I suppose. But this time the result was quite different. I forgot the exact words of the play. Cruelly, I continued, substituting my own words, getting laughter from the audience and completely throwing my fellow performers off, creating havoc with the script. I finished the scene to surprisingly warm—and certainly welcome—applause.

While hiding behind one of the make-believe bushes in our pantomime of not-too-brave soldiers in the premiere performance of *Peter and the Wolf*, my hat got caught on one of the branches and decided to stay there, to the giggles of the audience. The desperate stage whispers of our choreographer, Adolph Bolm, were to the effect that I had ruined his ballet. All was forgiven, however, when the curtain came down to numerous curtain calls and his acclaim.

Each choreographer had his own personality, his own devices to fascinate the audience, to make a dance better than one thought possible. From the first days I loved and worshipped Fokine, admired and was slightly afraid of Mordkin, was inspired by Nijinska, admired and tried my best for Bolm. But with Dolin and Antony Tudor it was always a challenge. Somehow our personalities clashed. I felt that they did not think I could do justice to their choreography. Therefore I did not do my best, and many times during rehearsals I made mistakes. Many times in our lives there are misunderstandings among people. It sometimes happens that one person's chemical makeup is just plain unpleasant to another. *C'est la vie!*

At the first rehearsal of Ballet Theatre Dolin appeared, making an entrance the way only a premier danseur would—a person who had complete confidence in his accomplishments. Vieux rose tights showed off his well-shaped legs, a sweater of pearl-gray cashmere was thrown over his shoulders, and the ever-present cigarette leaned at an angle from his thin, slightly sarcastic lips. His eyes, very bright and all-seeing, registered everything and everyone, while at the same time pinpointing someone that attracted his interest. His sense of humor, though very English, always contained a touch of the risqué. Dolin enjoyed pinpointing a mistake, making a joke that would shock some while amusing the others.

Over more than thirty years of knowing Dolin, I have felt every time I met him or worked with him that it was an event, even in the later years. Once in a play called *The Dancer* he proved his acting ability, using his theatrical sense to the best advantage. Another time, at a benefit for the Winter Garden, he danced *Hymn to the Sun,* leaving a lasting impression of self-assurance, showmanship, and the art of presentation of a self-admiring ego at its fascinating best. In the ballet of the *Fair of the Sorochinsk,* dancing *en pointe,* he realized the dream of many a male dancer—to perform in pointe shoes. He chose the right subject to impersonate—the devil. The toe shoes became hooves. His interpretation of Fokine's Bluebeard remains in my memory as one of the best performances of that role, which demands humorous qualities as well as the techniques of a premier danseur.

Our acquaintance over the years has consisted, for the most part, of occasional meetings. I have not forgotten—but it does not matter now—how I was hurt several times during our first rehearsals. One incident cost me a day's pay, as punishment for my insubordination. It was during a rehearsal of *Giselle,* which Dolin was setting for Ballet Theatre. I was constantly being corrected and told off, although I was by that time a very reliable, conscientious, hard-working dancer. I realized that there was going to be a "new member of the company," so at a general rehearsal I finally had "had it." Telling Mr. Dolin sarcastically that I was not "pretty enough" to be in his ballet, I made a reverence (a bow) and walked off the stage. The new member was put in my place and I was fined for disobedience—many were amused by the trouble I created.

But I had my revenge some time later by actually being begged to perform in *Giselle* at the Metropolitan Opera House. I had come in rather late because the first ballet was *Giselle* and I was scheduled only in the second ballet, *Graduation Ball.* The curtain had just gone up and Alicia Markova and Anton Dolin were already on the stage when our ballet master told me to go on. He knew I remembered all the steps. I rushed to dress; the costume had originally been made for me, so it fit perfectly. Two other dancers helped me dress, while the first pantomime and the pas de deux of Giselle and Albrecht were being performed on stage. I was ready to go on stage for the dance of the wine gatherers, and to my great satisfaction I danced without one mistake, proving that I was a dependable dancer. It just happened that night that action shots of the performance were taken and I have memo photos of that performance. Dolin had a humorous way of getting even with me some time later. I had invited to a chic restaurant called The Golden Horn our mutual friend Anna Ricarda, a lovely young society lady who was also a dancer just beginning her dancing career. Dolin joined us with his friend and proceeded to order everything a la carte. When the evening was over, I had to borrow money from Anna to pay the bill. Some time later I realized that Dolin had a good heart when he asked me to help him drive about and take care of Olga Spessivtzeva, the great ballerina of the past, who was not well and was almost forgotten by her old admirers and the public. What happened to Spessivtzeva can happen to any of us, I am sorry to say.

Dolin's devilishness sometimes would take the upper hand. I remember a few instances that occurred while he was performing the pas de deux with Alicia Markova while on the road with the Original Ballet Russe. Dolin and Markova were our guest artists, and their appearances improved the box-office intake. Dolin misbehaved a few times, just to break the monotony of one-night stands and probably for the benefit of all of us who stood in the wings to watch their performance. He would wink at us with a smile, and all of a sudden walk away from the spot where he was supposed to be. Poor Markova would have to improvise a few steps of her own. But during the coda he would dance with even more flair, finishing with a bravura that always brought down the house. Even though Markova would not talk to him for a day or two afterwards, she would eventually make peace with Dolin. They were a world-famous ballet team, equal only to Alicia Alonso and Igor Youskevitch, or to Margot Fonteyn and Rudolf Nureyev.

The exciting period which surrounded the first season of Ballet Theatre was noted especially for the intense concentration required of the young dancers, the anxious worries of having to remember the great variety of choreographic steps and styles, as well as a very natural concern with which costumes to wear for which ballet. Although three months of rehearsal was more time than most dancers get to prepare, the actual performances of all the ballets we learned were crowded into less than two weeks. Every evening was a premiere—a first for both the public and for us, the dancers.

In later years it was somewhat different when performing the same ballets with the Original Ballet Russe. Because I did not have to concentrate or worry how to perform the next step or how to dance the next movement of the symphony, it became almost automatic. We had danced the steps so often that the regular repetition made the combinations familiar, part of a "system." In many favorite role we could embellish—do more pirouettes for example—but the excitement and suspense never equaled that of the first weeks of Ballet Theatre. Only when we had to dance a world première of some ballet with the Ballet Russe would the familiar excitement fill the blood and the pulse quicken.

In later years, during the War, while experiencing the hopelessly empty, lonely nights in an army barracks or lying awake in a flapping tent somewhere in the tropical jungle of New Guinea, I did not concentrate on the misery of the surroundings but, rather, on remembering the ballets that I used to dance. I often fell asleep reconstructing the choreography and sequences of the ballet steps. I also kept my sanity through those days of military life by visiting, whenever possible, the U.S.O. centers, where I would listen to ballet recordings. All these efforts were doubly successful: I not only kept my sanity, but, when I was able to return to the beloved ballet world, I remembered the steps.

On one of his visits to New York from the Canal Zone in 1940, my friend of Balboa high school days, Jack Chase, arrived during the busy period of Ballet Theatre rehearsals. I had no time to show him around New York, and could only see him a few minutes at a time. So I asked Dorothy Hall, my friend and ex-partner from the concert days. "Dorothy, take care of Jack." She took such good care of Jack that he fell in love with her. When he left to return to the Canal Zone, Jack was really "all gone" for Dorothy. A correspondence started, continued, and finally resulted in a proposal of marriage. Dorothy was uncertain but fascinated by the offer, and contemplated the complete change that would have to be made in her life. To leave her parents, to give up her dancing career, her security, to move to a life far away in the tropics? But Jack was very persuasive; he had a boyish charm that was hard to resist.

Although I was a go-between, a match-maker, I refused to give advice, insisting that they had to make the decisions and then live by those decisions. After a year and a half, Dorothy and Jack were married. For over thirty years, with long intervals between each meeting, we would see each other. They are now grandparents, retired and living in Florida. They have had a full life—troubles, children, and now know the joy of grandchildren; and they're still living together, not apart. Dorothy had her glamorous days in ballet, dancing on Broadway in *On Your Toes,* doing solos in the Fokine Ballet, for Ballet Theatre, then teaching ballet in the Canal Zone. Thinking back, I am glad I was busy with those rehearsals.

Remembering now: This was just one of many marriages I have "arranged," willingly or by chance. It happened to a few other pupils and friends as well. I usually have a "feeling" when two people might be right for each other. A few times things did not turn out happily. Still, when I think it over, lives were lived more fully. Although problems were abundant, they replaced loneliness and frustration.

Someone may ask, "What about yourself?" Well, I prefer to be a loner, to have my freedom, to be on the sidelines watching the parade of human joys, problems, separations pass by. Life and the world around are so interesting I just enjoy being. . . .

The summer of 1940 was hysterically busy for me. Offers from summer theaters and the possibility of a few performances with Ballet Theatre at the stadiums in New York and Philadelphia forced nerve-racking decisions of what to do—which contracts to sign. I was actually busy in three places. After I signed a contract with the Suffern Summer Theatre, Ballet Theatre's manager, Richard Pleasant, sent me a telegram inviting me to sign a contract for extra performances with Ballet Theatre at Lewisohn Stadium in New York City and at Robin Hood Dell in Philadelphia. I drove to rehearsals for *Dr. Faustus* in Suffern (where I also had a job teaching dance as part of their summer theater school program) and then to New York to perform; then on weekends to Clinton, Conn., to rehearse a brand new show called *After the Ball*. Jacques Cartier was the choreographer, and Patricia Bowman, who was the star, had gotten me a part in the show.

The Suffern Summer Theatre was a new venture with big names, a lot of money and, as usual, extravagant expenditures. Rex Ingram was Lucifer, with Walter Armitage as Faustus. A special organ was bought and installed in the back of the theater to create the heavenly music and to accompany the hellish dancing when we danced to tempt the unfortunate Dr. Faustus.

The theater was in a very advantageous location near New York, and the combination of talent and some big names with important connections helped to open the doors for many to exciting performance opportunities. There were glamorous audiences which included such personalities as Flora Robson, Vivien Leigh, and Laurence Olivier. To this day I vividly remember the thrill of meeting and talking to these wonderful people, who were, and still are, in my mind and memory, a special kind of humanity.

In the repertory of the Suffern Summer Theater were a lot of very ambitious plans. Some very excellent performances were given by well-known artists who agreed to perform without pay because the plays provided good opportunities to be seen near New York by audiences and agents. On the faculty at Suffern was the fascinating, talented artist Margaret Severn, a lovely dancer. It was her "specialty" that made her famous. In her inimitable manner she created a new world of visual experience with her masks, which highlighted the characteristics of the roles she portrayed.

It was a magical time in Connecticut also, a time in which new talents were being discovered: Alfred Drake and Barbara Bel Geddes, both of whom later added luster to the marquees of Broadway, were in the cast.

Friendships were made and acquaintances enjoyed—a few of them have lasted a lifetime. Some of these friends stand out more vividly than others, mostly because of their special individuality and because, as happens once in a while when two personalities meet, something chemical happened: The minds clicked, blood ran faster, and the fusion of personalities created a new atmosphere for talk and feelings.

Yes, summer theater—theater in the woods, theater by the old mill, the barn theater. Country theater, somewhere right off the highway. Hot summer nights, cars parked on the lawn, among the trees, in the high grass alive with fireflies. After the show a short drive to the nearest lake for a swim in the nude, then resting out-of-breath on the anchored float, away from it all, with some melody drifting across the water from a radio or a bar.

The artists in these summer places are a combination of old-timers, new rising stars, enthusiastic young hopefuls, and movie idols making personal appearances for a few weeks in order to "get in touch with the public." Also you'll find a few of the young "smart set," with hopes of crashing into the limelight. There were always a few who were talented, a few handsome or pretty, a few pathetic leftovers from the "Good Old Days" with stories to tell of the past grandeur of the Theatre. These stories were exaggerated through the years by repetitious narration and the ever-rich imagination of the story-tellers, who by this time in their lives had become convinced that these exaggerated lies were truth. All these are a part of the exciting, friendly atmosphere, with no time to accumulate a feeling of routine or intrigue because one show replaces another in a week's time. So-called friendships are quickly made with sincere promises to meet someday again in the city; but promises were usually forgotten among the new impressions of the rush of following days and rehearsals for the weekly new shows.

*Though you are away, far away . . . the words that wanted to be said are unspoken . . . Your nearness is still felt, because within my heart you are ever-*

*present . . . The image of you, your ways and your habits, the smile on your
face, the look in your eyes are all alive, and the feelings I feel are memories
dear . . . From the past, all the things you have done and the emotions I felt
have created a pattern of an unforgettable design in my mind and heart . . .
Yes, yesterdays are a part of us, making us what we are today. . . .*

The try-out for *After the Ball* at the Clinton Summer Theater in Connecticut
was an eventful production because so many of the people involved "made
it" later. Performances by several established artists revealed new abilities,
new sides of their talents. A very touching interpretation by Patricia Bowman
of the heroine, Cinderella, was a delight. Her song to her only friend, a cat,
gave Patricia a chance to try her voice, which, although not large, was quite
pleasant. But the true delight, as usual, was her dancing, in which she was
partnered by Jacques Cartier. The powerful and experienced Marian War-
ring Manley, with her impressive dimensions and voice a la Tallulah Bankhead, created a new style for the Good Fairy. For the good-looking, beautifully voiced Alfred Drake, I believe he was only a step away on the ladder of
success to becoming a Broadway idol as Curly in *Oklahoma.* At Clinton,
Barbara Bel Geddes was one of the young girls who was eagerly learning
how to move on stage, and one could tell and predict that this aspiring actress would reach her desired goal. There were a few very good-looking
young men (I felt almost out of place among them, but I knew that one of the
reasons I was in the show was that I could dance better than they) who succeeded in becoming "somebody." These included the handsome Don Murray, who went on to Hollywood, and the good-looking Steve Brody, who for
years had his own artistic career as an actor before becoming an artistic
businessman, in creative jewelry.

My memories of this summer are unclear, not only because of the confusing rehearsals in Suffern and all the socializing and teaching I had to do,
but also because a part of my mind was on the performances with Ballet
Theatre, where changes were constantly being made. For instance, instead
of the Spanish approach of Fernandez to the *Goyescas* which we had done
in the winter season, we now had the glamorous, exotic dancer Tilly Losch.

As I remember, I had difficulty finding a place to stay in Clinton, but finally,
thanks to an offer from Steve Brody, shared a lovely cabin by the sea. While
in Suffern I had a real fight on my hands, refusing to dance "in drag"—as a
devil dressed as a woman. I won my argument by making the costume myself. It consisted of the tights that I wore in *Blue Bird,* a hat from *Prince Igor*
with two peacock feathers representing horns, and a strategically placed
sequined fringe giving the idea of a bra and G-string.

As the summer progressed, the Suffern Summer Theater was becoming more and more interesting, and before it came to its abrupt and untimely close, I was able to work with many fascinating people such as Mackay Morris, Ruth Weston, Kenneth Bates, Fanny Bradshaw, and my talented friend, the individual artist Margaret Severn. "Suffering with Margaret Severn in Suffern" became many a student's comment. Margaret was much more of a "slave driver" than I, getting the best out of the students. She became the one who was feared and respected. For me, it was one of my first instructing jobs. Margaret never rested. Even in the middle of hot afternoons we could hear her practicing her castanets somewhere in the high grass behind the theater. But when she performed a few times, I learned a lot from her artistry and dedication.

I wish I could remember all the fascinating stories narrated to us by that veteran of the stage, Mackay Morris, glamorous tales about the leading ladies of the theater when he had been a matinee idol. These tales were often told after the performances, somewhere during the drinking of wine and unwinding in one or another local café.

We were lucky to witness some grand up-staging between the stars as well as some of the practical jokes that were played during performances. For instance, during the run of *Mazepa,* Ruth Weston, as she was driven off the stage strapped to a *papier-mâché* horse, all of a sudden produced an American flag to wave goodbye, as a joke to break up Mackay Morris. The effect broke up everybody in the audience as well.

Kenny Bates amazed me with the variety of roles he could play, while being such a quiet, unassuming person in real life. Rex Ingram fascinated me with his size, his bigger-than-life behavior, and his exuberant personality. Walter Armitage, our boss, was the personification of a charmer who could accomplish anything. Being a good actor and flamboyant personality, hardly anyone could refuse him. This was his success and also his downfall. There was nothing that he could not have for that theater or for its productions, but he overstepped his good luck by spending too much, living too wildly. The parties were fantastic, but the local community was not ready for the kind of permissiveness and free behavior which is commonplace nowadays. The final result was the closing of the theater for moral and financial reasons.

At the same time as the summer theaters were going on, there was all the excitement of rushing to perform at Lewisohn Stadium in New York. This was Ballet Theatre's first experience with outdoor performances. I especially remember the second act of *Giselle,* so beautifully danced by Nana Gollner. In *Goyescas* the glamorous Tilly Losch, along with her well-known interpretive back-bends, demonstrated her ability to move her arms in such a manner as to create a Moorish feeling in the Spanish setting.

During this version of the ballet there were a lot of stationary moments, in which we had to stand in imitation of Goya paintings—without participating in the movement on stage. In one such moment I misbehaved—one of the few times in my career on the stage. I did something that I could never do even in real life. I pinched my partner Kirsten Valbor's behind. For this I was punished with silence from her for many weeks to come.

We traveled to Philadelphia to perform there in the park. Johnny Kriza was a new member of the company that summer. I remember how nice he was—and he remained so through all his life. I do believe he is the only dancer to become the leading dancer of a ballet company who was liked by everyone, and I personally have never heard anyone say one word against him. Leon Danielian and I were roommates during our stay in Philadelphia. I believe Johnny felt secure with me, because I was the "older" dancer. He was a shy teenager, and his self-assurance and sense of humor came later, with his success and growing up.

There were so many new impressions that summer of 1940, so many new faces, personalities, and friendships. The possibility of choosing and doing so many different things made my head spin. Even now I really do not know how I managed all the rehearsing and dancing and still maintained such an active "social" life. At that age one does not want to "miss" a thing. During those months the horizon of my experience was enlarged, and my growing up was enriched by those around me, creating a standard of artistry which to this day is hard to match.

At about the same time I managed to take flying lessons and get a pilot's license, crowning my activities and accomplishments with signing a contract with the Original Ballet Russe. I still have the contracts, with my signature and those of Col. de Basil and Sol Hurok.

Among this kaleidoscope of memories of the early 1940s the following moments are bright on the screen of my memory:

. . . Patricia Bowman tip toeing across the stage among imaginary after-rain puddles of water in *Voices of Spring,* on the Center Theatre stage . . .

. . . The opening night of *After the Ball* in Connecticut, filled with excitement equal to that of a Broadway opening with all the important personages "out front" . . .

. . . Fanny Bradshaw, a perfect lady speaking beautiful English, heading the gypsy camp of the Suffern Theatre, talking to me with her friendly smile and gentle manner . . .

. . . The fantastic, wild party and after-the-party swim in the pool, my head spinning with the excess of wine and merriment after the opening night in Suffern . . .

. . . Meeting and teaching Harold, the German boy, son of an opera singer in Berlin, who had fantastic stories to tell. He was a beautiful blond, "almost a victim" of the decadence that was reigning at that time in his native country. . . .

. . . The never-to-be-forgotten moment of feeling like a bird/superman, with tears of ecstasy in my eyes, alone in the air on my solo flight over Roosevelt Field that summer of 1940 . . .

. . . The anxious waiting for news of Paul Haakon, who was also on his solo flight. He ran out of gas and landed in a field not far from the airport. . . .

. . . Meeting one evening the legendary Tallulah Bankhead, although for just a moment, after driving one of her friends to her place in Clinton, Connecticut . . .

. . . In the Ballet *Mécanique* by Adolph Bolm, at the Center Theatre, going up and down on moving elevators, being part of machinery—a "gear"— and anxiously passing or throwing an over sized silver rubber ball while thinking, "This is dancing?" . . .

. . . One of the most satisfying memories that stands out is of dancing the Gypsy Dance in *La Fille Mal Gardée* by Bronislava Nijinska. Although we fell on the stage, completely exhausted, at the end of the performance, it was worth it because it was a smashing success. . . .

# 27

Sometime during 1940 Father again asked why I was not busy with something more worthwhile than dancing. Why did I not fly? Was I afraid? Upon answering that I was not afraid, but that flying costs too much money, Father replied that he would pay for my lessons. The wonderful thrill of being a human that can fly began to materialize.

My friend Paul Haakon, who was at the height of his career, also started to take lessons. Early in the mornings the two of us would head out to Roosevelt Field near Mitchell Field army base, and after a total of nine or ten hours of instruction we made solo flights. The unforgettable sensation of that first flight is indescribable. I do remember that my eyes filled with tears and my heart was ready to burst with the feeling of freedom; I hated to come down.

Before receiving the license to fly a passenger, the so-called "private license," many more hours had to be spent handling different problems and tests, such as figure-eight flight patterns and a seven-hundred-twenty-degree spin, which is a pirouette-like turning of two complete rotations of the plane. I loved it all except one exercise in which the plane had to go straight up until the motor stopped—a "stall." I felt uncomfortably helpless, so high in the sky with my engine dead; as the plane started to fall it had to be brought under control and the engine had to be started again.

As our flying improved, Paul and I decided to buy a plane. We bought one with the help of a friend who was my father's mechanic and co-pilot, Harry Georgieff, whom we called *Bratoushka*. He was everyone's favorite, not only because of his knowledge of flying but also because he had a beautiful singing voice. Bratoushka had a way of singing which was embellished by moods he created. Being a Bulgarian, there was a dash of gypsy, a Moorish melancholy and a Greek brightness—all this resulting in a "soul effect" as if something intimate were shining through, lending a touch of sadness and a special quality of an unknown color to everything he sang. Among the three of us we found a plane, and Paul and I were very happy owners of a 145 H.P. Fairchild.

Finally, it was time to take up a "first passenger." Paul and I agreed to be one another's first "victim." And we lived to talk about it later with much pride.

I have included here a personal narration of another passenger of Paul's and mine, Kirsten Valbor who was also my partner in many dancing events, and she is still (in 1979), after all our experiences and knowing each other for so many years, my best friend:

Orest and Paul were going to fly me down to Red Bank [New Jersey] in their jointly owned plane. I really don't remember how this plan actually came about, but the arrangements were that we would fly down and be met at the airport by my parents, Paul and Orest would lunch at my home in Rumson and then fly back to New York.

I had stayed the night with the Sergievskys in that great duplex apartment they had in the south tower of the El Dorado in New York City.

We had breakfast; it was a simply glorious day and the sun streamed into the dining room; but I recall nothing of eating—just racing about waiting for Paul to arrive as we had to drive out to Roosevelt Field where they kept the plane.

Paul arrived and we began our goodbyes. Orest's father embraced me, kissed me on both cheeks and said, "Goodbye," adding gravely, "You are very brave." The whole tone was one of such sad finality that I began to protest. He merely said again, "Goodbye."

We got to Roosevelt Field and piled into the plane. For this trip I was to sit in the back, Orest was the pilot, and Paul the co-pilot. The day was brilliant, clear and cloudless. The mechanic stationed himself at the propeller and we began that exciting routine of:

"Contact."

"Contact."

The propeller spun, the engine caught and we were off. Soon, below us was Brooklyn where I had been born. Although I had never flown over Brooklyn before, it was quite possible to recognize certain areas—the school, the old neighborhood. I looked out the window at Brooklyn on the one side, then out the window at Brooklyn on the other side. And then I looked *down*—through a hole in the floor—and there was Brooklyn at my feet.

"There is a hole in the bottom of this plane," I said.

Paul looked back and down and said, modestly surprised, "Oh yes, there *is* a hole."

Orest looked back and said, "Where?" The hole located, they both turned back to face front and we flew on.

We traversed almost the entire length of Brooklyn when Orest said, "Now where?"

Paul said, "South-southwest," or something which sounded equally professional.

"Where's that?" Orest replied.

"Use the compass," said Paul.

"Where's the compass?" asked Orest.

I thought of Orest's father saying to me, "You are very brave," and I said, "Let me out of here!"

We were over the Narrows when Orest said, "There it is," and indeed there the compass was right in front of him.

The flight from then on was relatively calm. I didn't put my feet down on the floor of the plane, but the hole didn't get any bigger either.

We approached the Red Bank Airport. Now I should interject that the word *airport* is perhaps a trifle grand sounding, as this was actually a meadow or field with a long brown dirt landing strip set in a field of weeds and grasses. The windsock was clearly visible as we circled the field and came in directly over the single building, one story high, that constituted terminal, waiting room and office. It was lodged right under some very tall, nice trees; we were right over them, too. We came in lower and lower and there dead on (what an unfortunate choice of words) was the strip—and directly below us were treetops and telephone wires. Orest's eyes, Paul's eyes, my eyes, and I later learned my father's too, were on the telephone wires.

"We made it," said Orest as he did a neat three point landing.

"We made it," Paul sighed.

"We made it," said I.

"They made it," said my father.

They made the trip back just fine too, in spite of—or perhaps because of—lots of Aquavit over lunch. They tipped their wings over my family's house as they flew past on their way back to Roosevelt Field—and they are still both around, and so am I and perfectly willing to try it again. (Orest's father said "brave," not "wise.")

I have also included here another letter from Kirsten. Her mentioning "behind the stove" recalls the time nearly forty years ago when she and I danced, to make extra money, at some affairs in some most unexpected places into which my insistent and anxious agent "booked" us. This particular event took place at New York City's Ansonia Hotel, and for some reason was called "Strawberry Festival." It was one of those affairs in which the dance act (us) was sandwiched between a violinist and a singer. In this particular case, we were also sandwiched between a hot stove and a screen that led into a big ballroom in which we were to dance as part of a floor-show. For a dignified ballet dancer, especially Kirsten, who had just arrived from performances with the Royal Danish Ballet in Copenhagen, dancing a waltz among the tables in a lovely gown was not the most desirable goal of a dancing career. But later on we were treated like royalty when we danced the same number in Stratford to the acclaim of the Russian colony there.

Her letter to me gives a glimpse into a past which we shared.

Dear Orest,

My colorful and very haughty bird [I had given her a bird of colored glass] sits and glowers out at the Holiday Inn—the noisy traffic and general disorder of 57th Street—but smiles beautifully whenever the sun shines upon him. I need nothing to remind me of you for you are a constant with me but now here in my *bedroom*! I have this additional delightful reminder.

I want for you so many things—love, comfort and peace of mind—surely you are not *that* Russian that you want only dark eyes and tearful songs about departed loves—I write that because I am suddenly reminded of that night spot (oh what an old-fashioned expression) we went to once when you were home on leave and that man danced with those rather dull-edged knives and the girl sang one plaintive Russian song after another and when you waxed so joyous I asked what the songs were about so you translated as she sang about one tragic affair after another—lost loves, tearful partings, dark eyes and woe and sadnesses and unrequited loves asunder. Your absolute and total enjoyment of these disasters has remained with me as a treasured memory. We even had a photo taken by one of those flash camera things and I know you have it somewhere. Don't show it to anyone. I recall it failed to capture our wondrous physical attributes (and no cracks).

Love from your friend from behind the stove at the Strawberry Festival—
Kirsten (as if you didn't know)

My reminiscing with Kirsten these days always seems to amuse and baffle our friends who listen. And no wonder. We talk about our favorite alligator; we remember taking him for walks on a leash from our apartment on the thirtieth floor. My family, at that time, lived in the building where people were rather stuffy, so Kirsten and I made them uncomfortable by warning them not to step on our alligator. We pretended to have a leash in our hand, and we walked and pantomimed as if we actually had such an animal with us. No one who watched us could even pretend to see the imaginary alligator. Even today, Kirsten and I often baffle people when we start talking some nonsense as a bar—nonsense that only the two of us can understand or imagine, making our neighbors uncomfortable, or getting looks of sympathy—all of them convinced that we are completely mad.

Another of the passengers I flew in our plane was a glamorous friend named Ralph Clanton, who was in the early 1940s a matinee idol, one of the leading men on Broadway, playing opposite Katherine Cornell and other leading ladies. I remember quite clearly the day we went for our ride. I wanted Ralph to see New York from the air, so I flew very low—so low that upon my return to the field I received a ticket and a fine. The number of my plane had been reported by someone who could read it from the ground. I had been flying lower than the legal minimum, which is 1000 feet. I had actually circled around the Empire State Building. I never paid the fine, because as we landed, we learned what had happened that morning in Hawaii—it was December 7th, 1941.

Bratoushka, the good friend who had helped Paul and me select the plane, was a charmer in many ways in his everyday life. Many times Paul and I stopped overnight at his apartment in Forest Hills on our way to flying lessons at Roosevelt Field early the next morning. When the war broke out he felt that he should do his part. Being too old to be in the Air Force, he applied for the "ferry" service—a very important service to deliver men, supplies, and ammunition, for which experienced pilots were needed. Bratoushka finally passed all the necessary tests, finished his test flights for heavy loads and was ready to make his first flight to England. But then, silence. We did not hear any news for a long time. When finally a word came through, it was not the message we had expected, it was not from him. He had been killed in an explosion on takeoff. It had been sabotage. The cargo he was flying was too important to be allowed by the enemy to reach England. Another life wasted, cut short for peace?

The changing fortunes in the ballet world are exciting. Often, unexpected upheavals and dramatic shake-ups result in splitting companies. In one of these historic changes, the Ballet Russe de Monte Carlo was reborn, but became "American"—supported by many Americans and given an infusion of "new blood" by taking on many American dancers. The Original Ballet Russe went on to travel in Canada, South America, and Mexico under the direction of Col. de Basil, the direct successor of the great Diaghilev. With him was Diaghilev's former regisseur Serge Grigoriev, who remembered most of the Diaghilev-period ballets and was able to organize the de Basil company along the lines of the "old" Ballet Russe. And Grigoriev's wife, the glamorous Lubov Tchernicheva, was always a welcome addition. But, for this company, they needed more dancers—and this was my chance! My hopes of being in the "real" Russian company, with all the old ballets I loved so much, now finally materialized. Having been in Ballet Theatre had been a valuable and wonderfully enriching addition to my store of knowledge, and there had also been some help from Mme. Dokoudovsky, the mother of Vladimir, who was an old friend of Col. de Basil. After signing the long-dreamed-of contract with de Basil and Sol Hurok, I traveled to Washington, D.C., to join the company.

One of the first rehearsals stands out in my mind because it was a "comeback" occasion for Vera Nemchinova, the famous Diaghilev ballerina. The ballet master, Anatole Oboukhov (Nemchinova's husband) gave a "warm-up" class before the rehearsal began. I was amused by how strict he was—almost cruel—forbidding Nemchinova to do more than two pirouettes and correcting her for holding the balance too long. Most members of the company were afraid of him. Thank God, I had had the experience of facing Mordkin's temper in class and the demands of "Papa" Fokine, so I was only nervous, not petrified like the others. Nemchinova rehearsed *Aurora's Wedding* (as we called the truncated fourth act of *Sleeping Beauty* in those days) and *Swan Lake* with her perfect partner Michel Panaieff. It was a memorable experience for me to watch them work, and later during the performance to hear Madame whispering a few words during the *adagio/pas de deux,* emphasizing her movements with: "Love me," "Embrace me," then, as she was to move away, "Don't touch me," as she *bourréed* across the floor.

As a "newcomer" to the old company, I was also an "outsider." It always seemed to be that way and it took quite a while for a new dancer to be accepted. Very seldom during rehearsals would anyone willingly give me help. As a result, I learned the steps from the regisseur, Grigoriev, but many times I did not know the exact direction in the design of the choreography that I was to follow. It proved almost a tragedy for me when during a performance, my *first* performance, I found myself in a line with all the girls—we were facing all the men. Somehow I managed to get over into the right place during the next few bars of music. The mistake could have been prevented had someone just whispered to me which way I was supposed to move. I had had only two hours of rehearsal for this complicated ballet, one of the so-called "symphonic ballets" by Massine called *Les Présages* to Tchaikovsky's Fifth, which lasted thirty-five or forty minutes. Later on, it became one of my favorites, as did Massine's other symphonic ballets: *Choreartium,* to Brahms' Fourth, and the *Symphonie Fantastique* to the Berlioz.

I remember how surprised I was when, asking who had composed the ballet *Choreartium,* one of the dancers who had been dancing it for years said that she did not know. On another occasion, Nana Gollner had to substitute for another ballerina in the leading role of The Beloved in the *Symphonie Fantastique* (I believe her partner was Anton Dolin). Nana had time to rehearse only the pas de deux, which left fully three-quarters or more of the ballet unrehearsed. So a few of us who knew the ballet well were stationed in the wings, directing Nana with a few whispered words: which way to go, whether it was a *bourrée* or a *grand jeté* that was to be used to cross the stage. The intended effect in this ballet was that The Beloved moved in and out through the whole ballet like a vision, never really "being there" for any length of time. This effect was beautifully achieved, the audience understanding the haunting feeling in the mind of the poet, the unreality of his dream-like state, and his melancholic moods due to the influence of opium.

Lubov Tchernicheva Grigoriev—a grand lady, ballerina and actress, the glamorous Zobeide in *Schéhérazade,* the tragically beautiful Francesca da Rimini—will be remembered vividly by anyone who saw her in de Basil's Original Ballet Russe. In the early years of Diaghilev's Ballets Russes she was described in books and reviews as an exciting ballerina in such ballets as *Three-Cornered Hat* and *Good-Humored Ladies.* But to me she was the grand dame of the de Basil Company, a wonderful teacher for the selected few fortunate enough to take lessons from her while on tour.

Anyone who has seen Tchernicheva's performance in *Schéhérazade* will remember favorite moments from her numerous performances: the beautiful line of her body, her face in profile accentuated by white feathers and pearls, her supplication as the proud wife, her suicide by stabbing at the feet of her shah. There was a particularly poignant, tragic moment during *Francesca da Rimini* when, with her back to the audience, her arms rose slowly, showing her agony in clutched wrists and fingers, and then as she sank to her knees, opening her dress to meet the deadly sword of her jealous husband.

I was fortunate to have known her well; in recent years I have visited Mme. Tchernicheva at her home on the outskirts of London where she now lives. Photos of her glamorous past, with inscriptions from Diaghilev, Nijinsky, Karsavina, along with many mementos, souvenirs, gifts, and programs, fill the emptiness of her present and warm her lonely days with pleasant memories. Tchernicheva is still very beautiful. Her blonde-grey hair is fixed in the same pageboy length; she still disarms you with those same fabulous eyes. She is somehow smaller, though still as straight-backed as she was when we traveled those seemingly endless hours from Mexico City to Guadalajara. In those days, Madame was an example to many younger dancers, showing them how to look like a lady even when exhausted.

One of my especially treasured memories is of a walk on a sun-drenched afternoon with Tchernicheva and her husband, Grigoriev. It was a special occasion for me because I had been asked to join them. I had been accepted as their friend. At first they had regarded me simply as a "ballet enthusiast," as Madame called me, because I wanted to learn everything and to dance in every piece. That afternoon we walked for hours, with many stops to admire the landscape or some picturesque ruins. Madame reminisced about when and with whom they had seen it first, and this was usually the starting point of some colorful reminiscence, which often led into another memory. For me it was wonderful, being able to hear—almost to see—such a wealth of fascinating people and events brought to life, enriching my knowledge and satisfying my curiosity about the foundation of the Ballet Russe.

Years later, whenever I visited Mme. Tchernicheva in her little cottage in London, we would reminisce; she often told me how nice the Royal Ballet had been to her, asking her to help with restaging of old ballets, and inviting her to see many of their performances. One time, when she was telling me about working with Rudolf Nureyev, she told me how good it was to help such a talented young dancer.

I believe that Madame during our years with Ballet Russe felt that I did understand, and so she called me to visit with her. On these occasions, with a sad voice, she would tell me: "Orestik, there is no use to put the face on, or to fix the hair . . . you understand . . . I feel lonely. Come, we will talk about the past." Yes, her one-time companions were not free anymore. They were too busy elsewhere. The last heartbreak was when Nana Gollner and Tchernicheva's former partner, Paul Petrov, teamed together in many ballets and later married. I would go over to Madame's and she would receive me in a lovely wrapper, a delicate scarf or a bit of lace covering her hair. She would order tea, and we would spend some time just gossiping or speaking of the people she used to like, whom she now missed. I do believe it helped.

When I wrote these lines about Mme. Tchernicheva, she was still well, even asking me to help her neighbor, a Russian ex-count. Now she is no more. But whenever I look at her photos and remember her, I am grateful for having been fortunate enough to have known her, for her having taught me and enriched my knowledge and love of the art of ballet. To me she was, and still is, the great lady of the ballet.

During our travels and performances in different cities, often appearing in some of the best university auditoriums, we would sometimes have to add a few "extras" to our own company to take part in the big ballets. In some cities, pupils from dancing schools were used, or acting studios sent us their promising students. A few balletomanes invariably found their way in to perform in the tableaux from *Aurora's Wedding*, *Le Coq d'Or*, *Giselle*, *Swan Lake*. In *Schéhérazade* the "extras" were used during the last dramatic moments of the staged massacre, the killing of lovers of unfaithful wives. Usually the "extras" were asked to rehearse with whomever they had to kill, rehearsing on stage in the spot the slaughter would happen.

I remember one time at Duke University the students were asked to come early in order to rehearse the killing scene. After the plot was explained to them and the action of the dancers was described, the "lovers" walked through the movements, demonstrating where we, the dancers, would be. I showed my future executioner where I would start and how I would hide, then run up the stairs to escape; that would be the moment he was supposed to "slash" me from behind with his rounded machete (made of wood, colored with silver). At the time of this demonstration, we were all dressed in everyday clothes, but later, with the make-up and body paint on, our identities changed dramatically. The "extras" were dressed in Oriental balloon-like pantaloons, with *chalmas* covering their heads, while we, the lovers, were almost naked, covered with copper-colored body make-up. Sparkling jewelry decorated our arms and chest, and transparent *shalvers* on our legs finished our transformation. When the dramatic moment of our deaths arrived, performed to the surging music of Rimsky-Korsakov, half of the lovers were already "dying."

I made my dash, but I saw my "killer" looking right past me. My whisper—"Kill me"—did not have any effect. I had to grab the sword from his hands and, running up the steps, commit suicide, stabbing myself, thus dying as I rolled down the steps and landed at the feet of my would-be executioner. When the curtain came down he was apologetic. He had not recognized me in my Oriental disguise. "Show-off" was the remark of some of my colleagues, because my dying had been so sensational.

The Ballet Russe tour of Mexico in 1942 was full of surprises and problems, especially for me. First of all, merely crossing the border presented a big headache for the management and a lot of work for the rest of us. Most of the dancers had been born during the Russian upheaval. Their parents had been refugees of the Revolution on their way to find a new "home." I knew a few dancers who were even born "on the way"—on a boat or a train. One of our leading dancers had been born on a French ship in Turkish waters off Constantinople; from there the family had finally settled in Paris. Many were without definite nationalities, traveling with temporary permits to perform with the Russian Ballet. Due to the war, going into other countries could be a problem, and many of our dancers were detained at the border.

Our company arrived in Mexico City minus twenty dancers. Some of them never rejoined us, others never left Mexico, remaining there until the end of the War. I will never forget the commotion surrounding our first performance. Everyone had to "double up"—dance his own part and at the same time fill in, dancing someone else's role as well. Even Mme. Tchernicheva had to dance a swan in the last line of *Swan Lake* and in *Prince Igor* to help the design of the choreographer. To add to our trouble, the high altitude of Mexico City made it very hard for some of us to breathe. We had to perform two days after our arrival; many of us passed out. If someone had to dance a fast solo or do a difficult step, it was certain that that person would have to be carried off stage. As the strenuous solos danced in *Graduation Ball* were finished, two of the girls fainted, and we had to carry them off the stage. My turn came in *Prodigal Son* (Lichine after Balanchine). All of a sudden I felt dizzy and the next thing I knew I was "coming to" with someone holding a cold bottle of Coca-Cola to my temples backstage.

I remember one rehearsal of *Le Spectre de la Rose* which lasted half the night. A young friend of Bernard, who was to conduct the ballet but had not had a rehearsal with the dancers, wanted to know the phrasing of the music to the steps. So I offered to demonstrate it for him. Thanks to my private lessons with Fokine, I knew *Spectre* well and many times helped the dancers who were to perform it. It is sad to think that if it had not been for the War I would have danced it myself—Grigoriev had almost promised me that.

A few special events stand out during our travels in Mexico; Easter Night, a bullring performance, Chapultepec Castle, the Popocatepetl and Chapala Waterfalls. I remember the drive from the train to our hotel, the aroma of the blooming flowers in the night, and the sound of distant mariachis. I was possessed by an enthusiasm to see and experience as much as I possibly could.

I therefore had to climb to the crater of the Popocatepetl. A few of my friends decided to join me in this effort, but soon gave up, lacking my enthusiasm. I continued to climb without them. It was too long and too slow to go the way tourists usually did; I decided to go straight up. Before long, it was so steep that I had to scale the steep grade on all fours. The wind became very strong and the sides of the mountain felt very cold, but in my stubbornness I kept climbing. Soon I had to crawl on my stomach, lizard-fashion. Whenever I recall the event now, I can still feel the icy surface near the top and the frightening dizziness as I looked back down—way down to where my friends were standing. They made signs for me to come back, and after a few more yards I lost my nerve. I turned once more to look back and lost my grip. I started to slide down. It was a fast and painful descent—not very graceful—and I ruined my clothes, tearing my trousers to shreds. There was no sympathy from my dancer friends, only the remark, "You could have killed yourself."

One night there was to be a special performance, not in the glamorous Bellas Artes Opera House, but in a bullfight ring. A new experience! When we arrived at the ring, the stage was just being set after the afternoon performance of the bullfight. A "wooden-horses" arrangement was being installed, but as the floor boards were put down, not all of them were nailed, as we discovered later. The effect during that performance was dangerously spectacular, and a bit of comedy was added where it did not belong. During the lively mazurka, while finishing a series of bravura steps, we had to stamp the floor. The steps were more effective than usual, because as we stamped the other end of the boards flew up, much to the surprise of the audience and to the discomfort of the dancers.

But it was completely different in another performance some time later. We were to dance in a movie filmed on the grounds of the Chapultepec Castle of Maximilian and Carlota. The leading star was the Viennese Miliza Korjus. We spent countless hours one weekend waiting for all the lights and arrangements to be fixed. During a lull in our activities, a few of us decided to find a place to rest. Sometime later I was awakened—one of the guards found me asleep, very comfortably. I was reprimanded because I had been sleeping in the royal bed of Maximilian and Carlota. I heard that that movie was very spectacular, but because it was made in German by a European company and was never released here, I have never seen it.

On our journey to Guadalajara over the Mil Combress, we passed an unforgettable landscape, on frightening roads with high precipices. We often had to stop and wait for herds of animals to pass or for a lazy cow to get up from the middle of a village road. As we passed by the Chapala Falls a rainbow decorated the falling waters, and the spray from the falls created an unforgettable sight. Upon arrival in Guadalajara, we fell in love with the old opera house, the Hidalgo Theatre—jewel-like, old-fashioned, very old world.

A sense of antiquity was very much in the air. Time seemed to have stopped here in the mountains far away from the modern tempo of the capital. I felt as if I were back in another time, especially one night—it was Easter. Someone had told us to be sure to come in the middle of the night for the service. The square was filled with native people all dressed up in old Mexican/Mayan costumes. Drums were heard and an almost dance-like procession and worship were taking place. I could hardly believe my eyes; it was religious, but pagan-like at the same time. The powerful feeling of Faith was in the air, but it was not church-like; it was strong, primitive, and very sincere.

When the bells in the tower started to ring, the mood changed. The bright colors started to disappear, as if they had faded. Black shawls covered the heads. The drums were silenced, fires extinguished, and candles began to flicker in the darkness; formal lines slowly moved to the steps of the cathedral, disappearing through the big doors into the inner sanctum.

The whole pageant was so dramatic in this picturesque setting that it left an unforgettable impression.

One of the most interesting persons I ever met, not only in Mexico, but anywhere in my life, was Bernard Priem. He was handsome, sexy, and talented, and meeting him was one of the good fortunes of my life. In addition to the pleasure of knowing this fascinating artist, he made it possible for me to further enrich my knowledge with experiences I would otherwise not have known. Because Bernard was a pupil of the great Mexican oil painter Orozco, and assisted in creating some of the great murals, I met the great painter himself and his young wife, and visited their home. I have seen many paintings otherwise unseen by ordinary tourists. If I had not met all these people, the visit to Mexico would not have been the same. During our time free from rehearsals and performances, and during the intervals between our engagements, Bernard was a guide to many places. He loved and lived in places and picturesque ruins of the incredibly rich past. One of the most memorable days was our visit to the Pyramid of the Moon and Sun. All that grandeur and the wonderful space of the past pageantry filled me with wonder and made my sentimental imagination just wallow in ecstasy. Imagining the costumes and the colors, I could almost see the ancient processions. When it was time to leave with the rest of the visitors, I just could not go. Patiently understanding my artistic "elevated" state, Bernard agreed to let me go up onto the top of the Pyramid of the Sun. There, as if possessed, I had to watch the sun slowly melt into the hazy mist as the wind made dust twisters, which were turning in pirouettes. Suddenly I had to offer my own ritual dance to the sun, around the sacrificial stone in the center of the top level. No costume or clothing would do. My civilized clothes were discarded. I wish I knew or could now remember what (or how) I danced—in the nude, worshipping Nature, the Sun, and the Wind, the past, and my own love of the dance. The only thing I do remember is the feeling of intoxication and dizziness, as if I were possessed by some spirit from antiquity.

The only other time I experienced close to the same "distant" feeling was on the last night, saying goodbye to my friends Bernard and Pepe, to Mexico and to my dancing. It was after midnight, on a bridge, with the sky full of the brightest stars; the whole universe seemed to spin in a wild whirlpool. It was a few hours before I left to report for military duty.

# 29

I can still feel the pain, the anger and helplessness which the telegram caused upon its arrival in Mexico City. American military forces needed—demanded—my return to the States! There was great pain in having to say goodbye to my beloved dancing. Although it had all been settled with military officials before by Col. de Bail on our departure from the States that I was free to tour in Mexico because our benefit performances did more good than my being a soldier, my father had told the draft board where I was. I felt helplessness at being swept by the currents of events which were uprooting my life and certainly not my choice.

Poignant goodbyes with friends, the last performances with my eyes brimming with tears; the last evening in Mexico City stretched into the dawn with two friends, Pepe Lemantour and Bernard Priem, standing beside me on the high bridge outside of Mexico City, looking up at the stars. The slow return to the hotel, the lingering farewells, and then on to the bus depot. These memories of my last days of "freedom" closed in around me and the longest, bleakest period of my life began—the army.

During the week-long bus ride to New York, I felt nothing but emptiness. My eyes recorded the beauty of the scenery, the colorful sets of the picturesque countryside of Mexico. I can still feel the numbed pain of my tired body sitting for countless hours by the window of the bus speeding through endless miles of open spaces, the colorless stops in Texas, and the sameness of signs and towns as we approached New York City. Upon my arrival, I was so tired physically and dead spiritually that I did not want to go to my father's home—or to see anyone. For a few days I stayed at Lanseer Hotel, across from the bus station, gathering will power for my last effort to say goodbye to civilian life, to my sister Kira, to Gertrude and Father. I do not remember the few days that I spent on Central Park West with the family, but I do remember the last evening at home, and saying goodbye to a small group of friends, which included Paul Haakon, who had come to see me off.

The nightmare of basic training at Fort Dix in New Jersey is familiar to many people who do not have military ardor in their blood. The idiotic rules and spirit-breaking "details" are *well* known. The rudeness and coarseness of army life are especially painful to a sensitive person—as if it were not enough that men were there against their will, turned away from private life, from life outside those army fences. In my case, going into the army meant saying goodbye to my dancing career. It is bad enough to be one of many insignificant people—especially after being on the stage—but now I had been stripped of dignity, as well. For example, I had to wait for hours to go to the toilet if I wanted any privacy—instead of sitting in a row of toilet seats as if I were among prisoners in a concentration camp. It is especially hard for people who have achieved something in life, who have become "individuals," to behave well in a herd. I was broken spiritually, and my personality, my sensitivity were bruised. It is very strange to write this, to reminisce about it now, rewriting and rereading my lines, recognizing what a terrible waste it all was, and still is.

During this period, in order to escape the unpleasantness of my daily existence, it became necessary for me to begin to write my thoughts about subjects which were pleasing to me. It is not exactly poetry, but rather what I call "beautiful expressions," and they did help to offset the ugliness of army life, to give some form to the tedious existence which I shared with the people around me.

Whenever I was free from my duties, I entered the world of my imagination and tried to forget—often by remembering things which had happened to me that day—in the USO, for example, or in the music room where I went to listen to ballet recordings. I found a refuge through self-expression, even when I described the places and people around me. Perhaps underneath it all there was a wish unknown to me at the time that someday, someone would share my emotions, would understand my longing. I never intended to write "poetry," although friends of mine have treated it as such; I just wanted to express in the most concise and aesthetically pleasing manner possible the thoughts, desires, the dreams, and moods which so frequently came upon me in my desolation and sense of loneliness.

These pieces were written during "free" time, on days off or late at night.

*Again, as I remember, how many nights or days ago?*
*How many sunsets and starlit evenings? It seems that it was so long*
      *ago.*
*So long ago that I cannot believe it was all true, memories of used-to-be.*
*Oh happy days, friendly smiles, charming evenings by the fire.*
*Lovely walks, the evening breeze, so refreshing with its coolness.*

Tramping feet, tired faces, half-smiles of lonely eyes.
You and I are equal now, the army "call" made us so.
The life of the past and loved faces seem to vanish into the past.
Tired mind, aching body brought to long day's journey at long last.
The midnight chill, starlight washed with dew, cool wind, the breath of
     night.
Rough voices of our guides, the army men, all so tired, exhausted,
     almost ready to drop dead.
We make our beds, fall half-conscious for a few moments of
     much-needed rest.
Just before the sunrise the bugle calls us to wake.
The new day, new worries start: "Fall out." "Get going." The new day
     is on its way.

In the evening, the subconscious mind wants to be away from all the
     army noise.
I need to find some peace and quietness of heart; finally I find peace.
In the sunset, in dogwood trembling in the breeze,
In the crimson clouds floating lightly in the tired day's departing smile.
Across the space to far away, to a distant land of sunshine and music,
Of moonlit nights and fragrance-filled air, my thoughts longingly steal
     away.
And once more, forgetting all, I am in the shade of the palms,
Gazing across the Mexican plains to snow-topped mountains.
Sun-drenched, dipped in melted gold, the palms stand breathless.
The perfume of jasmine, gardenias, makes the air heavy with its aroma.
Tilted over the eyes, sombreros, a splash of color, a bright serape—
Siesta time in Mexico.
Moonlight, starbright, dew-fresh, music melody tender,
Sadly elusive mariachis sing and touch the strings—evening time in
     Mexico. . . .

The war years were wasted time in my life. I lived, or rather existed, only with my body; my mind was in the past, not in the reality around me. I will only write about a few people I met, include some of the moody pieces I wrote then. Only at times would I wake out of my numbness reacting to someone's kind word or on noticing someone who needed attention or sympathy, or when I became conscious of the beauty of nature. But most of the time I was like a robot, my own "self" having withdrawn into a hibernation-like state. I guess human nature wisely takes care of that, keeping our machinery going while dulling our senses so that we do not go out of our minds. So, these few writings, written in free moments, were an escape for me, letting my emotions and moods out of my system, in writing instead of talking with someone. There were no someones to talk to, most of the time, no one who was understanding. Even today it is hard to find an individual who can be an understanding person and friend, who will listen to and try to understand a moody person like me. It takes a lot of giving and an unselfish person to be a good companion and a friend.

*The moon was rising rather embarrassed and slightly pink.*

*Another lonely evening, another lonely night wasting away to meet tomorrow, gray and joyless, so empty and so useless; but I still have my treasures; No one can take them away—my dreams, my memories.*

*The barracks smoking their pipes—the chimneys in the frosty air. A sudden whistle breaks the silence of the early morning into a million fragments.*

*The rain had long been crying, leaving tears on the window panes. Sad clouds, wet drapes, cover the horizon with their misty haze—but still there is a promise in these rainy days, a hope that these gray clouds will draw aside to let in the sun, and with the sun the spring will come to awaken the flowers, the new green grass, and the trees will dress in green lace mantillas of fresh, whispering leaves.*

*In the Past are memories.*
*Into the Future fly the dreams.*
*Wishes occupy the Present.*
*I loved, I kissed you, and filled my heart with happiness.*
*I dreamed a dream that I am pagan too.*
*As the hours were swiftly washed on the shores of time, I know it was but a dream.*
*In the morning light I beheld the ashes of my dream—an almost-dead gardenia.*

It was hard for me to learn to pick up cigarette butts at the command of a fat bully who was also a military-happy idiot. I was given a silly ''mental'' examination in which I was asked if I would have sex with an animal. I replied that I was particular and seldom had sex with a *human,* that I was *not* sick enough to have it with an animal, and that my examiner was sick in the head to ask me such a sick question. My answer did not please him much. Then, because of a disinterested clerk, I was given an induction card of the wrong color and herded, along with other newcomers, into a railroad car.

During the long, sleepless night ride, I discovered I was being sent to the field artillery at Fort Knox. Somehow, a few weeks later, perhaps after being overheard by someone, I was interviewed and, thanks to an Intelligence (S-2) officer, I was transferred to the air corps, although I had not been transferred soon enough to escape the exhausting road marches with gas masks—on which I passed out.

Liaison flight training (they found out that I knew how to fly) was followed by meteorological training and exams—readying me for shipment to Europe to be an interpreter! The Intelligence officer, a sensitive, patient man, started to teach me to type, and was planning to use me as a part of his staff in the Intelligence S-2 group in Europe. But while he was away ill for a few weeks "they" transferred me to another squadron. The officer who replaced him did not like my accent, and put me down for guard duty and KP. As the result of another inexcusable mistake and disinterest in high ranks, I found myself on the way to California, where I drank black widows (vodka, gin, and tequila) for a few hysterical days before sailing. I knew enough geography to realize that they were not sending me to Europe. We were heading south, somewhere in the Pacific. It was actually to the southwest Pacific—an area well called the *Hell-Hole*—New Guinea, Hollandia.

After a year-and-a-half of almost wasted energy there and in the Philippines, it was discovered in Washington that I should have been in Berlin! Even after the mistake was discovered, and the sergeant of our squadron called a special formation to say goodbye to "Murfie" (unable to pronounce my name correctly, they had given me this nickname), I was sent on my way. I had no traveling orders due to another foul-up—only the papers ordering me to report to Berlin.

Ft. Knox, 1943:
*The spring is nearing . . .*
*Wind softly whispers to Nature,*
*And as if in a hurry,*
*Slightly rustling empty branches,*
*Narrate the message to the trees.*
*Soon the black lace of their silhouette*
*Will be covered with tender leaves,*
*So creating deeper shadows.*
*Alone, these days the wind*
*With the breath of an early spring*
*Caresses then wanders on.*
*It seems to conquer time and space.*

*The time of awakening—the breath of promise of things to happen and to come—the time of early spring, when air, wind, and light blue sky, still cool with winter freshness, make the world intoxicated.*

> *There is a tender longing in the air,*
> *And clouds drape the sky*
> *In a transparent haze of colors. . . .*
> *In mantillas of light-green lace*
> *The trees are smartly dressing. . . .*
> > *As if unspoken words*
> > *Or an unfinished phrase . . .*
> > *As if half understood*
> > *Unanswered, uncertain*
> > *Is tender longing in the air.*

*Again, spring winds its way with the tentative fragrance and promise of flowers . . . an undecided, unknown quality in the air awakens dormant desires, dreams . . . there is a longing for something or someone . . . a restless spirit.*

*The human soul is without limits; the heart is bottomless. No one knows the depth of love. When it is powerful and the opportunity to prove it comes your way, in surprise you find how potent are the emotions in you. Love offers immeasurable treasures, yet most of it is unpredicted, as changeable as April wind.*

San Francisco, 1943:
> *Men, men, men. Loud voices, tramping feet.*
> *"Left, right, about face, count cadence!"*
> *Overhead the sky of tender blue*
> *With a light-white cloud to dress it up.*
> *Cool wind, that brings a message from woodland green.*
> *And in the evening,*
> *When dusk steals in quietly*
> *I closed my eyes and face the wind,*
> *Forgetting myself,*
> *Imagining and wishing it might be*
> *The wind that comes across the desert*
> *To pay its homage to old ruins*
> *In a strange land of ancient grandeur,*

*A land of flowers*
*Where ancient temples are full of shadows.*
*My wish is so strong that I almost believe,*
*If I open my eyes, that I will see*
*The dust in the distant golden sunset.*
*Near the holy altar*
*On the top of the pyramid,*
*The Pyramid of the Sun*
*Facing the Pyramid of the Moon,*
*In the heart of old Mexico.*

*Dreams are strange things,*
*So elusive yet so powerful,*
*So fantastic yet so possible.*
*They make our lives beautiful,*
*Yet bring much pain,*
*Because of broken castles in the air.*
*Memories are wonderful too,*
*Because they take us*
*To the land of used-to-be.*
*Into unknown future*
*Only dreams, which dare to fly beyond the horizon.*
*Wishes follow dreams*
*And so, the "fragile bridge of hope"*
*Unites the present with the future.*

*General confusion, but with a gaiety of its own. Smiling faces, friendly faces. Stately elderly women watching "on the lookout"; everybody is supposed to be "on good behavior." Skipping, a suggestion of flirtation. A word, a smile—U.S.O. social evening.*

*A touch of good, down-to-earth kindness and the healthy spirit of friendliness.*

*A welcome smile on the faces of the hostesses: "Go ahead and have a good time." Who knows who will die tomorrow.*

*Somewhere in the corner, with the illusion of seclusion, a couple are talking. He is trying to get a date. She is only permitted, authorized, and willing to give a good time in a spiritual, moral way. These are "nice girls," and sure enough they are. At the piano, someone reminisces; fingers glide along the keys in the almost forgotten pattern of the classics, while the radio blasts forth with a jazz version of a classical melody.*

# 30

He was of slight build, with a shadow of shyness about him, his straight blond hair framing his rather narrow face. The blue-blue eyes that lit his face were at times misty, as if distant thoughts were troubling him, or they were bright with the intensity of a vivid conversation. The feeling of sad gentleness about him was like the indefinite aroma of some unknown perfume.

While stationed at MacDill Air Field in Florida, we were allowed to take a ferry to Tampa or St. Petersburg in the evenings. During my stay there, coming back to the airfield one evening, I met Bill.

Out of a hundred G.I.'s looking out over the waters of the Tampa Bay, our sensitivity and loneliness unexplainably brought us together. After the ferry poured the uniformed humanity onto the military reservation, we two walked to the end of the air strip, where the tall pines made a strange whispering sound above us. We sat and talked until dawn. Somehow in our loneliness we found warmth, understanding, and a need for physical contact. First our arms were over each other's shoulders, then Bill's head was on my chest. Finally at the early light of dawn, before we went to our tents, we kissed—like two lonely beings who needed affection, the physical warmth of friendly lips.

Bill was an actor; the photos he showed me confirmed my intuitive feeling that he was good. He also painted beautifully. I believe that he had more than just talent; I am sure he approached being a genius. Tormented by some unrest, he rebelled against military life. Being an artist, his sensitivity was bruised by all the rudeness and roughness around him. As we talked, every time we met he told me that he was sure he was going to be killed on a flight mission. Twice I was shocked when Bill tried to end his life and had been prevented by fellow crewmen.

Occasionally we arranged to meet on a weekend; he would not show up until the very end of our free time, fighting the fact that he needed me as a companion and a friend. Some evenings he would spend getting drunk to forget—or at least to dull—the acute pain, the pain of the turmoil churning within him. On our days off, he would sometimes draw or sketch; he would often forget his drawing and a tormented look would come into his eyes, as if something were haunting him. I would try to chase that gloomy thought, talk or suggest a walk.

The last time we met he gave me his "wings"—the squadron insignia— and I gave him my ring. In our hearts we held a fragile wish that we would exchange them back when we met after the War; we did not have to express it in spoken words. That weekend Bill brought his sketching pad and asked me to pose; he also gave me some photographs, and later I received one of him playing Hamlet, sent to me by a friend of his.

*I was in love with love*
*Until I met you.*
*Now, in love with love*
*Became just loving you.*
   *The memories of you, so beautifully kept*
   *Forever fresh and fragrant—you were and are*
   *So many times repeated in the melody of a song,*
   *Or in the silence of the evening.*
   *I almost feel your nearness, the longing in my heart*
   *Is an answer to the memories, the times we spent together.*
*Waiting, with minutes that seem like hours*
*The heart repeating—in vain this waiting pain.*
*The empty loneliness ahead is re-echoing the Past.*
*The present is, by sorcery, in stillness.*
*But empty, silent: "WHY?"—drives the mind insane.*
*When all this will be over and peace will reign once more*
*I want to go beyond the horizon where the sky disappears into the sea.*
*There I will stay a while away from everydays*
*On some tropic island, forgetting troubles*
*Letting days go by just watching waves caress the sand,*
*Listening to the palms narrate the tales of tropic legends and of love.*

*The last breath of winter*
   *with its frosty air*
      *was filled this morning*
         *with dancing snowflakes.*
   *It makes me sad to see*
      *them touch the ground and melt away*
         *Losing their color of purity,*
            *So beautifully white.*

*The cold, wet kisses of the snowflakes*
  *Seemed to say goodbye*
*As with the last departing wishes*
  *They were melting out of view.*

*Tears of loneliness . . . the mist of a lonely heart . . . walking alone,*
*listening to the wind sighing in the tall trees . . . as if with its whisper the*
*wind could bring to life the naked emptiness of branches. . . . While up*
*above, through the torn curtain of the dull gray clouds, the stars and*
*pale moon, in all its splendor, were uncovered to vision.*

Philippines 1944:
*My lonely spirit with a sudden pain of desire united with the mind and*
*losing itself among the clouds drifted my thoughts to far away. . . .*

*A few empty glasses, with the foam of beer dried like a lace design,*
*smoke, loud talk. A few women giggling at the section near the bar, at*
*the bar a few men. A sailor, well-shaped, long and sinewy, with sad*
*eyes, stares at nothing. How empty and sad.*
  *(written during a free evening at some bar on a day off)*

Weeks later I lost his wings somewhere in the Pacific; I had an awful feeling
that he was dead. When six weeks later I found out that he was lost—shot
down over Germany—the date was the same as that of the day I lost the
wings.

I still treasure the photographs of Bill. They bring back his image, and
though it is sad, like the shadow of a cloud, I remember with gratitude that
my life was enriched by knowing him and having his friendship.

# 31

*Scattered thoughts in the early morn, wind-blown, rain-wet.*
*Just a few thoughts before the day arrives, chasing the mood away.*
*Hiding my memories in the sad shadows of my heart;*

*Though timid, they still warm my blood with the afterglow of the days*
     *gone by,*
*With memories of my friends and with the faint hope of possible*
     *tomorrows,*
*Of friendly smiles, brown orchids, gardenias, and blue champagne.*
*With trembling captive wings my spirit is in pain.*
*The freedom song is in my heart, but there is not a word upon my lips,*
*My eyes see horizons distant, my soul is in constant yearning.*
*Demanding, searching, being with trembling heart forever longing*
*To be in spirit free as the wind, to be as romantic as a moonlit night,*
*To be sincere in all my feelings,*
*Never to talk or act against, but to follow the truth wherever it may lead*
     *me.*

Guam, 1944:
*In space, above the clouds—the ocean immense and blue—I feel*
*remote, hardly living, just witnessing the cavalcade of many-formed*
*clouds. Ocean waves below seem just small ripples. A piece of land,*
*seen only once in many an hour, does not seem to belong to Earth, is*
*but a bit of green among the blue. The horizon, slowly retreating, my*
*journey sings its way. One more island, one more country to see,*
*remember, and explore. In every place I leave behind, I leave a part of*
*me. But, in exchange I take with me a memory.*

On the way to Clark Field / Manila, Philippines, 1944:
*Another island on blue horizon, with haze its hills are almost hidden,*
*The palms wave a welcome in the tropic air.*
*By the shoreline we stop to rest a while. Guam.*
*Dry palm leaves twisted, with bamboos for support—*
*The native huts, so fragile, and yet*
*So bravely withstanding rain, wind, and human wear.*
*Around them so intimately near, are proud palms and dusty*
*Banana, long-leafed trees. In the doorways, or almost hidden behind*
     *handmade screens,*
*The wistful faces of the Philippines.*
*Men, more wise than brave, while women, looking clean and proud*
*Almost ignore our curious, somewhat amazed stare.*
*As we swiftly pass on our wandering way*
*We see the natives walking steadily on their way*
*To distant market or to visit a nearby place*

*Where they will trade what they have for what they need.*
*The water buffaloes, with long horns, lazily, as if reflecting,*
*Chew their food—the dusty grass—or once in a while, against their will,*
*They pull a load, dragging it along the ground followed by an impassive*
*native.*
*Pagoda hats, so neatly made of straw and dried leaves,*
*Create a shadow, hiding the face from the scorching sun or a searching*
*look.*
*There is beauty in their line, with almond eyes beneath—*
*Those umbrella-like creations could be the envy of some fashion,*
*Where women like to dress to attract admiring males.*
*Many bright-eyed children are more cheerful than their elders.*
*Forgotten are the troubles of their past.*
*But older men and women look on in silence, watching the passing*
*cavalcade. Only once in a while does*
*A smile light a face.*
*In the evening, in the nearby village, the busy day begins to rest.*
*Native women with their children watch their men and boys*
*At play, relaxing in a newly learned game.*
*Some boys pass on and wave; with friendly smiles and husky voices*
*They say, "Hello, Joe," and are on their way.*
*The sun departs behind the clouds that drape the distant sky;*
*The backdrop of palms creates a theater-like setting.*
*Later on, dark silhouettes against the tropic sky,*
*The palms hold back the moonlight, while I, spellbound,*
*Admire Nature's panorama, trying to memorize all I see,*
*Admire, or feel in my heart.*
*And though I am sorry to be on my way again, I am anxious to see and*
*visit*
*New places beyond the horizon. And so again, I am on my way.*

Written while hitchhiking across the Pacific on my way to Berlin:
Fear? No. Anxiety? Yes. I suppose because of all the tragedy of that which I witnessed as a small boy during the Russian Revolution, I have no fear, that is, I am not "afraid for my skin," or of the termination of my existence. I do like the best things in life, but since it is not always the best, almost anything will do. I would not mind dying; I just do not want to be an incapacitated invalid depending upon others. That is why I am careful, taking care whenever possible to stay away from "troubles" and do not take unnecessary chances. I have received a few stars and a few ribbons and got them in the following manner.

On Christmas Eve our flotilla of landing crafts (LSTs) left New Guinea, Hollandia, under cover of darkness. There must have been twelve or more of these strange square-nosed boat/barges in an uneven line, each one keeping just ahead or to the side, in view. Before we were halfway to our destination, an airborne attack left only a few of the craft to continue on their way, in smoke-covered security. All I remember of this journey is praying a little, and with my theatrical sensibilities, somehow admiring the "show," the drama, of war, while my mind wondered with resigned numbness whether we were going to sink next. Our squadron lost all its equipment and upon our arrival at Biak Island we depended for many weeks upon the kindness and care of the "Aussies" there, who supplied us with food and the bare necessities of life's survival. For this ordeal, I received a star.

Biak, a small island off New Guinea, was a jumping-off place to other islands; only runways for reconnaissance planes. In the beginning, just as soon as a few tents could be put up, we had to be on guard all the time, because many stray bullets whistled by from nearby trees from which the last few enemy soldiers had not yet been shot down or taken prisoner. A few times a cry, "Down! Down!" saved us. Even in our tents, we would fall to the red clay floor, later to see a hole in the tent where we had just been standing. We received another star.

After a few weeks of calm, black nights, our squadron decided to have a movie show, to cheer up the low morale of the men. A piece of white cloth (I guess it was a white parachute) was stretched between two palm trees for a screen. The audience—the intelligence reconnaissance squadron, consisting of mechanics, pilots, and intelligence specialists—welcomed this event with the enthusiasm of small boys. I suppose the movie and equipment had been brought over to us from Australia by the "Aussies" along with our supply of food. (We had been without any supplies of our own for weeks, except for an occasional feast, even ice cream, when a Navy ship stopped by and treated us to the luxury of American food.) After a lazy afternoon of swimming in the lovely lagoon and an unexciting supper of powdered milk (blue), powdered potatoes (lavender), powdered eggs (slightly green) and a few pieces of fresh fruit (exchanged with the natives for a can of beer or a chocolate bar), we stretched out on the coral and gravel runway or leaned against palm trees to watch the long-awaited movie.

I do not remember what the movie was, because we ourselves became a spectacular show. It was so sudden, so fantastic in its effect, that only after it was over did I realize what had happened. An enemy plane had followed, undetected, our reconnaissance P-38 returning from a photographic mission, and sprayed our bivouac area with devastating gunfire. The gas tanks and ammunition exploded into flames all around us, creating a fantastic, nightmarish scene of desolation. I just sat there watching people jumping into foxholes, running away from the flaming inferno. Later on when I was asked why I did not run or jump into a foxhole, I really did not know what to say. I had not been scared; I just did not care, at that time, what happened to me, and the tragic show had been so sudden and so theatrical that I was stunned. One-third of the men in my squadron (perhaps as many as thirty) died; I received another star for my "bravery."

The only times I ever "lost blood" were when I cut my finger to the bone on KP at Ft. Knox and on Biak Island when I went to the hospital tent to give a blood transfusion to some of my fellow soldiers who needed it because of their wounds. Later on I received another star for my set of ribbons; I felt that I really did not deserve it. I had not experienced any so-called fear, the way most of the soldiers felt. Trying to analyze it now, I imagine it was my state of mind. I was so resigned and so depressed in my thoughts and feelings, thinking my life was finished because I did not expect to dance ever again, that the fear of death did not even enter my mind.

To this day, in 1979, I am not afraid to die—life is wonderful, yes, but it is also very troublesome, and I am tired. I have faith, and believe sincerely that there is an afterlife. I would never agree that with the destruction of our bodies we are finished, that we are nothing. The spirit, in some way, somehow, somewhere continues to live on, as in our hearts, thoughts, and memories, certain people, our dear ones, are still alive and somehow still exist as long as we continue to remember them and lovingly think of them.

September, Full of Departing Leaves and Wings:
>    *Again golden-threaded Autumn*
>    *With its multi-colored patchwork*
>    *Comes rustling in with fallen leaves.*
>    *And the Sun, as if tired*
>    *After summer's harvests,*
>    *Appears later every morning.*
>    *In the evenings, the breeze and the dew*
>    *Cools Nature, and somehow*
>    *Brings peace to the tired soul.*
>    *The burning desires of a few days past*
>    *Bring only a quicker tempo to the heart,*
>    *But not the all-consuming fire of passion.*
>    *The flame, though bright, is cooled with Autumn winds.*

Once in a while, with a sigh, I would turn my thoughts back to the wide and open spaces of the limitless steppes, to far away, beloved Russia. There the Tzarina, Winter, with her magic, sparkling mantle of snow-diamonds and the icicles, transparent frozen tears, cover the fir trees, dressing them in ermine, while in the cool distant sky, the clouds are chased by frosty winter winds. In the distance, ringing clearly, the quicksilver of youthful laughter in harmony with the musically melodious bells of racing troikas, riding swiftly, with snow flying from under the hooves. Eh! yamschik! What is the hurry? Sing a song! And from the heart, sad but beautifully melodious, a song of gone-but-not-forgotten days, of gypsy life so free and gay.

In the twilight of the early dawn, when the pageant of the sky begins its color play, the morning mist, like a transparent hazy curtain, hides the mystic sun. In the quiet of the evening with the gentleness of the night winging its way with its starry moonbeam-woven mantle to cover the nakedness of day, I wait impatiently for the coming of the evening or the quiet before the daylight of the early morning.

When my moody spirit is at play and loneliness grips my heart, I try to warm by the reflected glow of the happy yesterdays. When in the glamorous sparkling days in the tropics, the music-filled nights, my life was swiftly rushing by. Now, as if in a half-conscious state of mind, I am not quite sure if I am really here. Perhaps, any time now, I will wake up to find myself where my heart is longing to be.

Before my memory pales, before too many impressions crowd in, I will try to record in these lines my latest emotions, places and events. Not that I will ever forget them, but time does dull the color play as the cavalcade of new emotions thrills the heart and stirs the blood.

*Suspended, halted in between yesterday's sunset and tomorrow's*
*sunrise,*
*Tonight, today, stop in wonder, the hour hand seems to be at a*
*standstill.*
*And so . . . I remember yesterday and wonder of tomorrow. . . .*
*Yet the present moment is not real; away from everyone and all, I*
*doubt my existence,*
*And think: all this—is it not a dream? A dream remembered or*
*dreamed?*
*The things that will be remembered of my travels in the Pacific,*
*The sailing on the SS Monterey, where every morning at sunrise I was*
*true to the Art of Dance.*
*I practiced adagio and the port de bras; later, the marine day would*
*start:*

Descending to the hull for breakfast, suntanning on the deck,
Every once and a while, a few hard-working hours of KP, down there,
    below.
The journey of many weeks took us beyond the hot equator.
New Caledonia, so strange and distant, Australia, Brisbane with its
    smiling Aussies,
New Guinea, the steaming jungles, Hollandia, busy and important,
    active all through the day and night.
Then on Christmas Eve, an LST was our home—at sea.
It was a solemn evening, eleven or fifteen of the strange landing crafts
    in a long uneven line,
Gliding on the smooth waves to evade the submarines. . . .
Someone heard a rumor that we were bound for Biak.
When we finally landed, there were but half of the craft; an enemy
    attack had taken care of that. . . .
The sea before us, cliffs behind, a strip of coral runway in between,
A few palms which had withstood the fire and shelling of attack,
Some of the caves still inhabited by Nipponese skeletons.
New Year's Eve, lonely and so unfestive, so far away from all we
    love. . . .
On the first of the new year we were moved further up the island,
Where Nature was unspoiled and the shore was wonderful for
    swimming.
For a while it was calm living by the sea, the moonlit nights, sunburned
    days,
The lazy, dazed tropical living, until one night—a surprise attack
Reminded us with morbid clearness that there was war and death,
Not far away, but right there among us. . . .
Bright explosions, fire, smoke, many wounded, many dead.
After that, an alert was sounded many a night, reminding us
That Sons of Heaven were nearing to kill some more of our boys.


## MOONLIGHT MELODY

I want to put down on these pages a feeling, dream, and melody. . . .
I felt the dream and my heart sang the melody. . . .
A moonlight melody was born or created many moons ago. . . .
And now, reached me . . . through time and space. . . .
        To find an echo in my heart. . . .
            It takes a medium to transfer a sound,

It takes a heart to fall in love,
It takes a touch of moonlight to make a dream reality. . . .
And so . . . it happened . . . and is now with the past.
The magic of moonlight, and the caressing breeze
Will never touch me without awakening this longing . . . of moonlight
    melody and you.
I try to talk, to think, to feel, but futile is my effort.
My heart is conjured into stillness . . . remembering your nearness.
Your smile in the shadows, a touch of moonlight in your hair . . . and
    humble ebb tide at our feet. . . .
It might have been imagination, of lonely heart that dreams,
Moonlight does awaken fantasy . . . and dreams. . . .
The ocean was all silver,
Lost messenger—the breeze—from trade winds lost
Was caressing with its coolness.
We dipped our bodies naked, into the melted blue-silver of the waves,
And with our hearts and souls became one with Nature.
Across the waters reaching us, a melody was drifting,
But another melody was there before—the song of songs in our hearts—
Some people call it Love—some, Infatuation—or blissful Intoxication.
The evening passed into night.
At the bewitching hour of midnight we were in each other's arms,
With a tender kiss upon the lips.
    Whoever will someday read these lines, words, and phrases
    Will not understand, unless he too has been spellbound on a
        magic night like this.
    Only one who has walked up the path of moonbeams,
    Then remained suspended, as if resting on a cloud,
    Can understand and thrill to the song of Moonlight Melody.
And live above this world—two souls in perfect harmony.
    I wonder how Moonlight Romance began?
    How this intoxication started?
Closing my eyes, I step back, into the distant past.
    Once upon a time—long, long ago—
In the days when all was pure and silent,
    The Moon looked through the clouds
And saw this Earth and Ocean free. . . .
At first it glided over trees, looked into the fragrant flowers,
And then—suddenly—found its reflection in the silver
    mirror of the waters.

And so—moonbeams innocently kissing—
    Found response in silver waves, and all intoxicated
    Created the song of songs.
Ever since that day, human beings
Who find a reflection of their searching soul
    In another's heart repeated, hear this Moonlight Melody,
    Thrill, forgetting all around, they climb the moonlit stairway
    To live for a few brief moments above this Earth—like gods—
That is why we know aesthetic moments, because we see the reflection
    of each other's dream in our eyes and hearts,
That is why—we hear the song, the Moonlight Melody. . . .
Another moonlit night . . . but rather hazy—
Perhaps it's kind to me—it does not want
    To hurt me with its brilliance,
    Awakening the dream—making me sadder than I am.
The days past were so full with the joy of living—
    Now, empty days ahead will make me sadder still.
I did not want to stay, alone, to watch the sunset;
The beauty of the other evenings is too vital and too fragrant yet. . . .
Just now—I cannot enjoy, alone, the beauty that is around,
    Because we are apart. . . .
The time will pass, events and days will crowd in. . . .
New impressions will dull the pain of parting. . . .
Anyway, our emotions are not lasting
    That is why—I treasure them this way.
I walked away from the sparkling ocean,
    When the sun was yet high up in the sky.
Slowly, I walked on the dusty road
    From the place I learned so to treasure. . . .
    Leaving a part of me there on the shore. . . .
In waters of the tide, and in the shadows of the palms and the tropic
    trees.
Soon—in a little while—the night will kindly possess me. . . .
    Helping me to drift away from lonely sad reality. . . .
    Into the dreamland and make-believe. . . .
So . . . Closing another chapter, another door in the mansion of my life.
But I am grateful because often I will open this secret door—
Walking in, I will hear again my beloved Moonlight Melody. . . .
                           Aloha.

*But life goes on—and the calm tropics, the sea, the clouds, and the trees*
*Erase the fatal deeds, and days continue their sun-drenched journey.*
*Later on, at Palawan, Leyte, yes, as I remember. . . .*
*Just a few weeks ago it was Biak, with ocean blue and free,*
*The dusty ugliness of the island forgotten, while the new shore*
*In the shadow of the palms, or submerged in the waters clear, or*
    *sundrenched on the sand,*
*So being, living in the tropics' lazy daze.*
*Sometime later, the Philippines—busy days of working hard.*
*Many, many days and evenings busy with missions flown, photos filed,*
*Reports that have to be sent to the infantry.*
*With the help of our missions the war moves on successfully:*
*Formosa, Okinawa, China are on our daily list.*
*Strange names become familiar, far horizons become near.*

*Now to remember the Philippines and Manila:*
*The natives in their pagoda hats, women with high-sleeved dresses.*
*The cabby carts by ponies drawn, the husky singers of San Fernando,*
*The almond-eyed hussies of Tarlac, GI soldiers, suntanned and tired,*
    *but eager*
*To have fun, relax in drinking, forgetting last night's rendezvous with*
    *death.*
*At night, not far from the squadron area, guerrilla shots are heard in the*
    *dark.*
*A few more sons of Sun are killed—a few less to take shots at our boys.*
*After the cool night, the sky awakens, begins the multi-colored play of*
    *sunrise,*
*With clouds on parade, some of them reluctant to leave the*
    *mountainside*
*On which they have been resting overnight.*
*As morning brightens into day, the native boys and women*
*Start to come to visit us; some bring laundry, others sell or trade*
*Bananas, mangoes, and papayas for cigarettes, candy, or tobacco.*
*On days off, our trucks speed Manila-bound on the dusty road.*
*The panorama of peaceful life stretches mile after mile,*
*The carabao tilling the soil, or majestically, lazily, pulling a load,*
*Or standing motionless with native boys fast asleep on their broad gray*
    *backs.*
*The tragic pageant of Manila, draped in the ruins of past grandeur,*

Comes gradually back to life, like a wounded animal licking its many
    wounds.
At the outskirts of the main city, life tries to keep its tempo
Throbbing with every day's existence.
Soldiers, sailors, WACs and nurses, insignia of rank of many grades,
Walk about, snap photos, buy and bargain for souvenirs.
A mixture of yesterdays and tomorrows is present at every step.
Native dresses of pleasant colors, the graceful drape of the skirts, high
    embroidered sleeves,
Men in colorful shirts, or all in white, so very clean.
And there are many with suits abbreviated to shorts and cut-short shirts;
Most of the women wear native wooden, hand-carved, hand-colored,
    wedge sandals, stockingless, hatless,
Only once in a great while wearing a pagoda hat,
Combining the past with the present.
At night are heard gay voices, liquor-stained, but friendly,
Most of them unable to resist the offer of a native: "Eh, Joe—buy some
    whiskey."
Finally tired and exhausted, one finds his way home, to some place of
    rest,
Most likely some bombed-out building, without windows, doors, or roof,
But arranged with parts of tents so as to keep the rain out.
And so to sleep to the constant hum of heavy traffic all night long—
Trucks full of equipment or manpower to be delivered to the front—
While overhead the roar of planes assures us of the superiority and
    safety
Of our air power and men. . . .
And so goodbye to the Philippines. . . .
        now on my way across the ocean. . . .
What is next? Guam, Kwajelein, Hawaii, San Francisco, New York
    (home!), or Berlin?
Guam, all palm-leaved, with the sunset melting in the waves,
The air drenched in sweet aroma, star-dusted, sprinkled with fireflies.
Darkness hides the ugliness of the army tents, army buildings,
And softly, gently covers it all with the tropical night.
After GI "chow," unappetizing and cold, the tents welcome our sleep
For a few hours—until the sunrise when again, silver-winged,
We take off to Kwajelein, through the clouds, then into sunlight;
Over the blues and greens of the ocean, we fly our homeward way.
For a brief moment we are inside stormy clouds,

But the golden sun and ocean blue-green claim their own, very quickly.
Then, after many hours of light the plane is near the water's surface,
And out of the waves appears . . . sad, desolate, empty Kwajelein:
An airstrip, a few tents, a few barracks, a few desolate stumps of palms.
A few rows of airplanes on the runway, and the only life—a few human
   beings.
Again arises the same question: Was it worth it? So many human
   lives. . . .
As if to accentuate this doubtful thought, wounded men file out,
Pale and sick from newly fought battles, to board the plane for home,
Or to spend the rest of their broken lives in some hospital, forgotten.
Soon they are out of sight, but their comrades remain buried
Beneath symmetrical white lines, clear-cut, simple white crosses
Near the army chapel.
Soon our plane is ready to take off, saying goodbye to Kwajelein Island,
Without regret, but with a sad thought, remembering the war and its
   cruel price.
As I sketch these lines, the C-54 speeds through the night;
At times it shakes like an animal, shaken by the fury of the atmospheric
   elements.
Many thoughts crowd in, to be remembered or yet dreamed—
The past and the future are so unreal—the present so suspended. . . .
Perhaps it is all a dream, and awakened I will find all that has happened
Was but a nightmare, the imagination of a tired mind and lonely
   heart. . . .
But no—these people around me are too vital, too real;
They demand recognition . . . it is all true, and
I will be home in a day or two, as all this is being remembered
As I am on my way to new future days, a slow but welcome journey,
With the realization that I will be Home for a brief two weeks,
Then again to travel . . . again my Odyssey will take me to other parts
   of the universe.
I know all these travels are exciting, but somehow I take it all for
   granted.
How happy I will be to see and kiss the ones I love.
Times marches on, and so does Life.
Goodbye, Pacific; Hello, Atlantic . . . . Aloha, yesterdays; Greetings, fair
   tomorrow.

*May 9, 1945:*
I just reread these lines, these pages from the past. How right I was to say:
"Hello Atlantic!"—I am now sailing to Europe. "Fair tomorrow" was
yesterday—we heard, "War is over!" "Peace."

*Happy I am for the end of the killing and pray that the homecoming*
*For all the boys will be the end of loneliness, that it will be a joy.*
*And not bring disappointment or sorrow.*
*As for myself, I have a wish—that I will be free at last, out of this*
    *captivity.*
*In a few months back home, with the people I love. . . .*
*The Army thinks that my language ability will be of help, translating,*
*Interpreting to the Americans what the Russians have to say. . . .*
        *thus I am on my way,*
*Again, to other cities, with the prayer and the wish to be Home—soon.*
*Thoughts passing one another, racing through my head without order*
        *or reason,*
*Once in a while stopping, asking a question just to create more chaos.*
*But I would rather have these thoughts racing madly than the empty*
        *stillness*
*That is, at times, in my heart.*

Khata-Shack is written on the Russian-like gate leading to my porch at my
home on Fire Island Pines. Whenever I pass it, my memory goes back to the
original sign, 6,000 miles away, thirty-five years ago, on Biak Island. I had a
tent, lined with a used white parachute, there in the wilderness, surrounded
by the Southwest Pacific Ocean. I had a sign with two arrows pointing in
opposite directions: one to the left to Kiev, Russia; the other towards New
York, USA.

I later used the same sign on the Philippine Islands, but this time my tent
was bigger and had the luxury of a few extras, like a tripod with a clay bowl,
handmade by natives. My "cabin-boy," named Jesus-Narcissus, filled this
bowl with floating gardenias; Jesus often helped about the camp. He used to

carry my blanket for me to sit on while watching the movies, a task which made him the envy of other youths who were not employed. A few times pilots passing my tent were heard to question how I rated such a luxury. One of them remarked that even if he was not a ballet dancer he also admired beauty. The result was that, sometime later, a similar arrangement was installed beside his tent, as a surprise present from me.

On one occasion we were visited by the *Oklahoma!* company, sponsored by the USO. It was such a great pleasure to see my friends again, that momentarily I "came back to life," stimulated by the show tunes, the dancing and the show-biz conversations. It was good to react to the silly, bubbling conversation of "Mr. America"—Billy Webber, the ever-young eternally lovely chorus boy of Broadway, and especially to see and be with Kirsten, my ex-partner and friend.

My commanding officer had been only too happy to help with transportation and in welcoming the show and my friends when they arrived in the army planes at Clark Field. The parade of jeeps was like a gypsy caravan escorting the travelers to the half-ruined buildings where the performers were to be lodged. But my friends did not mind the wall-less, at times roofless, accommodations. They were happy to be above ground and out of the mud and dust of their previous accommodation, and welcomed the luxury (!) of a broken-down, bombed building. It was a nice change for them from the sleeping tents of the previous nights.

With my GI bag full of mementos of the Southwest Pacific (including small drums of native carving with snakeskin heads, shells, and native jewelry) I hitchhiked from island to island: Guam, Kwajelein (out in the ocean, a little strip of coral and sand, a few lonely palms, and countless rows of evenly spaced white crosses marking the lost lives of American boys), Midway, Hawaii.

*Clouds, clouds white and shining, clouds with silver edges, clouds—the*
   *caravan of the sky—clouds, I let my dreams, my wishes, and my*
   *thoughts sail far away with you.*
*Someday, some of you will reach the tropics, where with passion and*
   *abandon you will quench the tropics' thirst.*
*Others might on their way transform into starry snow to drape some*
   *distant mountain with a new and sparkling mantle. . . .*
*Or in some country after rainfall, some of the rain-dust will band into a*
   *magic rainbow*
*To show the way to where happiness and make-believe begins and*
   *ends.*

Then, for a few weeks, Camp Ritchie, in Maryland, before departing for Europe. For a short while, I found myself, miraculously, at home.

During the War, correspondence was mostly one-sided. It was strictly forbidden to tell in letters exactly where you were writing from. And you usually never knew, anyway, where you were going to be ordered next, or for how long; your whereabouts was strictly top secret. When I arrived back in the States, after "hitchhiking" across the Pacific, I was briefly assigned to Camp Ritchie, where I was being prepared to be sent to the European Theatre. During this time, I called my father's home in New York City and discovered that he was stationed in Europe—later, we were to be reunited there, under somewhat strained circumstances.

The "preparations" at Camp Ritchie were, for me, not only short, but frustrating. I was examined by an antagonistic know-it-all—an uneducated, slightly "pink" new Russian, who clearly resented my cultured Russian background. Our personalities clashed. It might have been my fault, because by that time I had had it with the army's bumbling mismanagement. Perhaps I only disliked that Russian because of his role in the army's officialdom; certainly class distinction had seldom in my life had anything to do with my relations with other people. Soon afterwards, I was dispatched to Europe.

I do not know exactly how my father succeeded in locating me. I was stationed in a chateau outside Paris. A message reached me, and a meeting was arranged through "higher ups," the high command, and I was informed to be on my way to meet him in Paris. Being too old for active duty, my father had been appointed an advisor, dealing with Air Force planes and places and supplies that had been recaptured. He held a very high rank, had a car with a chauffeur for traveling in France and Germany.

Upon my arrival in the city, I called him as instructed and we arranged to meet in front of L'Opéra. It was an emotional and very theatrical meeting. We had not seen one another for over four years. Both of us were in uniform; I forgot to salute him. We saw each other at quite a distance; he had just gotten out of his military car.

As usually happens at moments like this our bodies conveyed more meaning than words could ever have expressed. No demonstrative words or gestures were exchanged between us then—or ever had been for that matter. Father was too rigidly military in his bearing for that. This reserve was very difficult for me to control; I was, after all, a theater performer who was used to displaying my emotions. But even at this special moment, I held back in respect for his military-like, unemotional relationship with me. But at that moment I saw love in his eyes, and I think pride.

After he found out that I only had an overnight pass to stay away from the chateau in which I was staying, he immediately said that he would arrange for a pass for me to stay with him at least two days. We went to the Military Police, which was operating in L'Opéra itself; the backstage entrance was the headquarters.

It was strange for me to enter at the *Place de Diaghilev*—the stage entrance of L'Opéra in Paris—to get permission to be free from army life for two days.

After seeing a few high officials and making a few phone calls, it was all arranged. Father told me we were going to celebrate our reunion. He arranged to be free, too, and with a wink and a sparkle of mischievousness in his eye he said, "And I arranged to have an Army chauffeur be our transportation for our 'secret mission'." It was the first time I heard Edith Piaf. We went to the best restaurant in Paris, and drank champagne at the Bal Tabarin. It was one of the few times in our lives that Father and I were on more or less equal terms. It is nice to remember, although sad because this kind of association occurred only a few times.

After being with Father during that luxurious visit in Paris, returning to military routine was a dark reality. I soon received my orders to proceed to Berlin, and the journey there was very elemental, to say the least. A few of the cars on the railroad on which I had to travel seemed to have square wheels. Conditions were like a cattle-train. Only a few stops were of any interest, and whenever we spent a few days in a colorful, picturesque, old city, such as Marburg or Stuttgart, the ravages of war were everywhere— ruins, sad people, skeletons of vehicles—cruel, vivid witnesses to past madness.

Berlin! What a difference from the first time I was there: ruins everywhere, the sites of just-ended battles. The underground was partly flooded, and in a few places in the distance the remains of human clothing could still be seen hanging on electrical wires. Many times, trying to get somewhere on the underground, we had to get out of our train, go up to the surface, walk a few blocks, and descend again in order to reach the next station.

After many interviews, questions, and discussions, I was asked to sign up for another year or two in the service, with the promise of a promotion to the rank of Major or Captain. They were talking of making me a translator, and my rank in the army had to "balance off" with the Russian translators. I refused—I had had it.

The military personnel really did not know what to do with me, the European war was over; they were now settling the boundaries with the Russians and other nationalities. If I had still been in the South Pacific, all I could have hoped for would be a leave, a furlough, but I had accumulated enough time "points" from my two years in the Pacific that they would not make me sign the paper.

Just at this time, the Russians had finished presenting a gigantic show for the Allies; everyone was talking about it. Some Special Service personage suggested that the American sector should make a similar gesture—an American show.

The next thing I knew, I was summoned to the highest office. After some interrogation and further interviewing, I had a personal meeting with a few important officials, and finally a person-to-person visit with the dashing General Gavin. The result was, after a "talk" with even more officers, that I agreed to stage such a show, with the condition that I would be the one to decide (and receive support for) whatever I thought was artistically right and necessary. I was transferred again and became a member of the great, famous 82nd Airborne Paratrooper Division.

The show was to be "All-American," with some of the best available people directing and writing the music and the skits. It proved to be a grand experience, but also one with many problems. The *Berlin Sentinel* of October 20, 1945 wrote about the event:

If the quality of a musical comedy can be measured by the enthusiasm displayed by the cast, then the soldiers in the Berlin District are in for a treat early next month, when more than 60 enlisted men and WACs present their all-soldier show, "You Are On Your Way" at the Titania Palace. More than a dozen members of the company eligible for discharge have chosen to stay on and continue with rehearsals and the presentation. One GI hitchhiked 200 miles to get in on the proceedings.

The theme of the story revolves around a girl, a boy, the Tiergarten Post Exchange, and the trip west. In their third week of practice, morning rehearsals, intensified work on dance and song routines . . . army obligations have been hampering rehearsal attendance. . . . Louis Sgarro and Kay Lancaster have the male and female leads. . . . Dan Cestaro handles the comic side and Bob Keefer the tap dancing.

The show is under the direction of Orest Sergievsky, son of the noted test pilot for Sikorsky Aviation and himself a licensed flyer. Sergievsky, a Russian-born artist from Kiev, has studied ballet from experts in the field. He is assisted by a Stage Director—Bonnie Hawthorne, a Special Service hostess and graduate of Northwestern, who led little theatre productions before joining the Service. Nicolai Shutorev, the song director, has done choral work in Hollywood and with radio. Len Pabish and Lou Alexander combined to write the music and lyrics for the musical, which features five original tunes including the catchy theme, "You Are On Your Way."

TALENT-PACKED MUSICAL COMEDY
PLAYING BEFORE FOUR NATIONALITIES
"You Are On Your Way," the two-act all-soldier show which completed its run at the

Titania Palace is now playing for French troops and will soon entertain the British and Russian forces. It played to capacity houses. . . . It made amazing strides in later performances, steadily improving itself and giving GIs a show packed with laughs and good music . . . the whole show gives a little extra punch which made a hit with soldier audiences, and many of them come back again. Bob Keefer's interpretation of his dance "Conversation Boogie" and Tom Acosta's "Cape Dance" were very well done and had the attributes of the better dancers in the States. Lou Sgarro turned in a fine performance. The "Old Black Market" scene was perhaps the most effective in the show, with everyone on the stage turning in a bang-up job on that fast moving number. A "Dream Sequence" was also very well planned and enacted with no slackening of the pace, which made both numbers a hit.

These were write-ups in the newspaper, but I never saw the actual performance, because as soon as I finished with the rehearsals I was free to go. To be free, to be free to be my own self again.

It had been a wonderful experience for me, however, to put this show on and to work with some of the nicest people I have ever met. But it also had its nerve-racking moments. One of the most difficult things I had to face was keeping people together. For instance, keeping the pretty WACs and handsome paratroopers near the stage, because as I was rehearsing one group the rest would wander off into the shadows of the auditorium or into the privacy of the grand tier boxes. It took a lot of calling and searching to find them and get them back on stage. But as rehearsals continued and the spirit of the show grew, it became easier to control the new-born artists. Another trouble was making dancers out of six-foot athletes and girls who knew next to nothing about dance. I separated out the women who showed an ability to move gracefully and chose the more agile fellows who could learn a Russian dance or to handle a Spanish cape or just remember a square dance in the dream ballet. The fellow who walked 200 miles proved to be a natural; he could move and was a very good comedian. In Bob Keefer I found a talented dancer who did the "Conversation Boogie." Tom Acosta in a nightclub scene did a very good spoof of a bullfighter. The singing voice of Lou Sgarro was later recognized in the States, when he became a singer at the Metropolitan Opera House. The Black Market sequence gave many opportunities for the performers to show off their abilities in mime and group work. Bonnie Hawthorne and I became good friends, and our friendship still continues, although mostly over the telephone. I still see one of the paratroopers, who likes to reminisce about the time in Berlin.

While I was rehearsing the show, Paul Haakon visited Berlin with the USO show *Up in Central Park*. It was wonderful to see a friend so far away from home. We were almost persuaded to visit the Russian sector, but I backed out at the last minute—the memory of my life under their regime was enough to keep me in the safety of the American Zone. Somehow I found time to attend Berlin University as a GI in order to learn some German. Another memory of my stay in Berlin is attending a performance of the Berlin Philharmonic Orchestra; I still remember the wonderful unity and effectiveness of their performance.

The trip back home proved to be a nightmare. After my departure from Berlin, I had a brief wait in a lonely, colorless camp in the north of France. This was followed by a horrible sea voyage, under cruelly rough circumstances, with the December weather angrily tossing the Liberty ship this way and that for eight days. Inside the hull, the bunks in which we slept were four layers high. Stale food was served, combined with the smell of seasick soldiers. It was as if we had outlived our usefulness and were now expendable, unwanted surplus. The only consolation was that these were the last days of military life; this marked the end—and the freedom of civilian life lay just ahead.

It was possible, however, to climb out of the smelly hull and walk about in the cold drizzle on deck, braving wind and cold weather. Once in a while, you met a lonely soul such as yourself, and could exchange a few words or enter into conversation. At those times, we talked about the tentative plans for the unknown future. I am grateful for the chance meeting of Bill Thiel on that crossing; he was a sensitive human being who responded to my need for companionship, and he helped me regain my faith in friendship and humanity.

# 33

My official liberation from military "imprisonment" was at Fort Dix in New Jersey: It was full of unnecessary waiting and wasting precious days and hours before freedom was mine. I do not remember exactly how I made the transition; I do *not* remember acquiring civilian clothes, or what my first celebration of freedom was. I do know that I was welcome at home, and met a few of my friends; but coming back to life after years of misery was a slow process. My "mustering out" pay was spent partly in the lovely Barbary Room in the Drake Hotel on 56th Street. In those days the Barbary Room had seagreen and gray velvet-like furniture, soft lights, violin music, good drinks, a luxurious feeling of comfort and could provide a peaceful rest from the pressures and tensions of an alien outside world. Within two weeks I had spent over a thousand dollars drinking champagne and gradually finding myself. With the last check I received for my "military sojourn," I bought a beautiful folder on Atlantis, created by the curator of the Pittsburgh Academy of the Arts, Mr. Ovinoff. I realized at this time that I must again begin to earn my living.

In Carnegie Hall I found a refuge in and friendly help from Virginia Lee, who was and still is the all-powerful manager and keeper of the Ballet Arts Studio. The legendary Yeichi Nimura and Lisan Kay were the figureheads of Studio 61 where I used to rehearse with Fokine, where I had my first concert long ago, and where I used to study.

It was arranged: I was to teach approximately ten hours a week. Gradually, my past experience in teaching "warm-up" classes on the different stages of the theaters of our travels came back to me. In the past it had been a general habit to arrive at the theater, put a "foundation" of makeup on your face, and then go to "limber up" on the stage. A few groups were usually practicing already, and eventually a kind of class with a few followers of the particular person developed. I had a following because of having been a pupil of the great Fokine and Mordkin, and I had a variety of steps that interested some of the dancers. My gift of presenting them to others was the beginning of my teaching career.

During the years of my military service, the Original Ballet Russe had been in South America, and our impresario and director, Col. de Basil, was anxious to make a comeback, to bring the company back to the States. But he also needed dancers and experienced performers to maintain the old standard of high quality. During the War he lost many dancers. So de Basil returned to the States to recruit, to augment his company with new blood, and to try to get some of his former dancers to sign contracts again. While watching the class at Carnegie Hall for new people, he came over to me and greeted me with a question: Did I still remember the ballets I used to dance? I told him that I had kept my sanity in the military service during the war years by remembering my dances and listening to ballet recordings. He offered me a "comeback." Would I like to rejoin the Ballet Russe in Rio de Janeiro? I could hardly believe it. The "prodigal returns" would become a reality.

The journey on the fruit ship "Pocone" to South America, with a stop-over in Recife, was a new experience. Our group of about fifteen or twenty dancers, to whom were added a few leading dancers who had recently come to the States to visit and were now returning, were a colorful assortment of people who had not yet become as one family. Their personalities were different, and the stamp of harmonious unity of the "class" distinction between the corps de ballet and the soloists had not yet been enforced or become obvious. To create some appearance of discipline and order, we were herded together daily to have a class, learning parts of ballets in the company repertoire. About four o'clock, we were free and subject to—if we wished—the excitement of the casino. Our First Lady, Mme. Lubov Tchernicheva-Grigoriev would preside over the spinning wheel or *chemin de fer*. We were paid a few dollars for our workout or partial rehearsal in the early hours of the day and usually these earnings were spent on drinks and gambling. Most of us felt weakened and that we were living "dangerously," but, really, ours were innocent pleasures—and about the only things we could amuse ourselves with on shipboard.

Our arrival in picturesque Rio de Janeiro and my returning to the company were very wonderful. My friends Oleg Tupine and Kenneth Mackenzie welcomed me like a long-lost brother. The rest of the members were warm and kind. It really was like coming back to life. The first night I performed I could hardly believe it was true. Looking into the audience through a peephole in the curtain, I could not believe the glamour and chic of the Brazilian society. The first rows and the boxes were gleaming with precious jewels; the evening gowns, the head ornaments decorated with birds of paradise, and the fur capes of expensive skins gave the impression of a different world—one which I thought was in the past. The receptions backstage, presents, invitations, the admiration of many of the balletomanes created in me a headspinning effect. The same thing happened in São Paulo, where we enriched our souvenir collections with semi-precious stones for very little money. I still treasure a few of my buys from those days: smoky topaz, aquamarines, and an amethyst ring.

The sundrenched afternoons on the Copacabana Beach cannot be duplicated anywhere else. And the midnight swims were lots of fun. Once I decided to go swimming after a party; not having a bathing suit, but having had plenty of drinks, I decided to go in in my birthday suit. Needless to say, a police guard learned about it. It all ended without any unwanted publicity, thanks to my friends, who picked up my clothes and walked along the shore while I was swimming along the shoreline to a spot at a safe distance, where I could get out of the water.

Our first trip to Sugar Loaf was not very successful. Natalia Clare and her husband, Oleg Tupine, and I were all lost in the clouds, but we made up for it by stopping halfway up for a few drinks, and to watch the clouds roll by all around us.

Our stay in Rio was made even more pleasant and interesting due to the charming music critic and friend of the Arts—Mark, who was acting as a host, showing us around the magically beautiful places and introducing us to many interesting people who entertained us and demonstrated how very hospitable and kind the "natives" could be.

But we also learned the other side of the native people—the unrestrained abandon of their excited political changes. One day we were notified early in the morning by our hotel that the performance had been canceled, and that we were to stay in the hotel—indefinitely. On no condition were we to leave the hotel. We soon realized why. An explosion broke the windows in the ground floor cafeteria. Many voices and signs informed us that another anti-American and anti-foreign demonstration was in full force. We were in a state of seige for three days. It was very colorful, but I thought I had had enough of this kind of experience in my life. On the fourth day all was as if nothing had happened, and life and our performances continued as before, undisturbed by the easy *mañana por la mañana* way of life in the paradise of South America—the beautiful Rio.

Nowadays, looking at photographs of our lazy days on the Copa beach, and meeting with my friends of those days, like Martin Snyder and Ann Barlow and her husband, Jimmy Nygreen, we reminisce nostalgically, with wistful sighs, about the good old days when we were not only younger, but when being in a company like the Ballet Russe had more glamour than the bluejean, "no fancy trimmings" fashion of today. It is true that ballet is more popular these days, but it is also true that familiarity takes away from the aura of "romance." I personally miss the illusion and glamour of days gone by. The ballerinas now dress and look just like the *corps de ballet* girls, and most of the members of the ballet dress just like everyday beatniks—so sloppy that most of them look as if they should go home and change their clothes.

# 34

We stayed in Brazil for a long time, giving performances in Rio, then traveling to São Paolo. During the intervals between stops on the tour, we had time to visit interesting places—some of the balletomanes invited us for weekends, or took us to see the fantastic resort hotels up in the mountains. Once in a while a few chosen ones were invited to the special dinners cooked by the Colonel himself, on which occasions a real Russian dish would then be created and enjoyed by the lucky ones. During one of the seasons just before we were to leave for the States, we were all happy with the news that Irina Baronova was going to rejoin the company, after a long absence. It was wonderful to see her, ever beautiful, with her special charisma. But she had to work very hard to get back to the high standard of performance that the audience had learned to expect from her.

Finally, the day of departure arrived; it was with wistful glances that we said goodbye to the Teatro Municipal in Rio, to the breathtaking view of the harbor with the statue of Christ blessing the country around and below. The journey back was very active, with much rehearsing of new ballets for our première in the States. Yara was to be the South American novelty for our New York opening, and we would be dancing a new ballet by David Lichine, Cain and Abel. The new romance of my friends Kenneth and Milly finally came to a happy climax with a wedding, and I was presented by the couple with a carnival-like gift of a colorful elephant—they called me a Russian cupid. It was a happy time for me, dancing and being with my friends, feeling alive again.

The special excitement of the Ballet Russe opening night in New York at the Metropolitan Opera House was even more intense because it was a comeback performance, our first in four years. We had a few new ballets, and the world premiere of Yara was to be our gift to the audience, as a colorful taste of what South America could be like. The old legend of the competition between the sun and the moon in the plains of Brazil, set to the melodious carnival fiesta music of Villa-Lobos created the right atmosphere for our comeback.

Our long cross-country tour was successful; we were welcomed in most places with open arms and friendly smiles of friends and balletomanes. To assure box office success, Sol Hurok added as a special attraction in the big cities guest appearances by Alicia Markova and Anton Dolin, performing their famous pas de deux either from Sleeping Beauty or Don Quixote.

But as happy as I was to be back and to dance again, there was something missing. Finally the realization dawned on me, and as usual, my truthfulness to my own self became clear—the separation from the ballet for more than three years had taken its toll. I was not dancing as well as I had before; there was no hope of improving enough to advance, to dance better. My age was against me, and maturity cruelly advised me that it was time to stop. I respect the ballet too much to serve it half way, to stay, to try to "last a little longer."

For my own ego it was wrong—it took me two years to say goodbye. But during those last years I spent all possible time and effort learning everything I could possibly learn.

I decided to memorize as much as I was capable of, all the parts of other dancers, my favorite passages in the ballets, even the ones that I did not dance. I wanted to know all the solos and pas de deux danced by our leading dancers, to absorb all the "secrets" of individual personalities, all the tricks. In other words, I decided to store away as many of the treasures of ballet as I could possibly hold. Finally, each time I knew I was performing some ballet for the last occasion, I savored with a sad pain in my heart the pleasure of performance. I suppose it was very Russian to be sadly happy, but no one knew about my decision. It was my own battle, and I wanted my painful farewells to be in my own private world. When I finally decided to leave in 1948, hardly anyone believed I would. A European tour had been planned after our season in New York. I decided which performance was to be my last. Before I left there had to be a replacement; someone was found who had been in the company before, and I had to pay this dancer for his extra rehearsals to learn my parts. Bronislava Nijinska was very angry with me because she had just given me a nice spot to dance in *Pictures at an Exhibition,* and of course Maestro Grigoriev was furious, but Mme. Tchernicheva understood.

So a few days before the final performance at the Met, I left, after dancing in the gay *Graduation Ball.* There were real tears in my eyes and those of my partner, a dancer from Brazil, as she gave me the blue ribbon from her hair as we said goodbye on stage during the ballet. In the finale, as we—the cadets—were leaving the ball, I knew that I was walking off the stage for the last time. I still have the blue ribbon.

I wanted to say goodbye to a few of my friends in the company, because I made a point of leaving without a big fuss over farewells, so my friend Tania Chamié offered her studio for a small party. There were my close friends from the company and from the outside world, my friends from everyday life. I calculated how many persons I would have to feed and how much they would drink; all was well and the party half over when suddenly there was a knock at the door, and the all-powerful and much-admired and feared impresario Sol Hurok arrived with a few of his friends. It was for me a surprise and an honor; but I had to borrow money and send out for more refreshments. It was a grand finale to my dancing career.

# PART
# THREE

---

# Memories
of yesterdays

Above left: Gemze de Lappe. Above: Flower Hujer and Miller. Left: Natalie Conlon Tupine. Below: Evelyn Taylor.

Above left: "Chuck" Morell. Photo by
Maurice Seymour. Above: Fred Zotter. Photo
by Marcus Blechman. Left: Jack Hardwood.
Below: Bob St. Clair. Photo by Maurice
Seymour.

Opposite page:
Above left: Saul, Peggy and Jeanny,
"Balletomanes." Above right: Nancy Malone.
Left: Tom Kelly in Paris. Right: "Lili" and
"Chip" Bond-Lomas, dancer and composer.

Above: Dance Varieties benefit performance with
Marsha, Tom, Pat, Vivian and Roberta. Below: *The
Witch,* Tchaikovsky Benefit. Photo by V. Sladon.
Right: *The Dream* at Columbia University. Photo by
Fritz Hock.

Opposite page:
Studio party for José Greco. Left to right: Carola,
Tasha, Miss Ruth, Billy, Jimmy, Patsy, Orest,
Margaret, Charles, José, Louis. Photo by Paul D.
Perez.

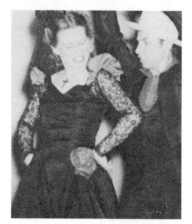

Top left: Tashamira in Mazurka. Top right: Margaret Severn in *Bullerias*. Above left: Winona Bimboni in a Spanish dance. Above: *Cape Dance*. Left: In Dance Varieties.

Opposite page: Tom Kelly.

Top left: Gayle Spear. Top right: Bill Galarno.
Left: Marina. Photo by Maurice Seymour.
Above: Nadira. Photo by Maurice Seymour.

Left: Dance Varieties opening number. Photo by A. J. Petersen. Below: *Foyer de la Danse.* Bottom: Finale, Miss Ruth cheered.

*Rosenkavalier Walzes.*
Photos by Maurice
Seymour and V. Sladon.

Opposite page:
Above: *Chopiniana.* Photo
by Maurice Seymour.
Below: *Can-Can.* Photo by
Maurice Seymour.

*Clair de Lune,* pas de deux with Roberta Banks and Tom Kelly. Photos by Maurice Seymour.

232

Above left: Lisan Kay. Above:
Bob, Flower and Tom. Left: Jack
Hardwood. Photo by Phil Belgard.
Below: Margaret Severn. Photo by
Boris Bakely.

234

Patricia Bowman in Fokine's *The Dying Swan*. Photos by W. H. Stephan.

Opposite page:
Above left: Lizabeth in *Degas*. Above right: Lillian Moore in *Auditioning at the Met*. Far left: Ron Murray and Gayle Spear. Photo by Stephan. Left: Ann Wilson. Photo by V. Sladon.

Left: Margaret Severn, Patricia Bowman and Orest at a party at the studio. Below: Patricia Bowman, Orest and Betty Bruce at a benefit. Bottom: Rita Cherisse and Tom Kelly at La Vie en Rose.

Opposite page:
Top left: Agnes deMille and David Nillo at the New York State Theatre. Top right: Dame Alicia Markova. Middle left: Hilda Butsova, at The Regency, Dance Magazine Awards. Middle right: Felia Doubrovska, at The Regency, Dance Magazine Awards. Right: Jean Gordon, Mr. & Mrs. Fischer and Rudolf Orthwein at Harkness House. Photos by V. Sladon.

Above left: Zara. Above: Orest by Gorlanoff. Left: Boychik and Billy. Photo by Maurice Seymour. Below: Rosano and Diablo. Photo by Margaret Sussman.

238

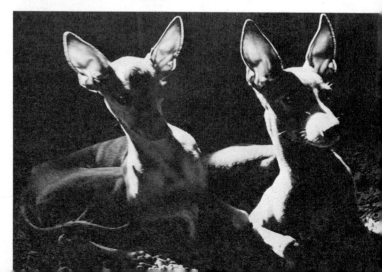

# 35

*1950:*

The next year was one of difficult adjustments and emptiness. Around eight o'clock each evening I would experience a terrible longing to hear the orchestra tuning up, to be in a dressing room applying make-up or warming up on stage—I missed these things more than the applause at the end of the performance.

I started to teach, in many places; invitations came requesting that I teach at different dance conventions—Dance Educators, Dance Masters—at private schools in Connecticut, Massachusetts, and Maryland.

I finally settled in the Dance Players' Studio on West 56th Street. Fortunately my neighbor was José Limón, a gentleman, a wonderful human being, and to me the best in modern dance. Somehow it was easier to adjust to my new life with a person like José Limón nearby, in the same surroundings.

I really do not remember how or who gave me the idea or the push to use my GI rights to go to Columbia University, but soon I was off to classes and getting more and more involved with activities in the Drama Department there.

Teaching a variety of humans is always a challenge, often depressing, and only at times inspiring. The laziness of people is well-known; only the dedicated or self-willed person can and will succeed in achieving recognizable results in the art of ballet. In America, where everything is hurried, and most things can be acquired in capsule form, simplified, or cut short, it is hard to persuade people that learning ballet is slow, self-sacrificing and very disciplined work. Many have the idea that after one pays, it is up to the instructor to make one work, to kindle some desire for the extra effort required for success with the hard-working, back-breaking technique.

In 1950, while teaching in rented studios, I was lucky to have among my pupils a few who were talented and devoted and fortunate in having parents who were helpful and sympathetic in their interests. So, I had a few teenaged dancers with whom I could really work, who came regularly to classes. At some of the conventions I was asked to teach some of the variations of ballets that I had danced. I was also asked to choreograph some new dances for the teachers, who needed material for their concerts or spring recitals. Trying out the new material on my pupils, I realized that they could perform well enough for paying audiences.

The next move was to have my own studio, a place in which I could rehearse. The members of my family were glad that I had given up my "gypsy" life and they were willing to help me financially to open my own studio on West 56th Street. I found a spacious loft over a garage, just across the street from the Dance Players. A studio floor of eighty feet long and more than twenty-five feet wide was laid to the ballet dancers' requirements, and mirrors were installed on one wall, with *barres* on the other.

So the Theatre Studio of Dance was born. It actually made history; right from the beginning things began to happen there. The opening was very social; my guest of honor I asked to be a dancer—comedienne Nancy Walker, who had just become the darling of New York in *Look Ma, I'm Dancin'*. One of the next events was a reception for the marriage of Maria Tallchief, the ex-Mrs. Balanchine, to my father's co-pilot.

Then good luck helped me with a rental demand from the *Show of Shows,* for which my friend Jimmy Starbuck was a choreographer. It worked out just right that when I was at Columbia University for my lectures, the studio was being used, paying almost all my rent.

Later on Jerome Robbins rehearsed and created his *King and I* there, and Don Saddler used my studio for rehearsal of *Wonderful Town,* during which I had the pleasure of becoming friends with Rosalind Russell and the bright and lovely Edie Adams. At the end of the rehearsals, before the show went on the road, I supplied a bottle of Russian vodka to wish them *bon voyage.* I remember, after a few vodkas, Ms. Russell remarked, "I do not know why I am being so friendly with all dancers, and the pretty young one who can really sing; you might steal the show." We assured her that with her personality and experience, and the admiration of the audience, she need not worry.

One of the rehearsals that took place in my studio was not so easy to take, although it was conducted by the well-known Jack Cole. It was for the show *Carnival in Flanders,* a Broadway version of the movie. He was such a slave driver that most of the dancers were almost crippled, and no wonder—for a whole week they rehearsed sixteen or thirty-two bars of music, the same steps over and over again until the ears and the muscles of the dancers were numb with fatigue.

One of the pleasant memories is of the time when a yet unknown, but very promising group of dancers rehearsed and auditioned, headed and inspired by Robert Joffrey.

In 1952, I arranged a welcome party for the triumphal return of José Greco, who had been away a long time, and finally returned to claim the admiration of the New York public. It was a wonderful party, with many celebrities headed by the legendary Ruth St. Denis, Charles Weidman, Patricia Bowman, and Tashamira.

Among my pupils at that time were many celebrities of today, including Peter Gennaro, Tina Louise, and most of the dancers from two Broadway hits, *Gentlemen Prefer Blondes* and Mike Todd's *Peep Show.*

Meanwhile my own lessons were very successful, and I started to choreograph and arrange performances for a group of my best dancers. There was a demand for benefit performances, especially from my friends in Stratford, for the Russian Church concerts and social affairs. I also remembered that I had promised myself not to forget the almost forgotten invalids in the hospitals, the unwanted part of our society who had been "put away," hidden, seldom remembered except at Christmas or Easter. So off we would drive to St. Vincent's Veterans (on 32nd St. in Manhattan), and then to others, such as the Goldwater Memorial Hospital in the Bronx two or three times a year.

From all that, and the accumulation of costumes of my concert group, Dance Varieties was born, and kept me busy for ten years until I had to give it up, because I was too tired to continue with the hectic schedule it demanded.

At the same time as I was creating Dance Varieties, I was finishing my studies at the Drama Department of Columbia University. Many times I was asked to help choreograph and stage productions there. Some of the students who took part in these productions came to my classes, and very often my pupils took part in the Columbia productions, most notably in *Drumlin Legend, City Madame,* and the ambitious *The Dream.* I also enjoyed creating the movements of Oriental quality for *The Clay Cart;* of course I "borrowed"

many of the movements I learned from Fokine in *Schéhérazade, Prince Igor* and *Le Coq d'Or.*

*The Dream* was the most ambitious and the most successful. It was a combination of *A Midsummer Night's Dream* and *The Faerie Queene,* with music by Purcell. It was a big success, playing to sold-out houses, and the presentations were extended for twice the number of days originally scheduled, which was unusual for Columbia productions. The dance leads were performed by my star pupils and two professional dancers—Gayle Spear, just back from Paris where she had danced in the Ballet de l'Etoile, and her partner Ron Murray, now Sequoia. It was a beautiful pas de deux. They appeared as swans; the headdresses were swan heads, producing a unique effect.

In *City Madame* I had to create a moving tableaux of masque-players, presenting the story of Orpheus and Eurydice; again my pupils took part and my little dancer Liza Ferguson was a lovely Eurydice.

As a result of all this activity and my willingness to cooperate with the drama teachers and the department, I was invited to become a member of the faculty upon my graduation with a Bachelor of Dramatic Arts degree. I had never dreamed of being a professor at Columbia University!

I must give my thanks to the wonderful teachers and instructors who were there at that time: Milton Smith, Gertrude Keller, Louise Gifford. They were the most inspiring and understanding faculty anyone could have wished for.

Teaching in the Columbia University drama department was a real challenge. Only after I gave it up did I realize how important it was in my life. The prestige, the honor of being a lecturer and teacher, and achieving the high status of professorship did not enter my mind until it was all over. I was too nervous, the work was too hard, and I was too busy. My own studio was large, and my involvement in the activities of Dance Varieties took most of my time and energy.

The three semesters that I taught at Columbia were very difficult, because every lesson I felt I had to prove myself to the pupils. The first part of the period was a lecture, with explanations and discussions. The hour-and-a-half of physical exercise was much easier, but even there it was a frustrating fight. Gradually my classes doubled and my value—rather, the value of what I was offering—was appreciated. But it was too late. My accent and my being a "ballet dancer" teaching rebellious youths had created problems. I had only a few professionals in the classes; the rest of them had to be made to listen and to do their homework. The actual demonstrations and "workouts" pleased some, but the fight to get them into practice clothes, and from the auditorium onto the stage of the Brander Mathews Theatre, and *then* do the walks, falls, and coordination exercises, were all a colossal problem. The challenge was good for me, and achieving success there gave me a certain satisfaction. I was proud to be asked to continue, and even to have two sessions a week in the future, but it was too late—I really was burned out. It all took too much out of me, and tied me down for eight months a year. After I stopped teaching at Columbia University, my own classes were enlarged by many of the Columbia students who were serious about their work. I was happy to teach them in my own studio under my own conditions.

I am glad that these days, finally, actors and singers are beginning to realize the importance of body movement and coordination. More and more of them study ballet, jazz, and modern dance. In those days I tried to teach how to move in different styles, how to sit or behave in a period costume. Though it was difficult to make them dance a minuet or walk to waltz music, the students realized what their bodies could do, and what they had to learn in order to be acceptably presentable in the roles they had to portray. It is a joy to see opera singers like Beverly Sills and Shirley Verrett move on the stage, and while singing, act with their bodies.

# 37

Dance Varieties—which kept me busy, exhausted me, and created a few moments of happy satisfaction—was my life for ten years. The beginning of it all goes back to concerts I had seen and in which later I was to dance. I saw Agnes de Mille in concert, and admired her determination to succeed and her talent for "telling the story"; I attended the concerts of Harald Kreutzberg, with his fantasy of presenting different characters of the past; the intense and colorful Angna Enters left an unforgettable impression on me with her interpretations of *Cardinal* and *Odalisque;* and there was the strength of Yeichi Nimura and Lisan Kay's Oriental fantasies. These provided the background for my own concerts in years to follow. In the beginning, I gave "intimate" concerts, usually for my grandmother and her friends, to show the progress of my studies. Later, the many benefit performances enriched my knowledge and experience. To all of those performances, I added the experiences and memorized material from over a hundred ballets that I danced during my years as a professional dancer.

The original format of my Dance Varieties grew out of my desire to dance. I had stopped my professional career early, at forty, so I decided to ask a few of my friends to help me to give a concert. Margaret Severn and I were to dance a rhapsody together; Jamie Jamieson, as a friendly gesture, consented to do his world-famous Scotch and Irish dances; and my friend Ralph Clanton, who was performing on Broadway at the time, agreed to be master of ceremonies. So the first Dance Varieties was performed in the Charles Weidman studio on 16th Street. It was a success, and proved to be the beginning of many "request" performances. In a year or two, Dance Varieties became a regular event. It was very time-consuming, energy-burning, and nerve-racking work. I had, most of the time, very good responses from the individual artists, but when I asked other studios or teachers to share the programs with me, the answer was no!, due to the ever-ugly presence of jealousy. After a few years it was really too much for me to create the entire program; I would have been only too glad to do parts of it, but others were afraid of competition, or were worried that I wanted to steal their pupils by using them in my concerts. Sad. But I did succeed in presenting some of the best dancers in solos which otherwise would not have been seen, such as Patricia Bowman's *Dying Swan,* or *Rainy Day in Tokyo* as danced by Lisan Kay.

After seeing one of my concerts, Mr. Koreff (father of the famous Nora Kaye), at that time the head of the Ballet Club of New York, asked me to choreograph two ballets for their program. I created the ballet *Foyer de la Dance,* the story written by Bonnie Hawthorne, based on a true event, with music from *Les Deux Pigeons.* I also choreographed my own "legend" ballet—*Legend of the River* for which Tashamira agreed to dance the lead, and the handsome dancer from the *Show of Shows,* Kevin Kelly, was her partner. In *Foyer de la Dance,* Harding Dorn from the Ballet Russe de Monte Carlo danced the lead, and my star pupil, Francesca Kawaguchi, created the role of the "other ballerina," who competes with Roberta Banks, a dancer from Radio City Music Hall. The backgrounds of these ballets were danced by my pupils, who though not professionals, were good enough to perform and for me to receive these notices from *The New York Times, Dance News,* and *Dance Magazine:* ". . . choreographer has visual imagination and a charming sense of lyricism . . ." ". . . showed the strongest command of his medium," and, "was sensitive to music. . . ."

Another "first" happened in my studio—the Ballet Negre. I was lucky to have a group of black pupils. 1950 was the beginning of the "break-through." Though most of them had danced in my shortened version of *Prince Igor* and other dances, and had also done solos (like Thelma Hill, who sang "Tenderly" so beautifully), there was a real need for a ballet especially for them. *Salome* was the answer, and the *Rosenkavalier Waltzes.* Cleo Quitman was just right for Herodias; "Bunky" was Herod; Thelma Hill the keeper of the veils; Tony Boss, the youth who kills himself; Betty Ann (later with the Music Hall Ballet for many years) was the Salome; and Jokanaan, the prophet, was beautifully danced by the tall, handsome Ward Fleming. The *Waltzes* I later rearranged, and it became one of the most successfully performed pieces.

Thanks to my previous work with character dances, I could create many different dances, and many times we called the program "Dancing Around the World" or "80 Minutes of Dances Around the World."

". . . Talented dance interpretation . . . as always, brings an exciting air of emotion to whatever he dances, the character dances of the old Russian school whose unaffected feeling for the stage is all too soon unfortunately disappearing . . ." ". . . O.S. should be complimented for the energy and thoughtfulness with which he has assembled a group of top notch performers and presented a pleasant, entertaining evening. . . ." These were the notices in *Dance News* and *Dance Magazine* as the result of my efforts and an occasional performance by myself, but the most satisfying feeling I had was when I succeeded in seeing my own pupils performing my choreographic creations. In these performances I found satisfaction and forgot the sadness caused by my not being a professional performer in ballet any longer. Today, of course, that sadness is all in the past, and I am actually glad to be outside the competition, the wild race to be "in the spotlight."

Other memories of evenings in the studio include visits by the legendary Ruth St. Denis. Miss Ruth spoke to the audience a few times, and invited me to be with her on one of her radio talks. I still have a tape of that radio program—a question-and-answer program on modern dance and ballet. I remember how we all bought a few boxes at Carnegie Hall for the big event of Miss Ruth performing *Salome*—a real experience. It was a time-defying presentation which disproved the theory that age and the dancer were incompatible.

Tashamira performed her modern interpretations of spirituals many times. There were also her wonderful dances from her South American repertoire (such as Sadie Thompson in *Rain* ), her lively Yugoslavian dances, and once in a while she would perform a mazurka with me. Margaret Severn graced my concerts, coming out of retirement. She let a whole younger generation witness her amazing artistry with masks, with which she created new images and brought drama to her interpretations. She made many people laugh at her wonderful caricatures of Spanish dancers, for example, or emotions such as envy. Flower Hujer created many new numbers with her group and some of my pupils. They performed these later with great success on concert tours. Zoya Liporsky amused and amazed many with her satirical mime numbers; they were my favorites—one really forgot one's troubles, and she brightened our lives with smiles which exploded into laughter. Lillian Moore contributed a great deal to the professional performances with her wonderful studies, such as *Supering at the Met.*

After a year or two, the studio concerts were so popular that I had to present the Dance Varieties in a better place, and the Carnegie Recital Hall became our "home" for many performances. As a result of the performances and the publicity, other offers began to come to me. One of the first was an offer to stage a pas de deux for *La Traviata* for the miniature Amato Opera Company. Lilibeth Williams and Fred Zoeter somehow managed to dance on the miniature stage at the Amato Theater; it was an experience for them and for me to do a professional job under the circumstances. I still have admiration for the people who undertake such big jobs, creating performances under such difficult conditions all in order to give the audience a glimpse and taste of grand music. Soon after that the Salmaggi Opera Company asked me to do the dances for the opera *Faust;* it was a difficult undertaking, but I had faith in my pupils (I also could not resist the desire to choreograph for the company in which I had danced fifteen years before). Only a person who had had experience with the opera could know, or even imagine, the difficulty of "cooperating" with the chorus, singers, and even the management. The ballet is looked upon as a necessary evil. Only one rehearsal with the company was allowed; every inch of space had to be won over from the immovable chorus to give the dancers an area in which to move.

I must confess, I had to do some "cheating," but it was for everyone's benefit. In my classes, being the pupil of Fokine, I always gave combinations from ballets of the Master, so my pupils were familiar with the steps and choreographic designs. Because of limited time, and to make sure that they would perform at their best, I told them to dance the part of the Valse Brilliante from *Les Sylphides.* It is a part for the *corps de ballet* in the finale, in which the choreographic design creates a beautiful continuity for the dancers to move from straight lines into a star-like formation. Then with a waltz, the dancers turn into two lines facing the audience. This choreographic pattern was perfect for the arrangement I wanted for the Fair dance. Whenever I can, I use combinations of steps I have previously learned, always thinking, checking myself to see if "Papa" would have approved if he had seen it.

My Dance Varieties could not have existed if it had not been for the participation and individuality of the performers. Thinking back, I would like to mention some of the names and their particular personalities. Some of them were and remained amateurs, although in my Dance Varieties they gave professional performances, dancing to the limit of their capabilities. Others, the professionals, were happy to help me, to perform just for the love of dancing, or to try new material in front of an audience. To all these people, I am grateful.

Memories of Gayle Spear dancing are still with me; particularly her interpretation of *Rhapsody on a theme of Paganini* by Rachmaninoff. The humor of Lillian Moore; her satrical mime and dances were highlighted whenever she performed. Julia Barashkova remains in my memory for her *Jealousy Tango*. Ann Wilson danced her *History of the Dance* with grace and authority, and delighted the audience with pas de deux in which she was partnered by Peter Nelson. Flower Hujer many times created excitement with her choreography and the exotic performances of her group which included a few of my pupils. Winona Bimboni, my friend from the Fokine days, danced the Spanish dance with me a few times, as well as her own solos. I was glad that I persuaded Haydee Morini to come out of retirement to dance her lovely *Viennese Waltz* and her amusing *After the Ball* number. Evelyn Taylor, who is now a wonderfully successful painter, graced my program a few times; I was happy to choreograph for her because she is such a faultless performer. Lisan Kay brought her art to the concert with the lovely dance with an umbrella, *Rainy Day in Tokyo*. The professional men that added strength and help were Ron Murray, Harding Dorn, Nat Horn, Bob St. Clair, and Gene Kevin; then there were my own pupils who became professionals, Fred Zoeter, and Tom Kelly. I was so proud when I saw them perform on the stage, being applauded by the audience. My baby ballerinas Francesca Kawaguchi, Marsha Blackman, Pat Marx, Lily Bancala, and Norma Lavore were indispensable, dancing in a *corps de ballet* number, then rushing to do solos.

I was lucky to have had the two Semaria sisters and their mother, Maria. While the girls were dancing in most of the numbers, the indispensable Maria was the backbone of the behind-the-scene help, creating the costumes, being the "backstage Mama" to everyone, and a real friend to me. Both of the sisters were studying Spanish dancing, so whenever a change of pace was needed in the program I choreographed Spanish numbers for them.

Felicia just recently helped me out; although she had not performed for many years, I persuaded her to dance at the Manhattan School of Music. A few years ago, after I successfully choreographed *Goyescas* for the Manhattan School of Music, they asked me to arrange the dance for the Vision Scene in *Thaïs*. I realized that I would need someone who knew my work, who could create a mood and give a professional performance. I also needed someone who would not be thrown by the difficulties of staging and lighting. I was right; by the time of the performance, only a true professional who had performed in the theater under every kind of condition could have given a performance on the limited eight-by-four platform in the dark, with only the glow of a spotlight. It was a very important moment in the opera, in which the priest dreams about the courtesan: The vision had to be strong, yet unreal. Upon my request to dance it, Felicia said *no,* but as usual, after my insistence that she and only she could do it, she did it—and was quite successful.

Vivian, the younger sister, was partner for Ernest Vasques in Spanish dances, but she also danced solos. Once, dancing the Prelude from *Les Sylphides* at one of the hospitals, she made such an impression on a poor handicapped girl that the invalid asked if she could touch her and her dress, because she could not believe that Vivian was real. Of course, it brought tears to the eyes of the few sentimentalists who were watching the show.

One of my best numbers was a pas de deux to the Debussy "Clair de Lune." Roberta Banks danced it with Tom Kelly. It was a big success, even in the Vets' Hospital where it was repeated. Roberta was my professional pupil from the Radio City Music Hall, and hers was the first of a series of marriages that happened among my pupils. Handsome Max Nivelon (Solomon in real life) danced in my concerts, and after some of the usual *yes* and *no* and finally *YES,* they were married.

It was fun arranging a "shower party" for my ever-faithful pupil Marsha Blackman-Kane—who was to marry instead of continuing her dance career.

One of the last marriages happened to my present pupils, Hillary (Pamela) and the wonderful mime Robert Molnar, who met in my studio.

Dolores was my devoted pupil, who had come to me after taking lessons with me at one of the conventions. She loved dancing, but was always petrified of performing; yet in the studio, like so many dancers, she had stamina and did the most difficult steps with pleasure and ease. It took a lot of persuasion to get her to perform, but she became my assistant for a long time. In the studio a very diligent pupil, Reinhold, and Dolores suddenly fell victim of a love bug and were married.

(At one of the dress rehearsals, with at least fifty people in the studio,

Dolores was dancing the Mazurka from *Les Sylphides*. After one of the jumps and a turn she suddenly stopped, looked frightened, and almost screamed: "I forgot to put on my pants," and rushed backstage. Of course, there was instantaneous laughter. Dolores did not get any sympathy from me—the show has to go on. My remark was: "Nobody would have known about it, because dancing in a long ballet skirt, who would have seen?")

Another of my dancers who made me proud is Lily Bancala. Very lovely to look at, a serious student, she danced in many of my dances, but as she always was a little unhappy on *pointe,* she finally started to take Spanish dancing lessons. Nowadays she is my pride, admired by many *gitanas* in Spain and other places for her arms. Lily is married to a wonderful guitar artist, Carlos Lomas. They have a home in Malaga, where I love to visit them. Whenever she is in New York, either performing or taking my lesson, I feel proud that I passed on the art of *port de bras* from "Papa" Fokine to my pupils.

My other pupil-dancers who performed in my *Salome, Rosenkavalier Waltzes,* and *Prince Igor* have been in many diverse places and situations: Thelma Hill was an advisor for the Dance Foundation before her death in 1977, as well as teaching at a university; Betty Ann has been with the Radio City Music Hall for over ten years; Ernestine "Fragil" Welch is an advisor in court procedures; Cleo Quitman is doing a night club act; Ward Fleming is dancing in Europe, Anthony Bosse is in the Ballets Trockadero; Charles Neal is teaching somewhere, and the bright, friendly Jean Hilzinger is teaching modern and jazz with a ballet flavor.

I was asked by Alan Banks to do a "white" number for his Brooklyn Academy Ballet Company. It was a very mixed-up time for me and the company; the travel from my studio between lessons and fitting in the rehearsal hours was a problem. Also, the journey by subway took a lot out of me, but finally the big day arrived. The performance was not of the first quality, due not to a lack of enthusiasm, but to the quality of the dancers. Although many of them were very good, their mental attitudes, as is often the case with dancers, prevented them from performing as well as they were capable. Why? Because most of them were "rejects." Their high quality and dedication were not enough. The spirit of defeat inside of these dancers caused them to be unable to give their best. The rejection, having not been accepted into the "companies," the big-time ballets, whichever they had tried to join, had killed that quality of high elation necessary for a dancer to perform. It is sad, but true.

To this performance came two of my most respected and esteemed friends: Maestro Robert Irving and the legendary "Miss Ruth" St. Denis. I was ever grateful for their consideration and effort in coming all the way from Manhattan to Brooklyn. Bob Irving excused himself, leaving after my ballet was performed. Miss Ruth, the grand lady that she was, was reading a book when not holding court to many admirers who came to greet her. She did not believe in wasting her time. She decided to leave after the intermission, so my father and family had to take her back to her hotel, although they wanted to see the rest of the program.

Which brings to mind: Once when I was to visit Miss Ruth in a hotel, as I knocked on the door she said to come in, but when I entered I could not see her. To my surprise her voice came to me from a direction where she could not at first be seen—then I realized that Miss Ruth was standing on her head in the corner of the room. With the words, "It is the best thing for you—I do it every day," she resumed a regular position and her beautiful poise.

I was lucky because I had had better opportunities than most of the dancers. My Granny, of course, tried to help me with my desire to dance and she instilled in me the understanding of discipline and the need to learn as much as I could master; and many times it was all a matter of my having been in the right place at the right time. I really doubt whether many other dancers had the good luck to have studied with so many great teachers, and to receive first-hand information from the best teachers that ballet has to offer: Lessons with Bronislava Nijinska in Kiev, Olga Preobrajenskaya in Paris, private lessons with "Papa" Fokine and Mikhail Mordkin in New York. And when I became professional, I continued over the years to take lessons from Anton Dolin, Adolph Bolm, Mathilde Kchessinskaya, Vecheslav Swoboda, Anatole Vilzak, Lubov Tchernicheva, Angel Cansino, Elizabeth Anderson-Ivantzova, Alexandra Danilova, Muriel Stuart, Hilda Butzova, and Helen Viola, among others. Most of my lessons were taken religiously; I was old enough to realize the importance of good training and respect for the art of the ballet.

All this training, taken with an almost religious zeal, was combined with my having danced in well over a hundred ballets. These I had to learn and perform, and in the course of this I worked with choreographers such as

Fokine, Mordkin, Massine, and Bolm. They all enriched my vocabulary of steps and combinations which I later was able to offer as a teacher, and which I passed on to a new generation of dancers. I am sorry to see that nowadays the blind, almost hypnotic faith and devotion which I believe it takes to work to the dancer's utmost ability is non-existent; the adoration of the teacher or dance itself can be found in only a few. Only the really dedicated can achieve that rarified plateau on which real dancers find the satisfaction, recognition, and justified admiration from the public. Nowadays there are few teachers left, such as the wonderful Edward Caton, who expects and demands high standards of learning.

This incident happened long ago, but it was so effective and right: Mr. Caton was teaching our class at the old Metropolitan Opera House. I do not remember which company or class it was, but I do remember that the class did not respond to his instructions, so, in his inimitable husky voice he told the class what he thought of us, threw the chair across the room, and left. His dramatic exit brought a few giggles, but most of us realized that we were wrong. Nowadays a teacher cannot do what, in most cases, he would like, due to money interests. In most places the pupil cannot be reprimanded because the money is needed to pay the rent. Permissiveness comes first, learning second; coffee break first, rehearsal or finishing what has to be done—second. The way I feel about it is old fashioned, but, believe me, it is sad that the standards today are different; the rules of life are not the same as they once were, and the younger generation with too much freedom is the loser.

I consider myself lucky to have "created" a few dancers and succeeded in producing a teacher or two. We must live with the realization that only one or two of one's pupils will "make it," that only once in a while there will be the excitement of a "find." The excitement and satisfaction when there is response and happy progress make up for all the frustration of the hardships and countless hours of teaching without the desired results. There were many who came to study with me during my twenty-five years of teaching who were talented but did not have the will power to continue, to face the hard work, to give up some of their social activities. But the few who did succeed were rewarded; this made me happy and proud. I usually ask newcomers: "Why do you study?" According to their answer, I begin to teach and correct them.

Fifteen years ago one of them answered, "I want to be something special." His name is Bill Galarno—and he is still with me. And he is something special. He's a very good actor and proves it by constantly working. He also sings, and gets jobs in musicals. Years ago when he made it into his first musical, *Hans the Tulip Boy,* I saw the talent and the possibility in this young man. Just recently, Bill passed an audition for a musical and was off to dance in the show in Amsterdam; it made me very proud. But I am writing about him now to prove that he is someone special—he has surpassed problems like no one else. About ten years ago he was operated on for trouble in his legs, and his blood vessels were cut. Three years of pain and being bedridden did not kill the spirit of his will to be "special"; he is performing, directing, and taking at least two classes a day, though many times he has to rest during class. Yes, he is altogether something special.

One of my lessons for adults gradually changed into two lessons a week, expressly for balletomanes. In the beginning, I taught for non-dancers who wanted to exercise and learn coordination. But before I knew it there were very serious students, singers, and actors. Eventually a dance critic, Saul, joined the class. Two sisters, Jean and Peggy, and another woman named Joanna—all balletomanes—became regulars, and during class they would ask me to show them a step or two from the ballet they were to see that week. Gradually they became knowledgeable and could distinguish many subtleties of performance. During the second year of the classes we were glad to welcome visitors who were professional dancers. I was especially happy when one of my favorite dancers, Herbert Bliss, visited the class. This gave me an opportunity to show my class how some steps were performed by a professional.

Other special pupils came to me by chance, or due to special circumstances, men like Bob St. Clair, Fred Zoeter, and Tom Kelly. They made my teaching worth the while, and as time passed, they have become part of my life.

During the gray days and empty evenings in the military army camps, there were fortunately friendly USO hostesses in the club rooms, to cheer us up and to give moral support, or just to listen to lonely men like me talk. One of the brightest of these was Shirley Watts, a woman with a big heart to go with the generous dimensions of her appearance. To distract us from our moody thoughts, she suggested that we re-do her office. A few of us created a mural on the wall of her room with a grape vine; this gave me an idea: The grapes would *have* to be painted with paint diluted with a bottle of champagne and, of course, another bottle of champagne was necessary to cheer us up. It was a very gay weekend, and working after hours made everyone forget for a while our sad states of mind. Somehow, years later, Miss Watts gave a note of introduction to me to a dancer from her native town in West Virginia. This dancer was Bob St. Clair, who was on his way to New York.

In 1950 or 1951, during the busy time of my running the Studio of Dance and rushing to Columbia University, I returned one day to the studio and found a young man asleep in the dressing room. While waiting for me, he had fallen asleep because he did not feel well. He did not know anyone in New York. Even before he gave me the note from Miss Watts, it was evident that he needed help. After my doctor examined Bob, we found that he had a temperature and needed a place to stay, to be taken care of. So Bobby was installed in the little private room adjacent to my studio, where the kindly mothers of my students nursed him back to health, giving him homemade bouillon or whatever else was needed. Before long, Bob was well and began taking lessons. Finally he passed an audition and one of his first jobs was in a tent theater on Cape Cod. I had to go and see the performances and it gave me great pleasure to see the product of my teaching and my friend's—Harding Dern's—choreography.

Later on, I found pleasure in hearing all the details of backstage problems and intrigues on Broadway. Bob became a favorite dancer of Bob Alton, and consequently danced in many Broadway musicals, including *My Fair Lady,* which lasted for years. Many times we would meet at the Russian Tea Room and I would vicariously live many exciting moments of the rehearsals for the show he was presently in, like the difficulties during the staging of *Me and Juliet,* which required precise timing for the attempted murder in which a sandbag had to be dropped at just the right moment.

After many other Broadway shows, Bob finally decided to change his profession, and one of our mutual friends—one of the nicest people I ever met—Henry Velez, who had also given up his acting career, helped Bob to get an assistant stage manager's job. Before long, Bob was the stage manager; these days he has another activity, that of art director for fashion magazines.

Every new show at Radio City for many years was a big event for me, because as a rule it was another "opening day" for Patricia Bowman. I was her willing page, and whenever I could and was free, I accompanied her to the early hours of rehearsal before the first show of the day. Then, during the run of the show, many times I would be given a pass and was able to watch the performance. One of the ushers was also enthusiastic about the dance and we had a few talks. Before long, he became my pupil and one more person who was to become my friend. I admired the serious and dedicated efforts which this young man—Fred Zoeter—was making to become a dancer. It was not easy for him to give up social activities and the hard-earned money from many hours on duty at the Music Hall in order to come to lessons between shows, or whenever else he could manage. By that time,

I was already involved in the staging of my Dance Varieties and a few other dance events which I was asked to do. Freddie had the quality and determination that helped him to improve very rapidly. He had no fear of trying anything, and stage-fright was unknown to him, at least not obviously. After a short time he was partnering a professional dancer—my little ballerina Lilibeth—in my studio performance, and when I was asked to do a number for the little Amato Opera Company in *La Traviata*, it was Freddie and Lilibeth who danced a pas de deux on the miniature stage. It was quite an experience for both them and me. They managed, although there was hardly room in which to dance. After a few summer jobs, such as in the Lambertville Playhouse, where many of my pupils performed, Fred was in musicals on Broadway. Finally the national company of *My Fair Lady* became the way of life for him for seven years. Many times Fred and his friend, John Greegas, who also studied with me once in a while, would persuade me to visit them in some city to see the show again and to visit with them. These two men had *joie de vivre* like no others; it was always a joy to see them.

*Friends; Gayle, 1943-1950-1960-1965:*
The first time I saw her she was a young girl of fourteen, with red hair flowing down to her waist. An innocent smile tempered the wisdom in her eyes, and she seemed untouched by the roughness of the army around her. Her laughter cheered many soldiers who came into the USO club for comfort and understanding talks with her mother, who was then a hostess of the Fort Knox club.

For one of the weekly shows, I taught Gayle a waltz, which we performed in several USO "floor shows."

The next time I saw her, she was a young lady, in an exclusive New York shop—correct, well-groomed, with the richness of her red hair piled up on top of her small head. She wanted to dance; we arranged ballet classes in one of the private studios with a well-known Russian ex-ballerina, Mme. Anderson-Ivantzova. In a few years, Gayle became a swan of a dancer, and through the proper channels was given a chance to join one of the leading ballet companies in Europe, where, in a short time, due to her perfect body and lovely appearance, top choreographers were creating dances for her. For seven years she lived, danced and matured as an artist in Europe. But the long absence from her native land created a change in heart and a longing to be back home.

I saw Gayle when she returned to New York—sophisticated, a bit sad because she had left part of her heart in France, but she was willing to work hard and start her life and career anew. But, as often happens in America, she was "too good," or so she was told by Lucia Chase (too good to be in the corps de ballet, but not well enough known to star in the Ballet Theatre company). Everywhere she was told to wait. Because of the necessity of financial survival, she took a job in a commercial review, in the Coliseum at Columbus Circle, advertising some material in an industrial show. It was wonderful but sad to see a lovely dancer with an aristocratic line and movement selling fabrics, dancing with yards of material in front of the disinterested customers with tired feet.

I later choreographed for her a pas de deux in a *Dream* production at Columbia University. She was a perfect swan, with her long neck, a small, lovely head, and a slender body. Gayle and her partner, Ron Murray (later Sequoia), were the high point of that production. After that, Gayle graced my Dance Varieties, dancing my interpretation of *Rhapsody on a Theme by Paganini* by Rachmaninoff. It was an artistic success.

Then came a time of new friends, and jobs that paid well enough for everyday living. She did summer theaters and teaching, but she tired of commercial dancing, and there was still no place for her in the real ballet world. Finally, marriage entered her life, followed by a child. Over the years, I always felt that Gayle was often on the edge of reality, a dreamer, like a bird in a cage, desiring to be free of the reality of everyday problems. Everyday life was all around her, but somehow never really a part of her. She was floating on the surface, but never diving into the mainstream. There was always an escape into the make-believe world of dance, or a lift from a vodka martini—a drink or two that we usually had to dilute—to ease the pressure of the day. Marriage and the child made her earthbound, and the brutal realization that her child was "not right" broke her heart and spirit.

She tried to be brave, to face it, but try as she may to live with that imperfect part of her being—her child—she was only half alive. Then when she failed again, losing her second child prematurely as she tried to take care of her first (who was by now too heavy for her to lift), Gayle gave up fighting and retreated into the world of escape—an asylum. We can never know the struggle which went on inside her. Her attempted suicide, seeing her in Bellevue in grey rags and broken-hearted, made my own heart ache.

Against some advice, I helped her to get out. For a while she seemed all right. I tried to arrange a different environment for her, a room of her own, a TV to distract her, to try to help her forget that her child was forever in some faraway hospital (he was deaf, blind, dumb, and could not sit up).

After a short while on her own in the new environment, she entered the hospital again. A telephone call from the Long Island mental institution informed me that she was again behind a fence, looking through bars at the world outside. When I visited her, Gayle seemed to like it there. She told me that she was teaching French and was free to move about; she was feeling well and she was glad there were no responsibilities. She told me why she had finally been brought there: Every time she went outside, she wanted to lose her identity. She knew what she was doing but could not stop. In taxis she would throw away all her papers of identification and money, and pretend she did not understand English, talking only in French. She would not tell the driver where she was living.

Later on, when she could leave the hospital for a day to visit, she looked almost well. On her visit to my place on Fire Island she slept for long intervals; at times she just sat looking ahead. I felt as if Gayle were trying to leave the present, as if she were wandering off to places unknown in time and space.

One day she called me, telling me that she was okay, that she was back with her husband; she promised to come to visit me at the studio one of these days. There was loneliness in her voice, and when I managed to make her laugh there was a sad sound to her laughter. But as is cruelly true, life in New York is selfish and busy. You let days pass, and you don't see the people you most want to see. Although not forgotten, they may wait for weeks to hear from you. Gayle never came to the studio; she called to tell that she had broken her ankle and had her leg in a cast.

It happened while I was away in Europe—Gayle had gone on a boat ride, the Circle Line, sailing around Manhattan. Days later her friends identified her in the morgue. There were no flowers or sentimental tears or eulogies at her funeral.

Now she is just a memory in a few hearts. But to the few who knew her, that memory is so vivid that she still exists. Her presence lingers on whenever I hear the music she danced to; all of a sudden her wistful, sad image drifts by, like a soft perfume of familiar shadow, real yet imagined. The sadness about Gayle is not deep because it only visits as she did—just passing through from somewhere to no-one-knows-where. Memories of her come to mind often; I feel that her past presence with us will be more real if I write these lines in her memory.

I often think of my friends these days. My thoughts are constantly with one of them. At times a certain melody, a song, a familiar phrase of music, or a mood brings back the past. One of you was a part of the music, the other made me think of a pagan island; one of you, with your vitality and merry laughter, made me forget the grayness of unhappy days. I have been lucky to have good friends who have been a part of my life because, without someone to occupy my thoughts, my life would otherwise be empty. To have a friend means to worry about, to work with, to look forward to seeing, to reach out, to make an effort to earn and sustain friendship—all these thoughts and feelings make life fuller and more interesting.

While stationed in Kentucky, near Louisville, many weekends were free; with a pass we could escape to the freedom of civilian life. It was not long before invitations to some private homes brightened our lives. One of these invitations was offered by Alice Givens, a charming person and lovely hostess who surrounded herself with many interesting people. I became a constant guest. Afterwards, throughout the years, we continued to correspond, and whenever possible I was only too happy to be included at her lively parties. Alice moved to the East Side of Manhattan near Sutton Place, and her apartment became a center for many show and fashion personalities. One evening I was there after seeing the Broadway show *Dark of the Moon*. I was talking to someone about how much I had enjoyed the performance. It was my kind of show—moody with a wonderful chance for the actor to do a lot with his own interpretation in creating the role of the witch-boy. Suddenly I saw the actor about whom I had been talking; he made a spectacular entrance in a floor-length bearskin coat, being greeted by Alice and applause of the guests.

It was Jimmy Lamphier, and later at the party he captivated everyone with his rendition of the "House of the Rising Sun." A few weeks later I persuaded Jimmy to perform in my Dance Varieties. I choreographed a solo number for one of the dancers to "illustrate" the sound of "The House of the Rising Sun" as Jimmy sang it. At one of my other concerts, Jimmy was narrator, the master of ceremonies.

His Broadway shows, *The Enchanted* and *Lady from the Sea* resulted in a contract with Hollywood, and still later TV. I hated to say goodbye to Jimmy, but I was grateful that we were friends, and I treasure the memory of having known such a charming person.

I was so impressed with *Dark of the Moon* that I chose as my scene for our class at the Columbia University Drama School the monologue of the witch-boy. Gertrude Lawrence was our teacher that year. It was during the run of *The King and I* that we were fortunate enough to study with this great lady of the theater. Always having trouble with my Russian accent, I was terribly nervous to perform before such a great person. What saved me was my ability to move. I almost choreographed a dance as I talked the lines of the play. I could see that Gertrude was amused. Afterwards, she was very kind: ". . . You moved beautifully. . . ." I assured her that I was not preparing to talk on the stage, but was taking drama courses to learn how to direct actors.

Another handsome actor friend of mine is Ralph Clanton. I still remember how I admired him in *Macbeth* (1940-41), with Judith Anderson and Maurice Evans; I went to see it several times. Then one evening at a very interesting party above the Blue Angel, where Margaret Whiting was singing, we were invited to hear Earl Wild play. He was giving a concert in a few days and liked to play for his friends—to warm up, and to watch their reaction. It was a real treat to be there listening to the "preview" of the program. All of a sudden Ralph Clanton walked in. I was only too happy to be introduced by the host and to express my admiration for his acting and good looks. When years later my first Dance Varieties was performed, I asked Ralph to be the narrator and he kindly consented. I had invited Ralph to fly with me over New York, as I wrote earlier, and our flight is well remembered because of the date—the 7th of December 1941. There were many wonderful evenings spent watching Ralph perform with the beautiful Katherine Cornell. In *Cyrano de Bergerac,* as the Count Guish, and in *The Stained Glass Window,* Ralph captured the colorful pageantry of the past, and nowadays whenever I see Ralph perform I give thanks that we still have actors who possess a polished technique which doesn't draw attention to itself.

As I look back, a wish enters my mind: Oh, to be a little younger! But then I immediately say, answering myself: Oh, no, definitely *no*—because if I were younger I would not have the dear memories that enrich my present, the memories and early experiences that helped to make me what I am.

During the busy years with all the activities in New York, I managed to teach and choreograph at the White Barn in Connecticut in 1953. The glamorous Lucille Lortell had invited me to be one of the instructors at her lovely summer theater. It was quite a challenge. There were many distractions and activities for the students, and therefore it was difficult to discipline and make them work as hard as I wished. The shows were always well attended, and opening nights were big social events. Beauteous Tina Louise was one of the pupils. It was fun. To get my paycheck, I had to go all the way up to the top of the Chrysler Building, and there in the inner sanctum, in a jewel of an office, I received my "hard-earned" salary. I am sorry that I did not continue to work at the White Barn, because a few years later Mme. Lortell acquired a small theater in Greenwich Village and produced one success after another, starting with a revival of *Three-Penny Opera*. But that is another "almost," of which our lives are often so full.

Patricia Bowman was part of my life for over forty years. At the beginning, I was full of admiration for her art as I watched the lessons at "Papa" Fokine's; later, during our performances at the stadiums, I elected myself to be her page, carrying her makeup box or her dancing costumes. As time went on, I was accepted in her entourage of admirers, and in a few years was a constant companion at social gatherings, and became a friend of the family. Mother Bowman, Annie, was a lady full of life, and an excuse to open a bottle of champagne was welcome. And there were countless occasions over the years. Usually, after concerts at the stadiums, even if we had been rained out, we would have a party at my father's apartment because he, too, was one of her admirers. Patricia suggested me for a part in *On Your Toes* in the St. Louis Municipal Opera and in *After the Ball* in Clinton, Conn. She even invited me to dance with her in the Copacabana in Rio de Janeiro, but I could not accept because I had just signed a contract with the Original Ballet Russe. Anyone who ever saw Patsy in *Voices of Spring* could not help but fall in love. She was the personification of the ideal ballerina, with glamour, dedication, a lovely figure, and sense of humor. The last twenty years we were sharing the same troubles over our having to teach and struggle to keep our studios going. Our mutual friend of long standing, Paul Haakon, and another friend from the "Papa" Fokine days, Eileen O'Connor—still a porcelain-like, fragile figure—would join us at our weekly get-togethers, and we would be happy to see each other and to talk about many happy moments of the past, and sometimes discuss our present troubles as well. My friendship with Patricia is a continuing silver lining to my everydays.

Paul Haakon is one of my best friends. Our learning to fly together, my admiration for his dancing, and many other shared experiences bound our friendship over many years. Paul arranged for me to be in the Littlefield Ballet which performed at the World's Fair of 1939—but it turned out to be a disastrous effort on my part. We had to rehearse in the basement of the Manhattan Center, with countless columns which were in the way of my learning to ride a bicycle. I resigned, saying that I had not learned to dance to do tricks on a bicycle. When I saw the Ballet on Wheels in *American Jubilee,* I had to admit that it was effective, because the huge three-hundred-foot-wide stage allowed a spectacular freedom and space for all kinds of innovations. But I was honest with myself, that I could not have done that ballet because I could never have learned to ride well enough.

Other memories of Paul go back to the Fokine Ballet, and later when he appeared in many engagements with Patricia Bowman and performances in the Persian Room at the Plaza Hotel. It was at one of these that I met Paul Draper and the wonderful Eddie Duchin. Many times I performed at the Plaza Ballroom for socials such as Russian benefits. As I walked from my dressing room, which was next to Mr. Duchin's, he often did a double take because I would be dressed as a tartar or as a boyar, in fantastic makeup and costumes. And then we often met again the next morning pushing baby carriages—I with my sister Kira, he with his son, Peter. We would stop and chat. In recent years, I've attended social events at which Peter Duchin is entertaining with his music, and I have had the desire to introduce myself and tell him that we have "met" before, that I remember him in the carriage in Central Park. But the New York way of life does not encourage such sentimental impulses.

As years go by, the few friends from the past, if you still have them, become even more appreciated. I am lucky to know the dancers I have partnered and to have them as my friends—Maia Hellas, a stylish, lovely woman, is one of them. About seven years ago as I was walking to the ocean at the Pines on Fire Island, I saw a familiar figure: "Maia, what are you doing here? I have not seen you for years!" She answered with the same question. We discovered that we had become neighbors. We recalled many pleasant memories: How we celebrated her first marriage after a performance of *Swan Lake* in Canada in a blackout during the war, how we danced *Schéhérazade* in Chicago and were told by friends to "cool it" for the matinees because of the children in the audience—evidently our love scene was too real. And I will always be grateful for partnering Maia in the symphonic ballets because she too was so very sentimental and allowed herself to be carried away by the mood of the melodies of Brahms and Tchaikovsky.

Another treasured friend is a lady of great charm—Natasha Molo—the backbone of the New York City Ballet. Through the years we met only occasionally, but nowadays our being neighbors on Fire Island makes it possible to share many pleasant afternoons and evenings. We have become understanding friends, sharing restful moments by the sea.

Through more years than she cares to admit, Kirsten Valbor has been my friend. Our friendship has withstood the test of time, and now it is enriched with understanding and the sharing of many memories. We have healthy arguments about the present; we have long since forgiven the many mis-happenings during our dancing together, and often have a good laugh about many things in the past.


*Now . . . about Jerry:*
He is an angel in human disguise. He was placed among us in just the right profession and at the right place; anywhere else, he would have been lost. Most of the time the people he helps do not even realize it. Many times he does not even know his own effect.

Where else but behind a bar would one find such an understanding heart hidden behind a tough, do-not-bother-me exterior? Where else would those of us who flee from troubles, problems, hopes, and disasters find momen-tary refuge before going out to face the rough sea of life again? Jerry, behind the bar, has a defensive front when necessary: As if he were saying, don't bother-me-get-lost-I-am-too-busy-what-do-you-want-from-me! But he also possesses a charm inside that will warm you. Shy but strong, a story-teller, a comedian when he wants to be, he can also be quite an unassuming fellow, just one of among many faces in a crowd, a regular guy.

Studying Jerry for over seventeen years has been one of my favorite "doing good to my heart" hobbies.

How does Jerry look? His physical appearance reveals his essence: Scotch-Irish, almost carrot-colored hair, quick moving in his action, conser-vative in attire, and generous in buying drinks for companions when "on the town" visiting some other bar.

And he was the first person I saw when I came out of unconscious anesthetic oblivion after a recent operation. I had forbidden anyone to visit me, but there he was, sitting by my bed in the hospital like an angel of mercy, welcoming me back to life.

One of my favorite people is Maestro Robert Irving. I have been an admirer of his ever since hearing him conduct the Royal Ballet at Covent Garden. I am grateful these days that my sense of humor is sharp enough to catch the wonderfully humorous asides that sparkle his conversation. It is a strange combination when the two of us have a conversation—my heavily Russian-flavored accent and the choice articulation of Maestro's immaculate English.

Saying goodbye is sad, but there is always a shadow of hope that perhaps somewhere, sometime there will be another meeting. Giving up, however, has more finality. At times it is admitting a defeat. In some instances, giving up can be a wise decision, which takes considerable willpower to admit and to execute. When I gave up my studios in Jackson Heights and Connecticut, I was too tired to continue to teach in so many places; but when I decided to give up the New York Studio of Dance, it was much more difficult—it was a part of me that was finished. Now that I have given up teaching for my dear friend Connie Moore, for whom I taught for fifteen years in Milford, Conn., I will miss seeing her—such a warm and kind person. And I will miss very much the music of my dear friend, Olga Antonuk; her musical accompaniment was a part of my life for many years. From the beginning, with her lessons, and then with her accompanying and her concerts, Olga was the soul of the Russian colony in Stratford. Following her graduation from the Conservatory of Music in Boston, she accompanied my ballet lessons for many years. She is now just a memory.

What is sadder still, I have given up fighting to maintain some of my close friendships. I have discovered that the effort is sometimes too great. If it is a one-sided attempt to continue the friendship, then something is wrong. To be self-sufficient is a great gift that my past life has given me, for which I am grateful.

The eyes were the first thing that impressed me when I met Tom Kelly. High-arched eyebrows sweep into the high forehead, a beautifully carved nose with fine nostrils, a handsome head of hair, good height, and a body that is disturbing but not perfect. His good legs, though not straight, are exciting, in later years beautified by ballet exercises. The main charms of Tom are his way of moving and behaving and, when one knows him, his honesty and good heart. The fascination to me was originally his background and his rebellious nature—to tune it and to direct it in an artistic direction became a challenge to me.

A Russian voice teacher called me one morning, asking if I would help a young talented fellow with a very good voice and a lot of promise. He needed to be "polished," this diamond in the rough. Another pupil of the voice teacher was already studying with me. So one evening a tough-looking young man came to the studio to watch a class. A few months later he told me that he was fascinated by what I could do with my feet and the way I moved, and because he skated he was very conscious of the line of the body. He felt he could do most of the steps. Well, it proved to be true. Tom started classes and in a few weeks had progressed so much that he started taking intermediate and soon afterwards advanced classes, which annoyed a few of my other pupils who had been studying much longer. Gradually Tom started coming in during his lunch hour, too, if he happened to be working nearby. I found out to my surprise that he worked as a roof-layer/ builder with his brothers. Before either of us realized it, he was taking six, sometimes more, lessons a week. Tom got hooked on ballet. In nine months, he was ready to perform. And after an audition he got his first professional job, a part in the dancing/singing chorus of the road company of *Gentlemen Prefer Blondes* with Marie Wilson.

Just before he left, I persuaded him to quit his roof-laying job. He had come to class all shaken up, wearing a torn jacket with all the buttons missing. Tom told me that a big concrete slab had fallen off the crane, and it was a miracle that his feet had not been crushed—he had managed to jump back enough to save himself. After some time passed, I suggested that he stay in the studio, in my dressing room where I had a couch, in order to save rent money—for that he would help me with the studio.

At that time I was teaching at Columbia, traveling to Connecticut on weekends to teach in two places, and the first Sunday of the month I was a guest teacher at the Marita Barker Ballet School in Worcester, Mass. I had already had my own studio for five years and been teaching for seven; I had by this time acquired some very good pupils and had turned out a few professionals. The idea of having my own group appealed to me very much, especially after I had used some of my best pupils in performances at Columbia University. From my adagio classes, I was able to choose enough dancers for performing in a concert group—and that is how my Dance Varieties came into existence.

I was able to use Tom in numbers and pas de deux. In some of the concerts he was in as many at twelve numbers. For instance, he sang a

French song and then joined a lively can-can number with six other dancers, or in a Spanish costume sang "Granada," and then performed a vivacious jota.

As the years went by, I kind of adopted Tom; not until the last few years of my Dance Varieties did I pay the performers, usually giving presents to my dancers instead. One summer I treated Tom to a week in Paris. It was an unforgettable experience for him, and he has not been the same since. Also, due to my busy schedule, the situation at home, the late hours I kept, and my mature age, it was time for me to be on my own. So I asked Tom to share an apartment with me. We found one not far from the studio.

To this day, after more than twenty years of living together, there are still many people who believe that we live together for reasons other than companionship. But our tastes and private lives are quite different, and our personalities would never survive a "close" relationship; one of the reasons that we are still together is that we always have separate bedrooms and spend very little time together, except during social engagements, going out to see a show or to the ballet with my sister.

# 41

*Friends, asking only for a caress:*
My earliest recollections are of Wright, a pointer; Nora, a spaniel; and later Mimosa. There was also an Irish setter, whose name I've forgotten. They were all my childhood friends. The Irish setter I imitated continuously, following him around all day and trying to sleep with him in his corner. Because I could not talk yet, my family understood my pantomime and supplied me with a tail—my uncle's belt. That was in Russia. In Stratford, there was Zara, a real lady, an Alsatian, whom I helped deliver of nine puppies; when Granny and I moved to New York, Zara presented us with a second set of nine offspring. Each day, in some way, she proved to us that she could understand almost everything we said to her. She misbehaved only when she was a puppy: For example, when I returned from classes at high school, I often had to search for my things. I would find my watch behind the couch, along with a sandal or some other article of attire; sometimes things would not surface for days after she had hidden them.

Zara lived in New York with my Granny and me for a long time. After Granny's death, a lady who used to help Granny during her illness took care of Zara because I had to travel with the ballet. Then I decided that, because the lady had a house in the country, she should take Zara permanently, which she was only too glad to do. Later, she moved to California and took Zara along. Zara was hurt, I heard, and they had to put her "to sleep."

Fifteen years later, when I settled in New York and had my own studio, I yielded to the temptation to have a dog-friend again. Bob St. Clair had an adorable Pomeranian named Stuffie who had a litter. Her first-born became my Boychik, but he was so small that I felt one dog was not enough, so I adopted his brother Billy, the runt of the litter. Though I called them "an excuse for dogs" because they were so small, they made up for their size with being bright and full of personality. For many years I took them with me to the conventions when I taught, and they were always the center of attention. They were quite obedient and could remain quietly with my things, wherever they might be; they amused a great many people.

Once, however, they did cause trouble. It was during a convention in Washington, D.C., at the Shoreham Hotel. Taking place in the same hotel during the Dance Masters of America convention, where I was teaching, there was also a gathering of archeologists—in the ballroom just across the hall. I had to leave the class, where as usual Boychik and Billy were settled in by the piano. As I returned and was about to enter the room where I had been teaching, I heard from across the hall explosions of laughter. Being curious about the source of so much merriment, I looked into the ballroom with the archeologists to discover that Boychik and Billy were walking down the aisle toward the lecturer, evidently looking for me.

As they grew older, Billy developed an unusual sickness. His system could not keep calcium in his little body and his bones became soft; his teeth fell out and finally I could not bear his being so incurably sick so I had the vet put him out of his misery. I insisted on holding him until he was dead—it was just as if he had fallen asleep. Boychik, now lonely and restless, stopped eating. The vet tried to help, but the poor little animal began shaking his head uncontrollably and banging against the furniture; it became evident that nothing could help. And, again, I had to hold the little creature and caress him until the breathing stopped. The vet at the ASPCA paid me a sad compliment—that I was the only person he had met who loved the animals enough to be with them during their last moments. Most people do not stay around to watch their animals die, he said, but have to leave.

I was very sad, of course, for many days afterwards. And then my friend Tom came in one night saying, "You do not have to keep this, just see how cute it is," and with that he gave me a little deer-like creature, an Italian miniature greyhound puppy, all legs and big ears. As with Boychik and Billy, one was not enough, so the next litter provided us with a second dog; the first, fawn-colored Rosano, was joined by Diablo, a slate-blue. For fourteen years Rosano and Diablo were admired and loved. They have been a source of a great deal of joy and company for me. After Diablo died, Rosano lived through a few traumatic weeks—but survived. Although old, he has become an aristocratic beauty. When Rosano dies, I do not plan to get any more dog friends. I have grown too old to say goodbye to friends such as these—it just hurts too much to go through it all again.

# 42

*Travelogue:*
Ever since I can remember, I have had a desire to travel, to see and to be in new places. At first, of course, I could only travel in my imagination, being a child and without means, but once I got started traveling, it became an obsession. I was bitten by wanderlust—the fascination of seeing, being, visiting, discovering, wondering what is beyond the new horizons.

After leaving Russia, I traveled for the first time across Europe, then to South America, and finally to the United States. When I joined the Ballet Russe, traveling became a way of life—the gypsy life of the dancing career. While in the Air Force, I was forever on the move, going all over the world. Only when my career as a dancer ended was I free and able to choose where or when and how I was to travel.

Traveling in the latter period of my life began on a tramp steamer in 1949. Since then, I've crossed the Atlantic at least fifty times, on many kinds of ships. Only when I travel with my sister Kira do I take a passenger liner, since I prefer the small slow boats when I travel alone. They have a more adventurous spirit to them, as well as providing extra days at sea. The irregularity of arrivals and departures adds to the charm of these journeys.

One trip I remember with special pleasure. It took twenty-one days to reach our destination, Alexandria, Egypt. Even the name of the Danish freighter had a romantic sound, The Silver Moon. We made several stops in the Mediterranean, one place being Tripoli, Libya. There, time seemed to stand still, the past became our present—the veiled women, the mosques, palm trees, all etched on a vivid, tropical background.

Just before our arrival in Alexandria, the captain asked if we would mind a four-day detour to Beirut, where he wanted to pick up some cargo; we also stopped at Port Said on the Suez Canal. Thanks to this change in our schedule—at no extra cost to us, incidentally—I was able to see that beautiful port city in Lebanon, which is also a witness to the ruinous political cruelty of man's inhumanity to his fellow man. Beirut, the land of milk and honey, had sweet-smelling air; in its ancient setting there were beautiful modern buildings painted in pastel colors, placed in a landscape of coral-colored mountains and waving palms. Nature provides very dramatic backgrounds for this part of the world, offering many strong contrasts. Modern homes next to antique sailboats in Biblical settings, for example; white sand and blue water, purple mountains, and dark green trees. All appears as if Hollywood had a hand in arranging the technicolor contrasts.

When, finally, we sailed into the historic harbor of Alexandria, I eagerly anticipated a trip which was to become the highlight of all my travel experience: to Karnak and the Valley of the Kings. This was a dream-come-true for me, a dream I had dreamt for forty years.

Alexandria is a city with a Grecian past, with pillars in a Pompeian style, with ruins of Roman baths. It is a mixture of practicality and grandeur, of modern luxury and extreme poverty. The modern homes were simplicity itself, set among the Arabian loveliness of minarets which suggested *A Thousand and One Nights*. Almost out of place in this were the ruins of ancient Egypt.

The pyramids look like the work of giants. They have been dated to B.C. 2,900—5,000 years old. Each stone weighs two and one half tons, and there are 2,300,000 of them. One stares, not believing what you see. Nearby, the mysterious sphinx keeps watch in tranquil wisdom, thoughts unknown by countless generations of men.

Traveling up the Nile to Karnak, one arrives in 100° temperatures. We were greeted by an 80-year-old guide named Magar—another experience. The Luxor temple with countless columns, the rows of impressive animals with the heads of rams and human expressions—it all seemed to be the setting for a dream from which I had not yet awakened.

Temple after temple contained beautiful writing on the walls which told stories from the past: Of self-admiring kings, of ambitious queens, of cruel victories of new rulers. Images of everyday life burst upon the imagination; and one had the feeling of being right there, of time rushing backwards, of our present becoming the past.

Crossing the Nile from Luxor, from Karnak with its ruins of ancient Thebes one passes into the Valley of the Kings. On the west bank of the Nile near the site of Thebes, there like two creatures from another world, the Colossuses which welcome—or rather command—you to be respectful at the entrance to the palace-temple of Hatshepsut.

After visiting the impressive tombs of Rameses and Nefertiti, one enters the tomb of Tutankhamen through the temple of Hatshepsut. Upon entering, the richness is unbelievable; the calm grandeur of the mummy's chamber is somehow undisturbed by the unwelcome visitors. At long last, my dream was realized: To be there and to witness the past, to be surrounded by what I have imagined and dreamed about since childhood. It was the most thrilling experience of my life.

Then I traveled from Alexandria to Piraeus, Greece. It was not only crossing the Mediterranean which caused a change, but also the shift from worshiping the dead to the worship of eroticism and a sense of life's joyousness. Worshiping the human body, and perfecting the aesthetic appreciation of the human form as the Greeks have done in their statuary—these qualities from Grecian antiquity spoke eloquently to the present. The acropolis, the Parthenon, the few graceful columns at Lindos, the lovely islands such as Hydra made me fall in love with the country. Once you have experienced the musical cheerfulness of the Greek personality, there will be the ever-present desire to return.

The most varied trip I have ever traveled was my first journey with American Express and a Eurail pass. I visited eleven countries; and it was tiring, but also very interesting.

In 1961 we covered the whole of Europe in a car; *we* being my sister Kira, my friend Tom, our friend Maria; the driver of the car was me. One remark made by my sister during the trip gives an idea of what kind of trip it turned out to be: "I wish I could sleep in the same bed just twice." I wanted to show my friends as much of Europe as possible—and probably succeeded. In later visits we could return to the places we had liked best, or so I planned at the time.

We arrived at the port of Antwerp in Belgium, where we were met by our car, a Citroen. The first stop was Brussels, with its gilded antique houses which surrounded a flower-filled square. Our plan was to follow the coast of France all the way to Spain; we usually drove until an hour or two before dinner, with a stop for lunch at some picturesque spot. Driving along the coast we passed many places of historical interest including Dunkirk and the fields of Normandy filled with red poppies (symbols of the battles fought there). The drive to Mont-Saint-Michel was unforgettable; it appeared in the distance like a mirage, and then gradually as we drove nearer became a beautiful reality, appearing to us through the mist. The climb to the top is steep and hard, but well worth the effort. Passing through Bordeaux, I was reminded of our departure to South America many years before. We did make some side trips, such as stopping in the city of Rouen in order to see the places where Joan of Arc had lived and died.

When we reached the border of Spain, we rested for two days at the seaside resort of Biarritz before starting our Spanish travels. Reinforced by our rest and refreshed after the wonderful swimming in the Atlantic, we first visited Madrid. We then journeyed by the coast to the Spanish "Riviera," Costa Brava. We began with Cadiz, Gibraltar. We spent a day each in Granada, Seville, and Cordova, but this was hardly enough time; it did give us an idea how colorful and dramatic old Spain could be. In those days there were only a few good hotels, and the stop in Malaga was especially pleasant and comfortable. In Valencia we went to see a bullfight, which is a cruel sport; but the pageantry is unforgettable. Barcelona was our last stop in Spain. In a way, I was glad that the driving on the Costa Brava was over, since the so-called highway did not have any barriers to prevent the car from going off the cliffsides; at times, it had been a nerve-racking experience.

In France, we traveled on the Côte d'Or, stopping for bouillabaisse in the colorful city of Marseille, then on the Côte d'Azur, where we stopped for ice cream on the boardwalk in Nice. A few years later I discovered a charming old-fashioned hotel named Le Beaux Rivage, which we have visited many times since. We hardly realized that before long we were entering the picturesque Italian Riviera—even more colorful, with unspoiled beauty due to fewer tourists, than the French Riviera had been. After admiring the art treasures in Florence and falling in love with the charm of that particular city, we continued on our way to Rome, where we were to join up with my mother, my sister Colette, and Colette's family.

The journey south took longer than I had expected, for it was dark by the time we reached the walls of the ancient city. Like many stubborn travelers, I kept driving in the hope of being able to find my own way, without proper maps. Finally, late in the evening, we found ourselves in a huge open area, which was surrounded by seemingly countless columns. In that dim twilight, we realized we were in the very heart of Rome, driving towards St. Peter's. But how were we to get to our destination where the family was waiting? A helpful cab driver was given the address and we followed behind in our own car; by midnight, we were all reunited and our worries were over.

While in Rome we were entertained by Grant Muradoff, an old friend of mine from the Metropolitan Opera days who had become important in the ballet world. After an emotional goodbye to my friend Tom, whom we left in the American hospital to recuperate from his appendix operation, we were on our way to France.

The journey north was uneventful, with many pleasant stops. We were now a caravan of two cars with our destination Edinburgh, Scotland, the home of my mother and sister. The last, long stretch from London to Scotland was difficult going. The familiar fog welcomed us as we crossed over the border from England to Scotland. Never before had I driven in such a mysterious void, or had such an uneasy feeling of the dark unknown. The hope that somehow we might soon be able to see or arrive somewhere, or that the wind might clear the mist gave us the strength to continue. We finally arrived, late but safe.

During our next trips to Europe, we selected just a few places to explore or visit again—often with the thought of enjoying more thoroughly our discoveries from previous journeys. Amsterdam is now on my regular list, as are Paris and London. The friendliness of Amsterdam is renowned, and it is very pleasant to glide comfortably in a glass-covered boat on the numerous canals in the evening while admiring the lighted bridges and lovely homes. Paris has an ageless charm which embraces you each time you return. London is a town where you could never see all the shows, even if you tried. Many times during stays in London I would see as many as nine shows in one week and leave the city feeling that, "Oh, I could have seen another play." Venice is like Rio de Janeiro—too beautiful; although you admire these cities, you can also live away from them.

These days, I travel every other year with my sister Kira. The years when I do not go with her, I travel alone, desirous of discovering new places and people, of seeing new art treasures and more historical sites. I often manage to return to my favorite spots, where I find old friends who have known me through many years of traveling.

Although I have lived in New York for a long time, Paris is where I feel most at home. I stay with Jean Imbert, a friend for thirty-five years, in his apartment in a fifth floor walkup at the foot of Sacré Coeur. Every morning before going to work, he grinds fresh coffee in an old-fashioned hand mill. As soon as I hear that sound, I rush out of bed, run down five flights of stairs, up the hill to a bakery and purchase freshly baked croissants and brioches. Then back to the apartment, where we have the fresh coffee and bakery goods and sit on the little balcony and watch the panorama of Paris around us. I sometimes go to the Place de l'Opéra or American Express to get the news from America. Later, maybe I'll sit at a bistro and watch the people pass by. In the evening, walking up the steps of the Sacré Coeur hill, I listen to countless musicians, who compete with one another; later I may walk along the Seine. A wonderful way to spend an evening.

# 43

1970:
The funeral of the second Mrs. Sergievsky (Shoura) was sad, but the sadness was *not* heart-felt. It was a sad occasion for my father because he was saying goodbye to the middle part of his life—the decades between the Russian Revolution and the Second World War. It was a sad occasion because nobody really cared that Shoura—Alexandra Kotchobey, ex-Mrs. Sergievsky—had died. Only a few persons with long faces—since it is the custom to be sad at funerals—were moving about and wondering: When will it be my turn? Who will be next to take that trip into the unknown accompanied by the melodious chanting of priests at a funeral service?

When I was asked what I wanted from the house in Stratford, where Shoura had lived for many years after the divorce, it was perhaps strange that I only asked for two things: a portrait of my grandfather and a bust of my father. A wistful thought crossed my mind: After all these years I had finally gotten my father back—his image in a handsome bust. My thoughts spanned the preceding fifty years, back to the time when I had felt much resentment toward Shoura for having taken my father away from me.

When I felt this resentment for the first time during the years 1915-1917, I could not possibly understand the tricks played on us by destiny, by political events far beyond our control. Alexandra had been a handsome woman, a good singer, and had had a jealous nature. She could also be a gracious and charming hostess who gave the appearance of loving fun and fine clothes. In the last years of her life she tried to make up for her selfish and occasionally unfair behavior towards me over the years, but these gestures came too late. She died a lonely woman. I always feel sad for people who are alone in the last years of their lives.

271

Death: It is the most violent experience. I want to be conscious when the end arrives. We die a little bit every minute of our lives. Few people want to think about it, but it is true.

Some people say "pass on," "to depart," or "sleep." Sleep? Hell, no, in sleep you wake up to reality. I want a change. Let it be just—some kind of a vibration in an unknown universe. I would not mind being part of the ocean. And my ashes will, I now hope, eventually find their resting place there. I have always found rest near the ocean, every time I've looked at it or walked by the shore.

Whenever I am troubled, long walks by the sea calm my nerves, quiet my restless spirit—almost solve my problems. The problems of everyday, when taken to the sea, become unimportant; emotional disturbances seem to change their colors. Black hopelessness becomes grey, a shade of melancholy becomes blue or light green, the color of waves.

Death itself does not frighten me because when I was small—before I had any concept of death's finality—it was all around me. The first time I met death face-on, it was very calm and it was an end to suffering; it was almost welcome. My Uncle Roman, dying in my arms, was finally released from the agony of his last illness. Later, when he was stiff and cold, with candles lighting his face, I was not afraid to pray near him—and probably felt a sense of peace surrounding the whole occasion. The first pain in my heart came when the wooden pine box was put in the ground, a few flowers thrown into the grave, and earth began to fill the open space. My grief then arose from the realization that I would never see him again on this earth.

Other deaths have created only a slight sense of emptiness, but they did not penetrate the heart. Sometimes the church service itself, with its lovely melodies and chanting, would bring a mist of tears; but this is a reaction of the eyes and not the heart. The final departure of an individual's spirit, leaving behind that immobile object in the coffin, has often caused a deep sense of resentment in me.

*Glances back:*

Life about me is moving faster than I am. I have been teaching myself not to rush after passing parades. Gradually I have begun to find pleasure in just relaxing, in remembering the past, and to find contentment with the things which I can still accomplish, such as painting, gardening, playing the piano, or reading. Many things which I once considered very important have somehow lost their urgency; they will wait.

My father died in 1971, after a short illness, at the age of eighty-three. It was sad, but in a way I was glad for him to leave. I did not want Father to experience the defeats of old age, because all his life he was, in a very real sense, the master of his own fate. He had been a hero in the First World War, when he was decorated with the St. George Cross and many other medals; for many years he had been the leading test pilot in this country, having established fourteen world records; and the charm of his personality and his good looks made his life splendid, interesting, and exciting. If Father had continued to live in an incapacitated condition, he would have been like a caged eagle; it would have been a losing battle, with ever-narrowing limitations and delusions of old age. Still, Father's death left behind a sense of emptiness and sadness.

The death of Gertrude, Father's third wife, in 1975 was harder to experience. Her lingering illness was painful to watch. The word *Why?* has a special meaning in her case, because Gertrude had been such a kind, thoughtful person; she had helped so many people, always guessing the needs of someone, always managing to be a real friend to many. It was not fair for her to suffer and to leave so soon.

But I still have my two sisters and my mother. The circumstances of politics and geography have separated us most of our lives, but I visit my mother and sister Colette every year in Scotland. Although old age had left its imprint on my mother, it is always pleasant to see her, to help her take a walk, to talk with her about the past. Often, in the evenings, as I fall asleep, I can hear my mother playing the piano softly—Russian melodies from long ago.

*Written on a cruise ship, winter 1975-76:*

*. . . and now my life has a meaning again: A responsibility and love for someone who is partly of my blood, the blood of the Sergievskys. Only we two are left—the last of the line—my sister Kira and I. To be needed, and loving to be needed—this is a rare and unselfish love. Many times it is a burden, but a burden which I am glad to shoulder, because it is a responsibility and duty, a family tie. Whenever I have to refuse some choreographic*

*engagement or cancel a lesson because of duty to the family, I remember that I had it all in the past. I am not upset when I have to do something because of "duty." I have chosen correctly, I know.*

I still have love in my life, the other kind of love, the chosen love, the love that just happens to enter the heart without being asked, without looking for it. This kind of love may leave without warning, the same way it entered the heart. As I write these lines, I am at peace. I have had a rich, full life, a lot of suffering and sorrow, a great many frustrations and troubles, but without them I could not have known the joy of success or the experience of happiness when I find an "echo" of my feelings in someone else's heart, or see a reflection of my own emotions in the eyes of someone dear to me.

*Fire Island Pines, 1963 to the present:*
In the winter this is a restful, peaceful place, with its continuous sound of waves on the shore, the miles of empty beach, the lonely cries of seagulls. The empty summer homes seem to intrude upon the natural beauty of the shore. At night the wind and stars take over; even the waves on the beach seem to calm down under their influence.

With the first warm rays of early spring, the voices of many birds cheerfully demand to be fed. The walks on the beach become pleasant strolls. The first greens in the cultivated part of the garden timidly announce the success of the autumn efforts with planting bulbs as they are awakened by spring.

As the days advance, the warmer afternoons invite home owners to come out to the island to see what the winter storms have done to their summer homes. At the end of April, the rush is on. Still, after the last ferry leaves in the early afternoon, peacefulness drifts in again, and the quiet mood relaxes the nerves. In May, the seasonal migration is in full force; squeaking carts, painting brushes, sweeping brooms, and friendly *hellos* establish the opening of the summer season. On weekends the wooden walks are crowded with tight pants, sandaled feet, pale faces, loud sweaters, colorful windbreakers, and picture frames; half-filled glasses are carried by half-drunken people going from house to house. At night, one can hear the sincere greetings of the neighboring home owners who ask with interest how everyone felt and fared during the winter exile.

In my little kingdom of birds and expectant flowers, it is peaceful. Many times each day I walk out to examine the green shoots, wondering what beauty is getting ready to blossom out, what miracle of nature will show itself. Anticipating the blossoms, I keep looking, admiring, wishing with wonder for the awakening of another spring.

# 45

Every place and person colors one's behavior. Surrounding atmospheres, vibrations of a particular moment cause most of us to behave in a different manner, rather than exposing our true selves.

The way I have lived is to be as honest as possible with myself, even though this has created problems, on occasions, for me as well as others. But I do believe that, in the end, this has been the best way. After all, when you are alone, that is when you know whether or not you are a nice person—when you can look into a mirror or your soul and feel good about what you see.

*At a "singles party" on the steamship S.S. Vandam, August 1976:*
The party is going on outside, on deck, while I sit at the bar having a second Beefeater gibson. I cannot make myself go out to the gathering; it is too nice in here alone, recuperating from another trip to Europe. As usual, I had to be many persons, assuming different personalities depending on circumstance; I seldom had time to be myself. So now I am recharging my batteries at last and, after six weeks, am beginning to get back in touch with myself.

With each person and situation, I have had to change my personality, never having time to be my own self, seldom having time to relax and see the places about me. This role playing is one of my idiosyncrasies. It is not a "put-on," because many times it is not even necessary; but my personality is made in such a way that I am somehow colored by the people I am with. It happens only with the people I care about or love. With people I have just met or don't care about, I often appear to be either snobbish or dull—or just an eccentric Russian.

So now I am on a trip to the Caribbean, to recover from the European trip; I'm alone, and enjoying the luxury of it. The people about me are colorfully dressed, but inwardly dull. I find it particularly nice to eat alone (I have a table by myself and a single cabin). I do not have to waste time with empty talk with anyone; I usually read while I eat, catching up on the books I like to read. I am like a fish out of water, belonging nowhere—just drifting, at times suffocating in my own loneliness; and yet I realize that I am just going through a period of having to adjust to my new age—65. I do not want to waste any more time on empty conversations or new acquaintances, although I do still enjoy talking with somebody who is interesting or wise. Whether at home or traveling, I find that there is never enough time for the things I want to do: read, paint, write, play the piano. Even when I relax, I do not waste time, but I find it fun to embroider as I watch television or as I sit in my home on Fire Island watching the countless birds as they eat the seed I put out for them. I love creating new designs for my countless pillows.

Many times I just remember treasured moments or personalities from the past, friends who enriched my yesterdays and became a part of my life. Early impressions and experiences became the standard for my future. Later events and influences may have compared, but they never repeated—I know better than to try to recapture the original past.

Life without love—or, at least, the memory of it—is just an existence without a heartbeat to create and regulate the tempo of daily life.

Like warm sunlight are the thoughts of someone I once loved. When I am far away, the need for someone's nearness is satisfied by memories. It is a fact that distance creates the illusion of perfection; one forgets the faults, and remembers only the pleasant, treasured moments.

*Today:*
Many people are not forgotten—they are remembered—but their names are not mentioned because some relationships and events were too intimate. They belong only in the world of memories and should not be exposed to the curiosity of strangers.

It is sunset time. The shadows have extended too far to keep their familiar shape. Soon darkness will cover everything in forgetfulness. I hope I will remember the starlight, and the sound of the sea, where my soul will find peace.

Thanks for the memory.